THE MESS.
TWO VOICES

To the Women who have made me the man I am.

My Mother who taught me so much but left me too soon.

Mary, married for ten good years, but we were too young.

Carla, the closest thing to family for a long time.

Debbie, who was a good friend from day one and was there at times when others weren't. You will always be part of my life. So glad your dreams have come true. Love you loads.

Janine, who loves me as much as I frustrate her. No-one has ever had my best interests at heart the way you do. I owe you so much.
Am certain you will meet the man of your dreams.

Table of Contents.

Chapter 41. Heaven.......
....And Beyond, The Twelfth Key.

PART ONE: THINGS WE NEED TO KNOW TO GET THROUGH LIFE.

Chapter One: An Introduction.

It is said that the hardest part of a difficult journey is the first step.
That journey doesn't need to be taken by car, plane, or train. It can be an inner journey, a spiritual trek to find ourselves.
For some it can be studying.
Others may focus more on self improvement: dieting, training to be physically and mentally fitter.
Forging a career path.
Or simply maintaining and nurturing family and the responsibilities that come with being a good husband, wife, daughter, son.
My journey is this book, and with a sigh of utter relief, I've taken the first step. More so because I would never claim to be a writer. I have always been interested in the process, always thought, 'what if'?
I will go as far as to say that I always knew I would write a book.
It's never happened before because essentially I've been scared witless. Carried that fear of failure like a yoke around my neck. Frightened of all the gremlins that exist, stored away in our subconscious, in the wardrobe, under the bed.
Hey, I've done half a page and it's therapeutic. I haven't broken out in cold sweats; time hasn't changed...but then again, much more on that later.
It's maybe not so bad because this particular

journey is shared.

Part of what I write comes from within; part of what I write is channelled.

Two voices accompanying one another.

Many of the earthly experiences are from my own life.

But this book goes much deeper than exploring this life and the world in which we live.

For the journey I write about is one that awaits us all and is essentially the ultimate journey.

Whilst we must never ignore the realities of this world, allow your mind the space to imagine something more.

I sometimes tell people that their mind, body, and spirit exist within a frame and that frame encompasses their lives.

Rule One: Remove The Frame.

Allow yourselves the luxury of expansion. Become open to the idea that what we believe to be a complete picture is little more than one piece in an infinite jigsaw puzzle.

As soon as we learn to accept this, we have immediately taken our first step in nurturing a desire to understand more of the world we live in and the worlds alongside and beyond this one.

My knowledge, as with most things we learn, comes from being taught. However my teachers aren't sitting in a classroom. They aren't scribbling on blackboards with chalk, or whiteboards with marker pen.

My teachers take up residence in my subconscious and connect to me through thought.

Everyone communicates with spiritual energy, most of you just don't realise it.

For those who are still scratching their heads, perplexed, I am a medium.

Maybe a medium with a bit of an added kick. The voices in my head aren't always connected to someone's dear departed but instead connect to a much higher plane of existence.

Basically though I'm little more than a go-between. A conduit between their dimension and ours.

Aside from my role as a medium I also like to think of myself as an average, normal person, though perhaps my life has been different from most, and some who know me would suggest I've never had a normal day in my life. Sometimes it's difficult not to agree with them, but I try hard to hold on to some sense of sanity amidst the chaos.

Perhaps if you read this book and follow the journey you'll make up your own mind.

It has taken me years to get to this point.

I knew from about twelve years old that there was a book to be written. At that time I was thinking fiction. In my formative teenage years I liked horror. James Herbert and Stephen King being my staple reading diet as I grew up. Then, as with most flights of fancy, the idea drifted into my subconscious to become a memory.

Aged twenty-four the urge briefly returned. That's when I realised I was never going to be some great scribe.

Then again in my thirties, thwarted this time by a self destruct switch, which was pretty much working overtime for a good few years. So every decade has come and gone etched in the frustration of knowing there is work to be done but not feeling able to begin.

Redemption comes in the knowledge that I was never ready to write this properly before now. The book in my head four years ago is not the same book that sits waiting to be unzipped today. But then even six months ago I didn't know, or understand, what I have a grasp of now.

So I ask you to dispel the beliefs you have nurtured about life and existence as you think you know it. Join me on a trek that is full of wonderment and mystery.

Life exists in universal balance. For everything positive there will be something negative. Everything good, something bad. From love to hate, joy to pain. Just as there is day and night, black and white, prosperity and poverty.

Rule Two: Keep It Simple.

People overcomplicate situations far too much. Too many what-ifs and maybes. While I know most things are never totally black and white, neither should they beyond a person's comprehension.

The tendency to overcomplicate arises because someone wants to make a scenario more about themselves than is necessary, or

there is something fundamentally wrong with
a situation, so they create smoke and mirrors
to camouflage the real picture.
So, no overly long chapters to baffle and confuse. In
fact my advice is to read this slowly. Allow things that
are new or maybe a little difficult to get your brain
around time to sink in. Don't take my word for
everything, ask questions in your own head.
Do this properly and you will get answers.
One question will arise I'm sure over and over.
Does this make sense?
I'm not asking anyone to dismiss science,
though science will probably dismiss me.
I'm suggesting that if what I explain resonates
in a simple way then there will be strong
foundations for a basis of truth.
Our journey will look at basic principles and
explain how they work, such as what gives us
psychic ability.
What happens and where do we go too
when we die?
Why are we here in the first place?
Why do some people's lives seem easier than
others?
How can some people's abilities to reach out
to spiritual energy differ from one person to
the next?
I'm going to attempt to put all of this
together and explain the meaning of life!
We won't stop there we will go much further.
To explore the possibilities of other life forms
and how they hold relevance to our own
existence, and trust me, the answers don't lie
a million light years away.
From the perspective of an afterlife it is the
usual belief, for those that do believe, that

there is this world, then the next.

The reality is a much richer tapestry. There are multiple layers of existences in the afterlife leading to what some would call Nirvana or Heaven.

We assume that heaven is the next port of call where we'll sit on fluffy white clouds playing golden harps. Think again.

Death leads only to the next rung on the ladder on a journey that concludes in reaching heaven.

We'll look at spirit guides, angels, everything in between the two and beyond. All the way to God, or whatever as individuals we choose to call the ultimate energy.

And for everything that I discuss from a spiritual perspective, I have also chosen to back it up by writing about my life. How I came to be who and what I am. The stories are all relevant to my life though I've changed some of the names to protect anyone who might not want to be associated with the book.

Just a little about me.

I currently reside in Harrogate, though I was born and grew up in Doncaster. I like to think of myself as a Yorkshire man through and through. Yorkshire being the county in England where these locations are.

There is no family to speak of. A half-brother is out there somewhere but there's been no contact in twenty-five years. My mother died when I was ten and I never knew my biological father. The man who brought me up, I bear his surname; we were chalk and cheese, and we hadn't spoken for years before he died.

I never met an Auntie or an Uncle who was blood as far as I'm aware. Neither did I meet a Grandparent. My mother was thirty-eight when she gave birth to me and back in 1960 that was considered old.

For ten years in the 80s I was married. A relationship that bore no children. As with most things in my life that end, I haven't seen or spoken to my ex-wife in a good fifteen years. I firmly believe that when something comes to a natural conclusion, you close the door and move on.

More than anything I wanted to be a Father but understand now that, to this juncture, God has had other plans for me.

My life is rich. Not financially - far from it - but I sleep well at night and generally feel all is well in my world.

I try to maintain balance and keep a happy medium, pardon the pun.

Just follow those basic rules.

Remove the frame to begin to expand your beliefs.

Keep it simple.

And there's a third rule. So easy, yet so hard.

Rule Three: Be Positive.

Create good energy and other positive energies will be drawn towards you.

Create negative energy and eventually things begin to go wrong.

In spiritual terms, positive attracts positive, negative attracts negative.

That's why when people enter a spiral of

depression it is very hard to find a way out.
So with my rules in place. My heart, mind,
and spirit fully charged, let's begin.

Chapter Two: Psychics, Mediums, What They Are And Mean To Us.

There are many people out there that don't know the difference between psychics and mediums.
This should go some way to answering those questions.

Intuition, Instinct, The Ability To Be Psychic.

We all have gut instincts.
Also consider situations that involve déjà vu.
Those times we think of someone who then rings us, or we bump into them.
These are both examples of psychic ability, though they can also be linked to mediumship.
The problem is that everyone thinks too much and that process gets people into trouble.
How many times have you thought, excessively, to a point where you've changed a situation in your head to fit what you want it too?
Those circumstances, being wrong, don't work out the way you would like, or maybe won't happen at all.
So more thinking is in order to slot yourselves back into your comfort zones.
But the more we think, generally speaking, the further away we get from the truth of our situation.
And all the while inside, our gut instinct

reaches out to us. Sending out messages of a reality we don't wish to hear or face up too. Thought comes from the conscious part of the brain, instinct from the subconscious.
I refer to this as creation's greatest anomaly. The conscious mind only takes up 5.75 percent of the workings of the brain, leaving the other 94.25 percent to the subconscious. I understand why this is so and the answer partly lies in our own humanity.
Also the brain serves as a portal to so much that we, as yet, cannot grasp.
We were created with a single mind, no conscious, subconscious split. I'm going back a few million years, to the beginning, or the beginning as we know it.
That time starts at the end of the Ice Age when we were first evolving into beings resembling something close to what we are today.
The same place where the Christian Bible begins.
We lived much simpler lives of course, and instinct was what helped us survive and further evolve.
Instinct was a more relevant sense than sight. That's why our eyes are sometimes referred to as the 'Windows of the Soul.' They were little more than an extension of that instinct, or intuition.
It's human nature to evolve through positive action, and, in balance, we devolve through negative responses.
One of our greatest weaknesses is laziness. In the bible it's reference to the eating of the forbidden fruit. A bloody woman's fault, as

usual.

Only kidding of course.

I believe Eve took the blame for getting Adam to have a nibble on that apple. Though only because the writer of that story was a man who had been getting an ear bashing from the wife while trying to write about creation.

But I'm getting away from the point.

After that apple, everything changed.

They noticed they were naked, so decided to clothe themselves resulting in expulsion from the Garden of Eden.

But this is what really happened - instinct and sight stopped working in harmony and the mind split, creating the conscious and subconscious.

All because we got lazy, cut corners, looked for an easier way.

And they weren't kicked out of any garden. They didn't turn up one day to find that someone had padlocked the entrance.

The 'Garden of Eden' is a euphemism for fertile land.

Instinct had always kept them there because it was safe. But, as we know, there are mountains and deserts, places far less hospitable, and while laziness caused the mind to split, another weakness made human kind relocate.

There's nothing wrong with a sense of adventure, but a compulsion to do something even though we know it's not healthy or right exists within most of us.

Yes, compulsion, or addiction in its strongest form.

Emotional compulsion can involve being with partners who aren't right for us.

Allowing people into our lives who bring nothing positive will, at the very least drain us, tire us out, and in more serious cases cause depression or a change of character.

Physical compulsions can be created through drink, drugs, even food, if we think in terms of comfort eating.

But physical/emotional compulsions throw everything into the mix. It can create a strong sense of adventure, but do we truly want to put our head in a lion's mouth or walk through a ring of fire?

The answer should be no of course, but all those thousands of years ago our ancestors left the safety of that fertile land to relocate to deserts and mountains because that compulsion to do something we know is wrong kicked in.

No thunder and lightening from above, just ordinary human behaviour. The free will to focus on what we want to see and what we want to believe, instead of listening to what our instincts are telling us.

Simply we are all psychic because we have instinct and intuition but those abilities are muted because we replace them with thought.

I'll spell it out again. Everyone thinks too much.

Instincts are powered by energy and the more open a person's mind the stronger that energy can become.

Everyone has an ability to be psychic but some will never evolve because they refuse to expand their mind.

How many out there will only accept what they understand or can be absolutely proven?

Then consider this.

How many times each month, weeks even, do we have an experience that we don't understand? Label as odd or weird?

If we just but admit it the answer is 'all the time'.

So expand your mind and try to begin to explore the possibilities created by the unknown. It's an ideal starting point.

So, simply, a psychic is someone who tries to live life by instinct, at least, as much as we live life through our thoughts.

Trust me, there is a place in your life for both and they are a good accompaniment to one another.

The Hows And Whys To Being A Medium.

Everybody in this world is a medium.

Why?

Because we have spiritual energies around us all the time, most of them trying to assist us.

We don't see them, generally speaking.

Many of you either don't know about them or refuse to accept them. But they are there all the same.

Energy can neither be created nor destroyed.

So before we were born the energy contained within us existed, and when we die it will continue to live on elsewhere.

A lot of people believe we come from the

earth and return to the earth and what we see and know is everything in existence.

I've seen far too much and constantly have experiences that prove unequivocally that this is not the case.

There are many theories as to why, as we get older, the years appear to pass by more quickly.

Our energies vibrate inside of us. While we age in time, those energies gradually speed up through out the course of our lives so that at the moment of passing, that energy is vibrating at a speed fast enough to leave the body.

For those of you who have watched someone die before them. It is impossible not to accept that it is as if something lifts from the body and that all is left is a shell.

Then once that energy is free of the body its vibration increases more rapidly.

I compare it to releasing a bird from a cage. Our bodies are the cage and the energy contained within is the bird. Once that bird is free of its cage it flies around in a much bigger space allowing its speed to increase. Once free of the body that energy vibrates faster than we can blink, that's why we can't naturally see them.

In fact they are moving at a rate faster than time.

Digital cameras take pictures with a shutter speed two thousand times faster than we blink. On many photographs we now get evidence of images known as 'spirit orbs'. So we can use that as an indication of how rapidly the energy is vibrating.

The secret to death lies in your dreams.
Dreams are created through your energy
and when the body is vacated, your dreams
become your new reality.
Certain groups of Aborigines believe that
'dreamtime' is the real life and the 'waking
time' is the illusion.
Maybe they have a point. After all the
'waking time' should last about four score
years by today's standards, but then
remember to take off at least a quarter of
that for 'dreamtime'.
Most of you will only physically die the once,
trust me on that one for now, we'll have
enough time to debate reincarnation later.
Anyway, in theory at least, who would be
mad enough to want to come back here if
we go somewhere better?
Essentially your dreamtime will be your new
reality for eternity.
Now lots of you will be thinking, shit, I don't
want to experience my nightmares for
eternity, and others will be screaming...but I
don't dream!!!!
Well, first off, everyone dreams. We just don't
always remember them.
Secondly, not all our dreams are what I call
reality dreams.
Each night the conscious and subconscious
minds communicate.
We have our spirit guides holding court in our
subconscious explaining to the conscious
mind all the things we are doing right, wrong,
and indifferent.
Our natural instinct is to go on the defensive.
Most people don't like to be told, especially

when we know we're wrong.

The resultant dreams can be confusing, frightening, frustrating, or just downright gobbledy gook.

You see we are working out our issues.

A more severe form of this is a nightmare.

Triggered by stress or the memory of a bad experience.

Then we have reality dreams.

If you dream of someone who has passed over, they are usually paying a visit. Some of these experiences can be more profound than others. It depends on how much energy the spirit possesses during the visit. The more energy he or she can muster, the stronger the connection.

Reality dreams can also be of our own creation.

Occasionally we tap deeper into other realities than we realise while asleep. These dreams translate into experiences where the recipient wakes up feeling wonderful. So much so that all they want to do is return to the dream. For most, a difficult, if not impossible, feat. Too much of a good thing stops being a treat after a while.

Essentially take that wonderful feeling, most of you will know what I mean, multiply that beautiful sensation ten fold, and you'll have some idea of what the after life feels like.

For most anyway.

Troubled souls don't always share the same rewards. Not to begin with.

Mediums communicate through spirit guides. Most relevant will be our emotional guides. They will usually be family members or people we had an affinity towards. It is not necessary to have met your guides for them to be around you.

Everyone has someone with them from the day you are born to the day you die.

Psychically we are linked to our mothers and genetically we carry traits from one or both of our parents. These bloodline links are meant to be more relevant in this world than the next.

Though children have spirit guides they can be less meaningful whilst growing up simply because children look to their parents for guidance, or so the theory goes.

Children who are orphaned or taken from their mothers will usually be more psychically and spiritually aware, albeit subconsciously, because their spirit guides will step in if necessary to help.

Likewise, children from unusual or difficult backgrounds usually evolve spiritually more quickly for the same reasons.

Ask a psychic about their childhood and most will have a tale to tell.

For most people however, emotional spirit guides take up residence once 'we cut the apron strings' and take our own path.

There are guides for other purposes.

A number of guides are educating me, providing the information that goes to make up this book.

Most creative people have a guide inspiring them. People in power, the caring professions, careers where people need to be in isolation or work alone.

Most commonly they send out messages that

effect us instinctively. They will put thoughts in our heads. Those Eureka moments that change our perceptions usually come from guides.

It's just that ego dictates that we will take credit for everything because it's too weird to contemplate anyone other worldly could be there pushing our buttons.

Random thoughts are usually put in place to try and encourage us to go in the right direction. Memories that cryptically resurface after any number of years are quite common.

We all have these experiences regularly, so we are all mediums.

It's just that some are more attuned than others in this art and more able to link in to their guides.

Those of you whose beliefs are absolute would still like nothing better than to be able to communicate, to get comfort from knowing your loved ones are still out there. Everyone can; it's all about evolving ones energy to become more attuned to those Spirits around us.

Alternatively you can visit someone who is closer to the finished article.

It's a question of finding the right person to fulfill your needs.

A psychic who links in to your energy, a medium who communicates with spiritual energy, or someone who does both, a clairvoyant.

Chapter Three: Doncaster, November 1970.

This is my starting point because, well there are obvious reasons that will become apparent, but from November 1970 to the Christmas of 1973 I had my first experiences of a spiritual nature.
If not for that time and those experiences, I may very well have followed a different path.

I was ten years old.
At that age, there is all future and very little past. I felt safe, oblivious to what was coming.
I lived with Mum, Dad, and this lovely old man called Danny.
Oh, and there was a brother, Ken.
Different fathers and he was eighteen years older.
Ken was a lot like Mum, just not as warm, or engaging. On reflection I think it must have been the age difference.
We lived on the edge of a council estate, across from a large factory, ICI fibres.
There was the time before and what followed afterwards. The time before is full of warmth, good memories.
So many memories before.
Waking up and seeing Gladys and Ernie, AKA Mum and Dad, asleep in bed. Remembering it clearly even though I could have been no older than two, staring out from my cot.
The first night in my own bed. A small framed picture of The Beatles on the bedroom wall. Something to look at, to help me get to

sleep.

'But I like Freddie and The Dreamers.'

Ungrateful little sod.

Mum used to sing a song most nights, one song before bedtime. Usually male performers though, Anthony Newley, The Bachelors. My favourite song of all, however, was 'Mr Blue'. Years later I came across a 7" single of 'Mr Blue' by Bobby Vinton tucked away in a drawer in one of the bedrooms. We didn't have a record player though, not til later.

First day at school. June 28th 1965, one day before my fifth birthday.

Dad worked hard, three shifts and most weekends. He was a fitter at 'International Harvesters.' They produced tractors.

Mum was a cleaner, on and off.

Old Danny was in his seventies. He'd go to his club every day, sometimes take me as a treat on a Saturday.

Though watching old men playing cards and dominoes isn't all it's cracked up to be.

Holidays. One week in Skegness, usually second week in June, Ingoldmells, adjacent to Butlins. I never got to go to Butlins and for years felt I'd missed out. A little like a poor relation.

But those memories were the best.

Falling off a wall and needing the biggest bandage in the world to stop the bleeding. Felt much better after Mum won me a cowboy rifle on the bingo. Would have been 1967.

Playing in the arcades whilst Mum and Dad went for a drink. Then sneaking into the club to sit with them and thinking nobody had noticed.

The Club Announcer telling everyone that 'The Flower People' would be arriving at midnight and one small child being taken home before he totally freaked out.

Hey, people cut their hair in my world; long hair was exclusively a girl thing.

So many memories.

The mirror on the wall strategically placed so Mum could see everyone's coming and goings.

A small black man would visit a house across the road most weeks. Mum would look up from her knitting, 'Florries having a bit of black pudding I see.'

Information is knowledge even to a seven year old and he became known as 'The Black Pudding Man.'

I once asked why 'The Back Pudding Man' didn't come to our house and got a thick ear for asking. You got a clout for being naughty in those days, even when you didn't know you were saying anything out of turn. And I reckon social services would have been handing out medals because that was good parenting.

Another lady who visited the neighbour two doors down. Little Shona. Fake fur coat, 4' 8" with bow legs.

Her place of worship was 'The Castle' and 'The Black Bull.' 'That's where that sort go,' Mum would explain. 'All fur coat and no knickers.'

I neither understood, nor dared ask. Why would someone who owned a fur coat not

be able to afford knickers?
One of childhoods enduring mysteries.
Years later I would drink in both
establishments and never found myself
accosted by strange, exotic women.
One question got answered though, very
much to my satisfaction.
'What happened to that lady mum, with the
funny legs?' Straight faced, that don't push it
look. 'Shipwrecked on a barrel love,
shipwrecked on a barrel.'
Another mystery surrounded my brother,
whom I never knew existed until he arrived.
Odd but true.
The best explanation can only be put down
to my Mother's quirkiness.
'How old are you mum?'
'Forty.'
That was it. Same answer year in, year out.
Then one day, about 1967/68 again.
'How old are you mum?.
'Fifty.'
She only drank two or three times a year.
Christmas, birthday, club outing.
Club outing was good and bad. Good
because it was usually anywhere but
Skegness, bad because of the travel sickness.
Quells, travel sickness tablets. I never worked
out what was worse. The sickness or the cure.
Only on bus journeys though, never on trains,
and we always went to 'Skeggy' on the train.
So the night Ken turned up it should have
been either mum's birthday, an event, or
Christmas, but I'm pretty sure it was none of
the above.
But dad had taken her out.

Twenty to ten on a Saturday night.

I'm happy as Larry because old Danny's looking after me and has let me stay up. And we've watched 'The Time Machine' starring Rod Taylor. Scariest film I'd ever seen but Danny said it was 'tripe' - his favourite word for things he thought were rubbish.

There was a knock on the front door.

People just used to walk in the back door, nobody knocked on the front.

I answered to a man who, while not tall, appeared powerfully built - like a bull.

'Is your mum in?'

'No. She's gone to the club with my dad.'

'Hello, I'm your brother, Ken.'

Now that bloody time machine was suddenly relegated to the 'whatevers'. Seven years old and finding you had a brother for the first time.

Nothing was ever explained to me and I never asked.

I pieced together that Ken had been in the marines. He'd also been living in Australia where he had a wife and a son who was a little older than me.

I realised later that I liked having a brother, but Ken was old enough to be of a different generation and didn't want the responsibility of a little brother hanging around. That's how it felt at the time.

Anyway he wasn't around long enough to make a difference.

Mum sent me to church every Sunday and I wasn't allowed out to play on that day. A woman would come and collect me and bring me back home afterwards. Church service and then Sunday school. I quite liked it.

School was different. I could sing, perform, possibly a family trait. Educationally I was little more than average. Every school report, A for music, C for everything else.

My entire school life became about avoiding confrontation, keeping my head down, I realised years later. Until it came to performing.

I appeared in every school production through junior school. Mum saw me play a sailor, an alien, Joseph in the nativity (fell off the stage). And the crème de la crème, got to do my own production, aged nine. Wrote the parts, sort of, designed the set, even more sort of, and starred in my very own adaptation of 'The Time Machine.'

The world of performing arts would have gasped had they seen the mastery of this production!

Ok it was alright for a nine year old.

The mystery, the enigma that was my mum. She had an illness which meant she had to avoid salt and was on medication for life. I think that's why she didn't drink all that often.

Her birthday was 29th February, a leap year baby. So technically she only had a birthday every four years anyway.

1970 was when my life changed forever. On the plus side there were three holidays, though little did I realise that it would be nine years before I got to go away again.

Not only was there the pilgrimage to Skegness, of course, but also a week in

Mablethorpe (rained all week and it felt like it was closed for four days), and a week away at Staithes with the school.

A holiday famous for my first real snog, Debbie James and she denied it for months afterwards, even though thirty kids and two teachers saw us on the back seat. Of course we got caught. She cried. I got slippered because 'young gentleman don't behave in that manner', and all I could think was 'please don't tell me Mother.'

She'd have had me down at that church before you could say 'Hail Mary', and we weren't even catholic.

It was the only time I ever got the slipper during my years of learning, but it was well worth it.

A bit of a downside was the world cup. Too young to appreciate it in 1966. I'd been encouraged to play upstairs with the neighbour's kids, doctors and nurses of course, and the first I knew we'd won anything was when they were dancing around the pitch with the cup.

So 1970 was the first biggy. Bastard Germans..bugger. Not all Germans of course, but football is football. Set a bit of a pattern did 1970. We'll not get into penalty shootouts. But then Mum went into hospital. She was in and out a few times. I never noticed the changes, but then I wasn't looking. She lost weight. In those days cancer usually meant a death sentence and she aged dramatically.

Both Mum and Dad were small in height, around five feet, and even at ten years old I was quickly catching up which, I suppose was my focus at that time.

I guess I was the only person not to notice. One day a kid across the dinner table in the school canteen smiled and said innocently, 'Your mum's dying. My dad says she'll be dead soon'.

By the time the dinner ladies got to us, the kid had a split lip, ripped shirt, cut on the head from a broken plate, not to mention copious amounts of mashed potato in his hair.

Funny, I got a clout for kissing a girl, but nobody did anything about the fight. I never even had to apologise.

Later I realised everyone knew what I hadn't been able to face up to; she wasn't going to be around much longer.

It was a Wednesday evening visit at the hospital.

The place made my skin crawl.

Dad was off talking to some Doctor and taking forever.

Ken was talking about 'a stripper' at the local club.

Betty, next door neighbour, had thrown her fish supper into the back of the coal fire in disgust.

Mum found this hysterical.

I noticed she looked much better. Glowing compared to everyone else anyway.

There were three other patients in the room and as far as I could tell they'd all had either an arm, leg, or both amputated.

Thank God that hadn't happened to mum.

When dad came back, he may as well have been out for a stroll to the pub. He never looked any different. Good or bad, his look was always one of indifference.

Shortly afterwards we left.

I remember thinking, looking like that she'll be home soon.

And I was right, sort of.

It was the middle of the night. Early hours of Saturday morning.

Dad said she was 'poorly' so I hadn't been allowed to visit her.

I thought that this was rubbish because she'd looked better and would be home soon.

Someone sat on my bed, ran a hand through my hair. I distinctly remember how cold the touch was, but there was no central heating in those days and this was the middle of the night.

I liked the curtains open and the moon shone through into my room.

She was framed perfectly in this half light.

Mum was home.

I smiled and she hugged me, squeezing me oh so tightly.

The breath drained from my small frame, because she was so cold. Probably because she was wearing one of her summer dresses in November.

For the first time I noticed she had been crying. She seemed to be putting on a brave face, but why?

She was home, here with me.

'You have to be grown up now.'

'I love you Mum.'

'I love you too.'

The tears returned.

'Look after your Dad and Danny.'

She got up to leave.
'See you in the morning Mum.'
I was suddenly alone.
Imagined it?
No, she was going back downstairs, singing quietly. I couldn't make out the tune, but desperately wanted to.
I got out of bed, ran to the door.
'Go back to bed, there's a good lad.'
'Night mum.'
I returned to my dreams with a smile.
The hospital people came at six twenty in the morning.
Got Dad and Danny up.
She had passed in her sleep around three in the morning. Pointless getting the house up sooner.
I was ten years old and lay listening to them talking downstairs. Couldn't move, couldn't breath.
It must have been a dream. Had to have been.
To this day I question the events of that night, some of them anyway. The one thing that would never leave me however was the smell of her perfume that still lingered in my room. Nothing exceptional, lavender, but it was something I could only associate with her.
I had undergone my first spiritual experience but was too young to understand.

Chapter Four: Sitting With Clients: Clairvoyance.

The first problem with clairvoyance, the primary reason it can carry a bad name, is because as many as ninety-five percent of those practicing clairvoyancey don't have a reasonable understanding of what they are doing.
To be accomplished at anything surely you have to know how your trade, or craft, works.
Appreciate what you have and be able to talk with confidence on your subject.
Everyone has some ability, but not everyone has the talents to read another person adequately.
This is a crucial facet of what we do because of the responsibility that comes with the job.
If people want to tell your fortune, talk about the future, then they should equally be able to tell you where their predictions are coming from.
And believe me, no-one in this physical realm can predict the future.
If I could I'd be a multimillionaire, with homes scattered around the world, and I wouldn't have to suffer the anguish of not knowing things.
Again we come back to psychics and mediums.
Many people claim to have psychic ability but not be mediums.
But as I've said everyone uses both abilities on a daily basis.
You see, while we cannot see the future, our

friends in spirit can see elements of what is to come for us.

Psychics usually use tools to help them make a connection to a person.

Tarot cards, though plain cards also can be used. Crystal balls, looking into a persons palm, ribbons, tea leaves, coffee beans, chicken bones.

The list is endless, though before we all start eyeing up those chickens running around the yard, you should be aware that all these tools really do is help us enhance our link to another person's energy.

We all link into each other's energy whenever we are around one another.

Being around some people can pick us up, others bring us down and tire us out.

Likewise, some people can make us feel warm or cold, trigger any one of the countless emotions contained within.

Sitting with another person will usually affect the way you feel for the time you are with them. The more sensitive you are the stronger the feelings.

Some people cannot be linked into in this manner.

If someone doesn't want to share their energy they can subconsciously create a blockage.

However that can be a good thing. If someone's in neutral they aren't going to cause you to drain in any way. Which is great, unless you are a psychic trying to link in to that person.

So if someone doesn't want to be read you will have difficulty forming a connection.

People have readings for many different reasons.

On a practical level it can be about careers, relationships, health. Though some are just curious, or skeptics not sure what they believe.

On a spiritual level everyone wants to contact a loved one, or are looking for proof that an afterlife exists. Whilst we aim to please, time has taught me that there's absolutely no guarantee of who is going to come through. Usually there is success but not always.

Anyone who's seen me professionally will tell you that I take my time. Not just with the reading itself, but the introductions too.

This is my preparation time. Clearing my head of anyone I've had recent contact with and linking in to my client's vibration.

If possible I step outside for ten minutes with music in my ears. Not always practical, but it helps me with my balance.

I always offer tea and encourage the client to relax. Light chatter from me and the chance for us both to settle down.

By the time I've completed this process I know whether I can read that person or not. I admit to being guilty of trying sometimes even though I know it just isn't going to work. I work through my subconscious mind and if I cannot link into that person, then there's nothing there.

Other problems can be created by the client's energies being reduced. Illness and hangovers the main obstacles. Tiredness through physical exertion another.

And let's not forget that I can have a bad day. All of the above equally apply to me and when my energies are at a low ebb I'm less efficient. I've become accustomed to cancelling clients if I get out of 'the wrong side of bed.'

And, despite popular belief, men are usually very easy to read. In fact there's probably only been half a dozen men in twenty years that I couldn't make a connection with.

You see while I cannot see your future, spiritual energy does have more of an insight. As explained earlier, once your energy is released from your body, the moment you die it speeds up at a rate faster than time as we know it.

So simply, we exist in time and they exist in a dimension beyond time.

So a gap forms between us and them in their realm, which will continue to expand as they evolve.

And that gap is our future.

Technically they cannot see the future, but they exist in a time beyond ours and can see aspects of our lives that haven't yet happened.

They describe it to me in these terms.

Our guides are stood on a tall hill.

We are on a path walking towards them.

That path is our life, or the life intended for us.

The point we are at is now.

Looking back we have the past and moving forward we have the future.

The more evolved our guides become, the further ahead they can see of our lives.

Spiritual evolution is obtained through

learning rather than the length of time passed. The more they learn the more energy they collect, the more they can build and evolve.

There are guides who will be able to see your life in its entirety and others that have a more restricted view.

Obvious question to some. If they can see our lives and the future, what's going to win the next Grand National and when can I have the National Lottery Numbers?

Did you imagine for one minute it would be that easy?

In order for material wealth to be part of the bigger picture then that path we are on needs to be clearly marked. Preferably with pound signs or jewel encrusted baubles.

For most of us that just isn't the case.

My own mother said something recently. She said; 'Certain events in life must happen. Other events will happen, and there are some events that can happen.'

This I found to be an odd statement. Mainly because my beliefs have always been that there is fate and free will and while certain events will happen, how we get between those points is where free will comes into play.

Certain points on life's path are clearly marked, events such as birth and death are obvious examples. However, there are more subtle fate-ruled points.

For a few years, in the 90's, I had it in my head that my path would change when I met a lady with a red Porsche. It happened and she was lovely, we just didn't have the right chemistry. She's now married with a baby and presumably very happy. The point is that she introduced me to Harrogate and if we hadn't met, I probably wouldn't be residing here now. And trust me, this is the place I now call home and hope to for a very long time. Fate.

Most people like to hold on to the ideals of free will because this gives them control. Power to decide for themselves.

Yet how many of those same people like to be led by the hand by others?

Worry about every decision they make? Feel so insecure that they inflict their will on loved ones to maintain power even though they know this is wrong?

Human nature makes us insecure and we are all children who need constant reassurances. We make wrong decisions based on control, or lack of it, and fear. Fear of failure, fear of the unknown. Fear of being found out. The shocking truth that we are mere mortals who will get things wrong.

So we make a detour, leaving the path that's meant for us and in doing so create circumstances and situations that we actually don't need to experience.

Then it's the job of our guides to help us right those wrongs.

We will get back on track because we have to return to have the opportunity to experience the events fate as in store for us. No-one's saying we won't make further mistakes and step off the path again. Far from it, I know that lots of people spend most of their life on the wrong path. There are some that would still get it wrong if the path was lit up with neon lights.

I've slightly gone off track here. Back to Mother's wise words.

So from the idea that there is fate and free will, we now have a third element. The leap from what has to happen to what will happen.

Simply, just as everything in existence has a hierarchy, so does fate. All things fate driven will happen. It's just that certain events need to be more precise than others.

If you are meant to marry your 'one true love' it is fated. The event will happen in the summer but could be any weekend as long as we're not still in the football world cup, or standing a chance of winning Wimbledon.

It's fate but not life or death.

Fate that will happen.

You've forgot your keys because you are thinking about last night and the argument with your partner. Absently you are further making yourself late having chased the cat round the garden because you caught it peeing on your plants. Two random events that mean you'll just be passing the house at the end of the street when the windows explode and a fire erupts. The right place and the right time to save the occupants who were not fated to die in fore said fireball.

Fate that has to happen.

There, however, is another kind of fate.

Missed fate.

This aspect of fate is huge in the sense of what it can do to our lives, not just in this world but the next. And it becomes more relevant later on, so please hold on to that thought for now.

With clients I follow one simple rule. If their guides tell me something, I can repeat it. Lots of people don't want to hear anything negative.

Well knowledge is power.

If there's anything bad that person already knows about then we can look for a solution. If there is anything bad that we don't yet know about, but can be avoided, then forearmed is forewarned.

Finally, if there's anything bad a person shouldn't know, then their guides aren't usually going to talk about it anyway.

If the news is all good you would think 'happy days' but then you might be wrong.

People do avoid good things as well. Usually, again, through fear, or the interference of others.

Another fact I've learnt over the years is that while I can get it wrong, Spirit Guides are always right.

Information, if not given with total clarity, can come down to interpretation. It only takes a spirit to be talking too quickly or not concisely enough for information to be misread.

When talking about the past, present, and future. I only know of a client what their guides choose to share with me, and their knowledge of what is happening far surpasses what you can read in a person psychically.

When you link into a person psychically, you are feeling what they are going through at that moment. Those feelings can change quite quickly, based on their mood.

I have a close friend who will tell you till she's blue in the face that she's not a medium. Yet she's very good at what she does, which is reading cards mainly. So I quiz her about her understanding of the future and she claims to see the future through people's auras.

Hands up if you've seen an aura.

Exactly. Not that many of you.

Some will never have an open enough mind to ever see anything of that nature. I don't see them naturally that often, but lots of clients see mine when I'm working.

The thing is that the aura is a reflection of your energy at that moment. The colours react and change tied to your emotions and general well being. So common sense dictates that as your persona changes so will your aura. In other words what you see is only relevant for that moment and not for the next number of weeks, months, or years.

So hopefully you can accept that our spirit guides are best placed to help us through life.

There are another few pointers to discuss however.

Everyone communicates with spirit.

They come in through our subconscious mind. When I sit with someone I've usually forgotten everything we've discussed within an hour of that person leaving.

In order to maintain a successful connection the conscious and subconscious minds move closer into alignment for the time that you are working. Then part again when you switch down. It is essential to switch down because the longer your energy is in alignment, the more drained your physical being becomes.

There is only one sure way to develop spiritually to become a medium.

That is through meditation.

Meditation comes in two parts. Intention and belief.

A person has to become committed to the learning process, as with any other subject we want to be taught.

I meditate twice a day, most days. Usually I fall asleep at some point but that is good. During sleep the two minds draw closer together anyway in order to create dream state. So nodding off is all part of the process. Plus it also serves as a way of resting the body.

There are many different types of meditation out there. In fact every time we lose ourselves in thought we are meditating. Meditation is all about finding a happy place in our mind. A place we can go to in order to feel safe from life's trials and tribulations, at least for a short while.

To talk to a spirit we simply have to think about them.

Through the process of thought we create the energy that allows them to come forward.

We visualise someone or something and in our minds eye that visualization becomes real. It needn't be a person either. It can be an object such as a toy, anything inanimate, as long it makes us feel safe and happy. Everyone can 'think talk.'

We talk to ourselves in our minds constantly. So just picture yourself talking to someone who's passed over and trust me, they will be there, listening.

To begin with it will be mainly your own thoughts running around your head. Sometimes you will think they're telling you things you want to hear. Events that may never happen.

Eventually though, you will learn to understand the difference between your thoughts and their words. It may be hit and miss for years. Sorry, there is no easy route to making the connection stronger other than the speed in which you develop. Then one day, you might not even notice, but these communication skills will have become second nature.

If we listen properly, learn to take the bad with the good, then our emotional balance can vastly improve and our true perceptions of life and people becomes stronger.

In other words, we can see what's happening around us more clearly.

You could visualise anyone but our emotional spirit guides are usually family members or close friends.

Visualising Elvis isn't going to give you the answers to your emotional problems. He doesn't know you, and if there's no connection, it's unlikely there'll be a signal anyway. Unless he wanted to talk to you.

But your Great Grandmother, even if you never met her, may well still be a strong link due to the emotional family ties connected to you both.

Another assumption people make is that once we cross over we become 'all-knowing.' This presumption can be a dangerous one to make.

There are actually a number of levels of existence beyond our own. I've written about this in terms of travelling through a number of different doors, though the shift, in reality, is more subtle and based on learning.

As we progress, our energies further increase in vibration to allow us to embrace our new circumstances.

If we imagine life, and death, as a video game containing eight levels, well we're on level one.

Spiritually, my guides talk about twelve keys, but we'll focus on this in good time.

Our spirit guides, on an emotional level, hover around levels three and four.

Whilst they don't lie, they can deceive us if we're not meant to see everything. Also they certainly aren't 'all-knowing.' Most, to begin with, anyway, are no different to when they were alive. The same beliefs, prejudices, and opinions.

Each new level of 'The Game' is reached through collecting knowledge, learning how to better ourselves, working with our energy, in order to ascend.

This, fundamentally is taken up by part two of this book, 'Everything you need to know to get to Heaven.'

Finally, when it comes to mediumship, it's each to their own. Different people teach different methods. Everyone wants their method to be right of course, because we all know best. Or our egos do.

If you find a teacher, or a development group, that works for you then stick with it. However, don't be afraid to change direction once that group has outgrown its usefulness. Everyone develops at a different pace and you'll know when it's time to move on. If something being taught doesn't feel right then don't do it. What works perfectly for one person might not work at all for another.

Take my own mediumship.

We are taught to open up and close down. I don't.

We expand more energy turning a light bulb on and off than leaving it running. So I switch down not off.

The benefit of keeping the links open is that I can draw in more energies during a sitting than most other mediums. Also each session lasts up to two hours. The theory being, if someone comes to visit you don't expect them to leave after ten minutes.

Another thing I don't do as a rule is use protection. Most mediums wrap themselves in a ball of light to keep anything negative out. A few years ago I would get caught out by this, but not any more.

If you tell yourself you have to protect yourself then surely you are giving energy, through thought, to a presence you need to protect yourself from.

But again, everyone to their own.

So that's how I do what I do. We are still only touching the tip of the Iceberg though. We will eventually visit those worlds of yet we

have no perceptions but not before we've
explored every avenue of this world and why
we are here.

Chapter Five: Dealing With Loss And Old Danny.

The world had evolved around myself and
my mother, through my young eyes anyway.
Everyone else was bit-part players.
So what happens when the female lead is
suddenly no more?
All those characters on the peripheral start to
grow or, as in some cases closer to home,
diminish in stature.
What more can we say of my small world? I
had never been allowed to venture very far.
Mum had chosen who I should or shouldn't
associate with. My friends were few but
'safe.' She had been over protective, but, to
her mind anyway, with good reason.
Next door lived Bill and Betty.
Sorry, I'd have got a thick ear for that.
Uncle Bill and Aunty Betty. Remember the
lady who had a dislike for strippers?.
There was a daughter who in turn had two
girls of her own, all living in the same house.
The eldest girl was my own age. The second
sister was two years younger; we fell in and
out like most kids do, but they were my
salvation for a while.
Several families had lived the other side of us,
but not for too long.
By the time mum died, a middle aged
woman had moved there and taken in a
couple of lodgers.
At some stage the year my mum had fallen ill
I'd started taking myself off too 'The Saturday
Club.' Kids pictures, under sixteens only.

The idea of a ten year old being allowed to get on a bus and go into town - alone - was much more common in those days. Normally she'd have gone into meltdown, but this was 'Saturday Club' and nothing bad ever happened there.

And that's where I went the morning my Mother died.

Going downstairs, the front room in darkness, three men sat in silence. Dad, Danny and Ken.

All of them keen to avoid eye contact with me.

It felt like I was the only one that knew what had happened, the events of the previous night fresh in my mind.

I'm ten years old, have just lost my mum and I had a better handle on things than anyone else. It was like role play and I had to pretend not to know, to go through the pain of being told.

To Dad, ' What's happened, why are the curtains shut?'

I'll never forget his discomfort. 'Your mum's gone to sleep.'

I wanted to say, 'Look I know she's died, I saw her last night before she left for heaven.' But what came out was, 'When's she going to wake up. Can we go and see her later?'

Was I being cruel, frustrated at being talked too like a five year old?

'She was very poorly and she went to sleep.' His brother's input. No better. No comfort anywhere in the room.

I remember looking to Danny for some sign of solace, but today he looked what he was, an

old man. Tears ran down his cheeks' Clearly he'd been crying for some time.
Enough of the game, if only for Danny.
God knows how the words came out, 'You mean she's dead. '
The tension was replaced by momentary relief.
Then, 'Can I still go to the pictures?'
Can't remember who replied, but 'Yes.'
Kids were a lot more innocent back then. But everything was clear beyond my years. These men could offer no compassion to a little boy. Whatever grief they felt was reserved for themselves. How the bloody hell could they comfort a child, especially one that had never had a hug or a cuddle off any of them?
That had been her domain. Maybe it wasn't their fault, after all she'd protected me almost zealously.
So I did them all a favour and went to the pictures. No debate, no argument, I got ready and left.
I held it together too, at least to begin with. Grief is an unusual emotion.
I never told any of my friends what had happened. Laughed and joked my way all the way to the cinema. As fresh as yesterday I remember I couldn't sit with my friends because the row filled up and I was last in line. So I found myself sat in a corner next to a little kid I knew from school.
That little boy did more for me than any adult during or after the event. He was about seven, wore glasses, birthmark on his face.
The boy's sister had a Saturday job there, at

the cinema. She was older than me, but I remember trying to get off with her years later and failing miserably.

Turning to this startled 'little 'un, unable to hold it in any longer, I said. 'Look, my mum died this morning and you best not tell anybody.'

I then cried through the entire morning picture show.

No-one heard the quiet sobbing but this little lad, you know what he did? After a while, he took my hand and gave it a squeeze. Some seven year old stranger had more of a clue than a room full of men who didn't know their emotional arse from their even less emotional elbow.

There was never an acknowledgment, nor a thank you.

Our social circles were very different. We weren't at the same school for that long; he transferred to the local grammar. He's probably forgotten, but for all my future faults and failings I would never forget the kindness I was shown that Saturday morning.

And no-one ever saw me crying over my mother again.

Not even during the funeral. Whilst everyone else wept buckets, I remained calm.

Not one of them deserved to share in my grief, or so I believed.

Mum had come to me that last night. My secret, something I couldn't begin to explain, knew they wouldn't understand.

Others talked about my behaviour.

One day, some months later, the neighbour's daughter during a fight said, 'You didn't care

about your mother. You couldn't cry at her funeral.'
I was usually accomplished with my comebacks but not that time.
Though deep down I knew it had nothing to do with anyone else.
Anyway there were new battles to be won.
Perhaps a child's resilience, my 'bounce back' ability came into play.
I reached out to my Father. Obviously he loved his only son, so everything would be well with the world again.
But there was another reality to face up to, something really obvious but unspoken. I was tall for my age. Dark, striking even. Everyone commented on me becoming a six footer for sure. Well whilst mum was dark in complexion, she was no more than five foot in height and dad was just about the same height if he stood on tiptoes. What's more, he was fair haired.
People saw me as outgoing, a chatterbox who saw the good in everything.
Dad was shy, antisocial unless he'd had a drink, and could sulk for England. Behaviour that became known as 'The Silent Treatment.'
So subconsciously my attention and small affections were transferred to a series of men who became father figures.
At some stage before mum died, Ken had taken up with the neighbour's daughter.
Every time I tried reaching out to him I was pushed away in favour of the girls,
particularly the younger one.
They all moved the following summer, setting

up home together. In one fail swoop I lost my brother and my close friends.

The one thing I did keep up was going to the local church. I found a certain comfort in the surroundings. And it was something mum would have wanted. I would do anything to maintain her memory. I even started visiting her old friends. After a while they may have got fed up of my turning up, but if so they never said. Every Sunday I'd go see mum's best friend, Aunty Dorothy, after church. It became a ritual for a while.

There was also a method to the madness. Danny had been in the First World War. He was eighty years old in 1970.

My everlasting memory was of an old man who would scream in his sleep. Cry out to whoever was listening in the ether. Over fifty years after that conflict and he still had nightmares.

After mum's death they became more frequent, or so it appeared.

Then one day, the same summer everyone moved away, I was sat watching television with him one evening.

I glanced across and was overcome with an icy chill.

Danny would be leaving too, very soon.

He smiled and sucked on his pipe blissfully unaware of what was to come, but I just knew.

So not being around home at weekends became a priority.

Dad wasn't all bad. I was clothed, fed, kept clean, allowed to do almost anything I wanted.

To quote him, at the time, 'Well he's a
sensible lad. Not much trouble.'
Out of sight, out of mind more like.
I was allowed to have a little transistor radio
in my bedroom. Jimmy Saville on a Sunday.
Top ten from five, ten, fifteen, and twenty
years ago, depending on the week. Listening
out for mum's music.
But what it was all really about was a desire
to know she was still there.
If she was, why hadn't she been back to visit?
My dreams, well they were just that. Nothing
special. No fantasy scene where angels with
harps announce her arrival. Nada.
I started to feel betrayed. A knowledge
locked away that there was something
missing. Quite a lot actually. Like a jigsaw
with only half the pieces on show.
Then I did have a dream I wished I hadn't.
Nothing earth shattering but it left me shaking
all the same.
I was sat waiting to see the family Doctor.
There's two, Burns and Hayes. I wanted
Doctor Burns who, while Scottish and scary,
always managed a smile and gave me a
toffee afterwards.
Hayes, to me anyway, was a twat. Ok, it
meant 'pregnant goldfish' but it was a new
word going round at school and it made me
laugh. Hayes never smiled and appeared not
to like children.
My name was called and I went into the
surgery to be greeted by Doctor Burns. He
didn't ask what was wrong but took my
temperature, checked my chest with a
stethoscope, and then looked solemnly into

my eyes.

'Now there's something I want you to remember. Don't let anyone tell you any different, your mother was a proper lady. You know you cannot see her but she isn't dead, not really. And she will come and visit you when she can. It's just that she's really busy looking after other little boys and girls. She always takes them to the two penny rush you know.'

I woke up sweating through to the bones and was off school for a week and the Doctor had to be called out.

Doctor Hayes, twatty twat twat.

The idea that she was actually alive was ridiculous but something I held onto from time to time. All the time the resentment towards my dad growing, for surely if she was alive he must have made her go away.

That day the Doctor saw two patients in the same house.

I was diagnosed with an unusual bout of flu for September, but the other patient had cancer in his lungs.

Unlike mum, however, Danny wasn't going into no hospital, not under gunfire. He'd survived two world wars and was going to go out his way.

He claimed the Second World War because the Germans bombed Sheffield and Doncaster wasn't that far away. The bombing was so intense it blew the windows out, or so the story goes.

If there was a medal specially designed for the dignity he showed, well he'd have been worth a bucket full.

Despite the growing pain we would sit together watching television. Me, lounging on the sofa, Danny, in his old chair. Puffing on that pipe that was a part of him, well what did it bloody matter now?

I remember feeling frightened, unable to look in his direction sometimes, knowing what would happen in the end, and wishing I could be somewhere else.

Selfish maybe but I had already suffered more loss than many others of my age.

In the end he was confined to bed, Danny's small family and his few friends constantly coming and going from the house.

The night before he passed I saw him for the last time.

I was going to bed. School was an escape even though it was cross country running, for I had games the next day.

Danny was stood outside his bedroom door. Pyjamas covering his emancipated frame, barefoot on a piece of oil cloth positioned between two carpets adjoined his bedroom and the stairs. Hopping from one foot to the other, grinning like a Cheshire cat.

I was alarmed but also found the scenario amusing. So much so that it was only later that I realised how wasted he'd become.

'What are you doing? You should be in bed.'

'The cold in me feet stops me thinking about me pain.'

Danny's smile widened, 'Your mum says she's going to take me t'two penny rush when I get there.'

A million questions tumbled through my young head.

For a father who never seemed to be there when it mattered, his timing was crap.

Bursting through his bedroom door.' Get to bed lad, Danny doesn't need to listen to your mithering.'

For all my frustration and resentment I hadn't yet got to the stage where I answered him back.

Danny passed the next day while I was getting wet and muddied on a school run. Though to call it running would be a gross exaggeration.

Fast forward to the funeral.

Danny's Son-in-Law saying a few words.

I was listening intently. More so than mum's funeral, almost a year earlier which had passed in a blur.

He'd been wounded twice during the Great War. Always been a character. He'd been a well known bookmaker at Doncaster race course, and a good husband.

I had never considered he'd been married, but he must have been.

His wife used to tease him when she was alive because of his simple tastes. He'd gone to the same club for sixty years and nowhere else. Never to a restaurant, never to a cinema, never to a pub, just the same bloody club.

Them were the days; he would have said. Once he was going to go to the cinema with Gladys and her boy but cried off at the box office. Stubborn to the end.

My ears pricked up. He was talking about me and mum.

More information. More knowledge.

'Your mum says she's going to take me t'two penny rush when I get there.'

There was a revelation to this cryptic comment; I found out much later.

When she was a teenager, every Saturday morning, mum used to take all the local children to the 'two penny rush', which was basically kids pictures and everyone rushed to get there and it cost two old pence to get in.

While I couldn't grasp it at that moment, mum was out there somewhere helping children who had passed and needed help settling.

I have often imagined old Danny sat in a cinema next to my mum and a hundred excited children. Though it would have to be a proper film and none of that tripe they make these days.

His words not mine.

Chapter Six: Energy And Vibration.

Why are so many people troubled in their lives?
Even when nothing is really wrong, we still worry, look for something hiding under the bed or around a corner.
Why do so many people go from relationship to relationship only to find they keep picking the wrong partners?
Why do we doubt our abilities, even those out there who can call themselves successful?
So many questions.
Everyday situations that most people carry, as a burden, throughout their lives and never understand why.
The answer, if not the solution, is simple.
Once again it's all about energy and its vibration.
As with everything in life, part of our journey is to work things out for ourselves, though I always think a little insight works.
Imagine a volume control on a television.
Now we'll remove the term 'Volume' and replace it with 'Energy.'
Now remove the image of the television and replace it with yourself.
Walking, talking, sleeping, eating, drinking, and all these actions being predetermined by your energy control.
You can't see it, smell it, taste it, hear it, or touch it. Because it's not one of the main five senses. Neither is it one of the many minor

senses we also use.

Essentially we are talking about an engine room that powers all of the above.

The most important facet of all it can empower or impair all of the main senses and be the root cause of many of the minor senses. Such as joy and pain and many more of the different emotional responses that we adhere too.

So lets look at our energy control and introduce some settings.

First of all divide the control into three groups, so we have black, blue, and white. Each of the three sections is marked with the numbers one to ten.

Blue is the middle setting and most relevant because that is the range where our everyday energy operates.

Black is the lower setting and represents negative energy.

White is the upper range and represents our connection to our happy places.

Let's start with our 'Blue' Settings.

Our everyday existence.

You wake up having had a restful night, and you're fully charged, so you're a nine at least. Maybe ten if you're fully healthy in mind and body.

Obviously as the day goes on we all begin to drain as the stresses and strains take hold. So gradually your energy control reduces. You might be a seven by lunchtime, a five by teatime, and all the way down to a one at bedtime. A lot of people need an afternoon nap or a pick me up later in the day to recover some of that lost energy.

But there is another important factor to take into consideration.

That is interaction.

For every person we come into contact with there is a knock on effect to our energy. We've all experienced this. After half an hour we can't be around that person anymore because they've tired us out. Alternatively we get together with someone and only after they've gone do we realise just how good we feel.

And this is because we share energy.

Even passing someone in the street can affect our mood without us even realising it's happened. Imagine taking a trip into town shopping. You feel really good. However, the longer you spend around lots of other shoppers your mood begins to unravel. You begin to lose patience, can't find what you're looking for, and lose interest until you just end up going home. Wondering why you feel so tired and haven't even got that one purchase you'd gone looking for in the first place.

Obviously it doesn't happen every time you go out, but it does happen. Beware the Christmas rush.

The reason for this is that energy is transferred from person to person, only a very small amount, but you imagine being happy and then mingling with fifty people who aren't. You only need to rub shoulders with them for some of their negativity to transfer to you. Likewise, you go on a party night out with a thousand other people all feeling great, I imagine your energies will keep revitalising through until dawn.

So we all have a blue energy control that governs our basic everyday actions.

Now lay the other controls either side of the blue. Black to the left, white to the right.

A little like bass and treble on a stereo. The settings on these controls don't drain the same as with the blue. They represent the negative and positive aspects of our lives and rise and fall depending on factors pertaining to our general emotional well being.

Ideally we want the black to be set low and the white high. If only life was a simple as flipping a switch.

We will be in the black and the white at the same time. Simply because there are aspects to our lives we are happy with and others we aren't.

Professionally you might have the best job in the world. Your friends might be the most supportive group imaginable, so your white count is high. Happy days.

At the same time, however, your marriage is falling apart. You have a medical problem which leads to mood swings, so your black count is equally high.

And this can again be equated to interaction. Like attract like.

If you are an eight in the white and a nine in the black you will be drawn to other people with similar energy. As the old adage goes, Birds of a feather flock together.

Opposing this we have someone whose black and white energies are both low, say a two or a three. These people are neither particularly happy nor sad. Just in balance. They will find it difficult to relate to someone with high end black and white energy. What they haven't experienced they can't fully comprehend.

Another thing to take into account is what happens when your energy alters. If you suddenly become much calmer you won't be hanging around those other negative people for very long, because you'll lose your connection to them. What was fun only a short time ago will suddenly become tiresome. You will want to connect to people who have an energy similar to yours and these friends will change depending on your balance.

I know lots of people have a real mixture of acquaintances who they just keep separate from each other. That's because they have people for all occasions and these are the people who are most changeable. 'Ruled by the moon' if you like.

So, I hear you ask. How do I get my white count high and my black count to reduce? Meditate.

Focus on the things that trouble you and ask in your head for help. That's what your guides are there for.

Clearly no-one's going to wave a magic wand and all becomes well with the world, but we all know when something's wrong, albeit subconsciously so we have the abilities to right our wrongs. It's just that personal choice comes into play and most people are afraid of the consequences of change.

Let's take this to a deeper level.

The psychic link we have to our Mothers as a child suggests that, during our early years, we will share similar energy settings.
And we do but only in a middle range. We have our own ups and downs.
Adolescent angst.
And that's where parental clashes really come to the fore.
If either mother or child go through a crisis and one of their energies becomes increasingly more negative than the other, then the child will have a personality shift.
This will be recognised either by the child playing up or becoming more withdrawn.
And trust me Mother, it will always occur when you least want it too, because the reason it's happening is due to some crisis that is threatening to break your psychic connection..
The next relevant link that can be similar to this occurs during relationships.
Two people meet.
Love is in the air....or not. I refer to this initial connection between two people as 'Emotional Heroin.'
Most people have been there. One night with a stranger and its got that 'Oh my God' factor written all over it. We've known each other forever; we must have met in a previous life.
Suddenly no-one else matters and your energy connects to your new found picture of perfection.
Then two weeks later the drugs have worn off and the prince/princess has returned to his/her previous incarnation as a frog.

This has happened to millions of people in millions of different ways, so why?

We all need a little excitement, something different now and again.

Most people aren't happy with their lot even when it's good. We get bored, become complacent. Even if you're all the way up there in the white and almost zero in the black, you'll still get fed up.

If things stay the same then we have nothing to compare like for like. So subconsciously we send out a wish/want signal into the ether. Make something happen.

Then we connect to a new potential partner, and the connection initially causes our white energy count to spike. So instead of a gradual shift it leaps.

We assume this is love.

Sorry to disappoint but love begins when those energy spikes have settled, and if your white counter has risen In the happy stakes then you might be onto a winner. That one special person you maybe can grow old with.

Most of the time though you'll wake up one morning, feeling like a total plonker, wondering where the rose tinted glasses had appeared from - again.

More tragically, though we all secretly love it, emotional heroin can really mess up our lives, looking for the next emotional high. That excited feeling created by doing something naughty. Looking for that certain someone who can give us that emotional spike, dismissing what we believe to be mediocre. That's why loads of women love 'The

Bastard,' and to keep balance in a man's case 'The Bitch.'

Nice steady guy comes along. Everything your parents would want for you. Treats you nice, says all the right things, loved by your friends. And you think, 'you like him, you can have him.' Common sense says, he's the one.

Emotional Heroin tells you a different story. Your white count might rise after awhile, but he does nothing to make it spike. You won't get your thrill, the fix isn't there. So the nice guy is cast aside in favour of the type of boys you were brought up to avoid..

And everyone knows the type.

That is also why some people never settle. If emotional heroin really takes hold then we can wander through life, from relationship to relationship, trying to recreate that excited feeling, believing it to be love. Then one day we're not young anymore and less attractive and we'll think back. Not to -the 'bastards', but all the good people we dismissed for their lack of excitement. You won't want to grow old with a bastard, at least not through choice.

But in old age we become more refined and so do our emotional addictions.

We go from searching for excitement to something more sedate. So yesterday's nice guy becomes today's most desirable option. Problem is, then they are all taken. Even though nice guys don't thrive in the single stakes they, almost always meet their heart's desire if they stay positive and believe.

Next we have the positive, and negative,

effects a longer term relationship can have on energy.

I always say to people who have partners, be there for each other but give the other space to be who they are. I also say that couples need to constantly communicate and should have at least one night every week for each other. Sod the kids for one night, if possible. We will all make time for a boys/girls night out, or to pursue our hobbies/obsessions. We can become workaholics. We'll let our respective families rule us; it's par for the course after all these years you'll say.

Your partner is always going to be the most important person in your life. And if they are not, then you need to look very closely at your priorities and whether you should even be together at all.

The problem is this. Usually one partner's energy is more dominant than the others. This can create changes in your submissive other. Great, if that dominant partner's energy is good and it empowers the other.

But what if that dominant partner's energy is depressive?

What if everything around them is negative? Then they'll drag their partner down with them. Strip away their own positive traits and drain them of what good they do have. The end result usually involves a lack of confidence and a total dependence on the more dominant personality.

The good news is that this effect rarely lasts forever.

Not many relationships last forever, and I don't believe they are always meant to. We can certainly love more than one person in a life time; it's just not that healthy trying to love two people in the same way, at the same time.

Gone are the days when women stayed with their men for fear of being judged harshly by others. No-one has to put up with bad relationships anymore. They never had too in the first place; it's just that third party doctrines dictated life's path.

Outside influences such as family history and perhaps more relevantly, religion.

On the down side, couples in bad marriages who do stay together are never happy. They are just too afraid to do anything about it. These are the people whose children and children's children can equally be affected through learned behaviour.

So we've done the family, the relationship, the marriage. So what about death, when a loved one goes into spirit?

Simply, the energy connection remains intact to begin with, though it changes.

Obviously we grieve, which affects the black energy levels, but keeps us connected to our loved ones.

Whilst we never forget that person, many love the departed as much as when they were alive, our energy connection does eventually loosen.

There's no reason to feel guilt; you're not falling out of love, and it's just that their energy is speeding up, the vibration is altering as they ascend. A distance is forming between you and your dearest departed to allow you to continue living your earthly life unhindered.

The same three energy meters. Black, blue, white.
The same settings one through to ten. But the size of the meters increases because the spirit has more energy than a physical being. And these meters will continue to increase in size throughout eternity as the spirit continues to grow through ascension.
One of the learning processes on the first spirit levels is to create balance and the white and black meters dictate our lives even more than they do here.
We carry good and bad within all of us.
The idea is to create balance, that way we appreciate the good, and learn to deal with the consequences of the bad.
And now, with no desire to further complicate matters, I'll introduce a fourth energy meter. This one serves as a link between all things physical and everything that exists beyond this realm and more besides.
The Golden Meter.

Chapter Seven: Friends, Neighbours, And Things Not Understood.

I'm sat on the front lawn doing my
homework.
Early summer 1972.
Dads on afternoon shift, 2-10pm.
Dinner is in the oven, prepared for me before
he went to work.
In lots of ways he was good. Life would have
been much easier if I wasn't around, but
there was never any suggestion of deserting
me.
 In later years, I would remember this, tendrils
of guilt creeping through my mind, because
whilst I wasn't cast out at any time,
eventually I would turn my back on him.
There were no more holidays or trips out
anywhere.
No real effort made at Christmas or birthdays.
Dad was good at the basics but not much
else, as though the bare minimum was all
that mattered.
Life is never black and white and the grey
areas can be difficult to grasp when you are
young and single minded.
After Danny's death, dad started drinking
more.
Don't get the wrong idea, this man was a
bloody hard worker and only had one
weekend off in three coming off the night
shift. But when he did go out he always came
home drunk. He didn't become a monster.
There was no abuse or beatings handed out;

he would just go to bed to sleep it off. But, not understanding the change, I grew to dread these moments.

A new experience and I didn't like to see him acting this way.

Yet another dimension came into play. Suddenly different women would start coming home with him -from the club. Always smelling of booze, cigarettes and cheap perfume.

When dad went out, for a while, I started going to bed early. Sacrificing the joy of the late night horror film for fear of listening to his antics if he chose not to come home alone.

One Sunday lunchtime, taking a page from dad's book, I was suffering a rare bout of sulking.

Those bed springs had worked too hard into the small hours, and this one had been very vocal. They were always gone the next morning though. Small mercies.

Perhaps he was more perceptive than I thought. 'I get lonely.'

One short sentence that was supposed to explain everything. Well tough.

But who it was actually 'tough' on, there lies the question.

Then there was the other great mystery which continued to perplex me greatly.

I continued to grow, in height and width, and was definitely going to be handsome. Mum had been pretty in her own way. From old pictures she'd had a look of Ingrid Bergman and the actress certainly had a look of mum when she was older. I loved 'The Inn of Sixth Happiness' not least because Bergman's character was called 'Gladys. Only this was Gladys Aylward the famous missionary, who ironically died the same year as mum.

I know I've already talked about this, but Dad was small and fair. We couldn't have been any more different in looks nor personality, and this niggled me, like a stone in my shoe. It just wouldn't go away.

Then, about a month earlier, I was playing football on the street with some other kids. Footballs were like gold dust. Oh everyone had one, but they were usually flat or had been burst. If it went in someone's garden, and it always did, eventually the ball would be confiscated, never to be seen again. So whoever had a proper football was popular. Today they were playing with a ball that I had acquired. People tended to give me my ball back when I asked, and didn't seem to mind me going in their gardens quite so much. Perhaps they felt sorry for me.

This day I was in goal, well not so much a goal as the width of the street. I wasn't that good at football anyway and being in goal was a no win situation. Not much happened and when it did it usually involved getting abuse for letting the opposition score. Only this day all the action was at the other end of the short stretch of street laid out between two junctions.

A voice, quiet but faintly recognisable. 'He's not your dad, but you know that.'

Looking round, surprised. No-one there.

My attention was drawn to the front bedroom window.

Old Danny watching me. Sucking on his pipe,

smiling down on me.

I felt the tears begin to flow. I became transfixed, rooted to the spot. Not sure which revelation to take in first. That my dad wasn't my dad or that Danny was back.

Then something flew past my head. The football. I returned to the real world to be greeted by half dozen voices screaming abuse at my stupidity for conceding the goal.

Ignoring them I looked up towards the bedroom. Danny was no longer there.

So whenever possible I've taken to sitting on the front lawn doing my homework. Casting a glance up in the hope that Danny will hear my silent pleas and show himself again.

I suppose I could have done my homework in his room, but that would have been too creepy.

The idea that my dad wasn't my biological father didn't register and was relegated to the back of my mind, though the stone remained firmly lodged in that shoe.

Anyone with half decent sight would see the obvious, but I chose to wear blinkers in those days. Always looking for the safest path to follow.

It was a while before I saw, or heard from, Danny again.

My affections were transferred elsewhere. Betty's husband Bill worked as a security guard at a factory ten minutes walk away. They'd always lived next door. Betty had been mum's friend, and of course my brother had moved away with the rest of that family. Ken visited Betty and Bill quite often but never looked in on us.

Frequently I would run errands for the neighbours. To the local shops or take a flask and sandwiches up to Bill at work.

In return Betty used to bake bread and cakes which she would send round to us.

The factory didn't have security as you would imagine today. No, this was little more than a mission hut where Bill listened to the radio and read the newspaper. In fact that seemed to sum up his job description quite well. Oh and he'd sign wagons in and out and check the factory was secure after hours.

Bill was in his sixties and we had nothing in common but that didn't stop us sitting together in the little hut for hours. I'd read comics whilst he lost himself in his newspaper. I had to make myself scarce if the factory bosses were around, but that wasn't too often.

It was a new escape from the everyday routine.

School was school, no angst there. My dad's behaviour troubled me, when it was happening.

This small hut, however, served as a sanctuary. It was great to be busy doing nothing. There was a sense of calm to this, equilibrium in the silence.

If I'd have known the word for this it would have been 'meditation.'

There were friends from school I mixed with irregularly. The local kids were a bit of a split between my school and the local Catholic equivalent. I quickly became aware that I was just about the only kid who didn't have a brother or sister close to my own age. Also that if I fell out with other kids they always seemed to have an older sibling or cousin to gang up on me. At times, it felt like it was me against the world. Keeping my head down, staying out of trouble.

Kids my mother wouldn't have allowed me to mix with under any circumstances suddenly came onto my radar, and whilst I always never felt that I quite fitted in, a boy has to have friends.

Many years later I would reflect on how different I really was. There was this sense of right and wrong that surpassed my tender years. It was second nature to be polite, put others first. The other kids picked up on this and teased me all the time.

There was always a sense of calm that would overcome me when I got upset that would translate itself into my dreams.

Even in my darkest hours, I always slept well, not least because of dreams that would take me to a wondrous place. I loved the Narnia books, and although I'd moved on to other texts, my dreams would transport me to this safe haven.

No, I don't mean Narnia.

Although this place that I escaped to existed in a world outside of our own.

A house. Who's size was beyond anything I'd ever seen.

I'd never go inside but would wonder around the gardens and walk alongside a river that ran along the left side of the house.

I was sometimes aware of other people

being there but never saw anyone.

There was another 'magical place' I soon discovered, this one very real.

Whilst the area's somewhat changed these days, thirty/forty years ago, Wheatley Hall Road was a hive of Industry. ICI Fibres (formerly Nylon Spinners) International Harversters, Sunshine Bakery. There was also a paper recycling plant and various other lesser known companies operating down there. Sam worked at one such place. Further down, opposite side of the road, there were other factories, not relevant to the tale.

Today, I am told the area has been overrun by car showrooms and retail outlets.

Every council estate has its dodgy families. The estate I lived on was no different. It may have changed since, but back then they'd move troublesome families onto the estate if no one else would put up with them. There were many more good families than bad mind you, but it was a tough place to live. Especially with no brothers or cousins to back you up.

So I became drawn into various petty larcenous activities or just plain stupid past times. I drew the line and never went beyond acting as look out, anyway I was a big lad and stuck out like a sore thumb. Most of the other kids were smaller, more nimble. Better equipped for running away from Sunshine bakery with trays laden with loaves of bread and confectionaries.

Further drawing a line, I would never accept any of this produce. Compared to today's activities this was mild, but in those days it was a big deal.

There was no drugs to be dealt, no legs to be broken as part of some protection racket, but we did a great deal of business with the vanilla slices.

Another hoot was to tunnel into the mountain of baled paper, until there was a network of tunnels running through it.

How no-one got crushed to death, on reflection, was a matter of wonderment.

Then one night someone had the bright idea of finding out what was round the back of the ICI Fibres.

Knowing this endeavour was wrong would normally have had me looking for excuses to cry off. This evening, however, I felt a surge of excitement run through me.

There were two brothers I hung around with, Steven and John. Good lads but my mum would never have let me hang out with them. They knew exactly where the hole in the fence was, in full view of the residents opposite.

It was a time without the means of communication we have today. Hardly anyone had a telephone in their own home. The nearest call box could mean a fifteen minute walk to some. So no-one could ring the factory complaining that boys were going onto their land. It would mean jumping in the car and going to the factory, and three boys weren't just worth the trouble. Anyway, as with the telephone, not many people on that estate could afford a car, not in those days.

I made sure I went last. More people would

see me loitering but if either of the others got caught, or worse snatched, I could do a runner.

Once under the fence we pushed through a high hedgerow into...a playground. Swings, a slide, climbing frame, one of those round-a-abouts someone had to push to keep moving.

A bit of an anticlimax really. Off to one side was a large hut and a bordered lawn surrounded by smaller hedges. This was the work's bowling club. The playground for the worker's children to keep them occupied, presumably, whilst mum or dad indulged in a spot of crown green. There was also a tennis court and beyond that a wide open expanse of green I recognised. Football and rugby posts were visible and in the summer I knew they played cricket on here.

Ken had thought it would be a good idea to bring me here in one of his more generous brotherly moments.

Beyond the playground there was an area of woodland. Well trod paths wove their way into the trees, and it was this place that became another haven for me.

Steven and John's interest didn't go much beyond the swings, but I wondered off into the wood before I even realised where I was going.

My knowledge of nature, even now, years later, could be reproduced onto a postage stamp. What struck me most was the peace and quiet, especially the further into the labyrinth I ventured. The evening sun was beginning to set, soft shadows falling across the places where the trees hung over the path. Eventually I came to a clearing on the side of what, at first, I thought was a river bank. In the distance, moving away, I spotted a barge. So this wasn't the river, it was the canal.

Instinct told me the river was situated the other side just beyond the canal. I discovered later that I was right.

Set off to the right I discovered an old air raid shelter that had been left abandoned for many years. It stank of all sorts and I never ventured inside more than a few times.

That particular summer I spent some part of almost every day there, at least for a few hours. I tried to go alone, avoided other kids when I saw them hanging around.

There was an oddity. The security men, unlike Sam they wore uniforms and had dogs, would be almost hell bent on removing all unwanted trespassers, especially kids.

I lost count of how many times they saw me, yet I was never asked for an explanation as to what I was doing there. Almost as though I was wearing an invisible cloak, the security men even walked by me on occasion. The dogs didn't even bark.

Years later I wondered if they'd felt sorry for me or whether there really was something more magical happening.

Dad didn't seem to miss me. Probably was thankful I'd found an interest.

For a few months at least I had some real peace in my life.

My time with Bill in the little hut and my time wandering around the sanctuary that existed

on my own doorstep were sheer bliss. Hey life
wasn't maybe so bad.
Even dad's idea of having fun was something
I learnt to cope with.
The dreams helped. They weren't real; I knew
that, but some nights I couldn't wait to get to
bed.
All was well with the world, but of course
nothing ever stays the same, and those
feelings were never going to last forever.

Chapter Eight: The Golden Meter, Often Tarnished.

There are many occasions when the content of this book has made me want to head for the hills. Trust me, I haven't just sat down and started typing. The concepts have taken a very long time to settle with me. Certain ideals and beliefs have been swept away, their replacements more mind boggling than you can imagine.

Everything worth doing well takes time, I've learnt that one.

The number of occasions I've put a time limit on completing this work, well, i've disappointed myself on countless occasions. The bottom line is, it takes as long as it takes. My subconscious mind will have always known; my guides will have told me.

Human nature, my stubborn side, dictates that I would fight this idea. A target's good as a guideline, just as long as it's my target not there's.

Three months was my estimate; that's the length of time I thought it would take to complete this work.

Reality is that the concept started as a germ in my head nine years ago. We can actually go back to childhood because I knew I was always going to write a book even then.

The point is that this book is channelled.

The practical detail is provided by high level energy. On our scale of one to eight, they are on levels six or seven.

Energies that were once people, just like you

and me, who have evolved, or ascended on the road to heaven.

Some so close they can see 'The Pearly Gates.'

Take the stories relating to my childhood, anybody out there want to adopt me?

Some of the more surreal details to these stories are provided by spirits who were around at the time, and even first hand in several cases.

The spirits providing this information exist on those lower levels, level three, maybe four. I refer to people like Bill and Danny. My mother, my stepfather.

You see it is assumed that there is this world and the next.

That is so far from the truth.

Let's go back to the concept that this world and every dimension beyond is like a video game, albeit an elaborate one.

Retain the concept of eight levels and the idea of the game is to get to the top level.

We exist on level one.

This is the only physical level.

Physical, because our energy is housed in our body.

Beyond this level our energy will reform to take on a physical appearance, but this will purely be an illusion. If you pass on at ninety years old you will be able to reform to take on the appearance of any age you choose.

One hundred years ago they weren't able to drive around in fast cars.

Until an object is physically created in this dimension they cannot have access to it there.

That is one of the more basic meanings to this life.

To invent, create, be inspired, so the rest of eternity can reap the benefit.

Each of the next six levels are all spiritually based and takes us through the realms of existence all the way to level eight which we know more commonly as heaven.

So if you hold on to the ideology that we go straight up to some divine place, well think again.

And yes, of course I'm going to explain all the different levels, just be patient. As Betty would tell you when baking, the ingredients have to go in the right order for a perfect pie.

Let's focus on our emotional guides.

They exist, usually on level three but sometimes can be higher energies depending on their own development.

Why not level two? I hear you ask.

Again, patience dear reader, all will be explained.

This leads us to another fundamental problem with our guides. The higher level guides have a much stronger perception of life than those not yet evolved.

So, in turn, our own perceptions will be effected.

Basically, the more evolved our guides become the better our understanding of life becomes. Their role is to share that knowledge or understanding, hopefully, to help make us better people.

But most of our guides hover around level three; they believe with good reason, so they aren't helping us the way they could be. I can see you all skipping to the relevant chapter now regarding this, well please don't, we'll get there when the time is right and not before.

Level two is the first stop off point, not for everyone, but those who were more troubled in this life.

Some of these energies will be there very briefly. Others, sadly, for eternity.

It can be a holding place for those who have taken their own lives or passed through actions of their own creation, eventually moving on at the time that was allotted for them.

It can be where individuals with mental health illnesses, or just plain antisocial problems go, in order to work through their issues before beginning their true spiritual journey.

Our loved ones can be around us, but initial access is limited until we've learnt those valuable lessons.

But this allows for an anomaly.

These spirits can still communicate with us, in some cases, and can cause trouble. I'm not referring to what you might think of as evil, though keep those Ouija boards under lock and key boys and girls.

These are souls of the troubled variety who struggle to move on.

We assume that spiritual energy is all knowing, wise. Well eventually yes, in principle, higher energies can be wiser than wise. Initially though we are not that much different than when we were here. No-one waves a magic wand and we're suddenly omnipotent.

We have to develop. So to begin with we will have the same views and opinions we carried through out life.

The only advantage spiritual energy has that can help is their ability to see further ahead than us, the future.

Even then it can be difficult to estimate a time period to go with these events.

They may see an outcome but not the where and when. They may assume it's next month when it could be five years hence.

Higher level energies don't make the same mistake.

This is where 'The Golden Meter' comes into play. While we interact with each other, our energies mixing and melding; we also interact with spiritual energy every day. Spiritual energy can push us way up on the white energy levels, but they can also adversely push us way up into the black as well.

Even those of you who have never believed in anything since the day you were born have to concede that, from time to time, someone can be overcome with feelings of euphoria on one hand, and pushed into the deepest pits of despair on the other. Yet there is no apparent reason or purpose to these mood swings.

They come and go with no rhyme nor reason. This is because it is not just like minded people who are drawn to us; certain spirits will give us energy to help us whilst others will take our energy to feed themselves.

And it's not the strong helping the weak and

vice versa. Unlike the properties of a battery, you have to understand that positive attracts positive and negative feeds off negative.
Take someone who has had a wonderful day, but feels a little tired as the evening draws in. Your spirit guides, or whoever has been around you, will give you the boost you need to continue because they will want you to spread the joy.
The idea being that they want us to fill the world with light. To build up a momentum so positive energy outways the negative and we all feel good.
Lower end spirits who simply refuse to evolve, feed off the negativity created in the physical world.
Imagine the millions of people who believe that when we die, we die. Nothing beyond this world.
Then they pass over and realise they were wrong. Well, still having many of their physical personality traits, they create a new set of beliefs.
It's great that I can look young again; there's no ill health, I can create a home, occasionally see my family, though didn't have anything much to do with the buggers in the first place.
But this is it now; there can't be anything beyond this.
This is just an example of course, but essentially that individual may never evolve beyond the level they arrive at.
Bloody minded in this world, bloody minded in the next.
Hopefully they will eventually get bored and

start to search for something more. After all, eternity's a long time.

Or maybe they'll come across this book, after all once we have it here, they then have access to it there.

The more energy they collect the more they can create, or build. The house needs a lick of paint, collect more energy to create the illusion.

But on level two, energy is limited and they use it to work through their issues. What's more, they'll be forever drained because that energy runs down so quickly.

This is why everyone's sense of timing is different over there. Everyone takes on the properties of rechargeable batteries.

As we journey through the realms of existence we are constantly expanding our energy source. We need to, there is also work to be done. The more energy we collect the longer we can operate, but equally the longer it takes to recharge fully.

In earth terms, the idea is to operate for sixteen hours and recharge for eight.

If we imagine our spiritual counterparts operate on a like for like basis, lower end energies may still work on the same ratio. Then they evolve and start to collect more energy. The levels on which they operate might rise to one week. A whole week without sleep, never feeling tired, at least until they start to drain. Then they will need to recharge, and this may take the equivalent of two to three days. So it's all comparable but the timing changes.

Higher end energies may be able to function

for tens of years without rest but then not be around for a few years while they recharge. This is why spirit's sense of timing is different from ourselves and each others. No two energies are vibrating at exactly the same rate.

But let's get back to those lower end spirits. They will steal your energy to use for themselves. They will feed off negative energies but can only be around a person who is sending out those dark vibes. They link in to worry, stress, addiction, which can lead to depression, or more severe mental health issues.

Lower end energies can even set up home in someone's subconscious and at its worst take temporary control over the host.

I know there is no scientific foundation to this, but then no one's ever explored this as a possible solution.

Multiple personality disorder can be created by a group of unwanted spirits setting up home in a persons mind. Allowed to do so because that individual, for any number of reasons, is energetically set at a constantly high level on the black meter.

Whether this ever will be considered as a reason for mental health disorders, well that's questionable, but trying telling me it doesn't make sense.

Make the unwanted guests leave and you are removing that personality trait which wasn't the hosts in the first place.

Enough doom and gloom. Very little is bad. While mental health disorders are very relevant to those experiencing them, they are in the minority.

For the best part, spiritual energy is there to help us. Carefully moving us from point to point in time to fulfill whatever fate has in store. Equally trying to help us in our decision making so we make the right choices.

For our part, we have to do little more than learn to listen to our instincts more.

Keep everything in life as simple as you possibly can. We don't need telling when something is right or wrong, but we tend to ignore the obvious for something that fits better in our minds, sits well in our comfort zone. Even though the situation we find ourselves in is far from that.

Also remember that positive attracts other positives.

Something that should be so easy, yet we all make heavy weather of such a simple principle.

Remaining positive.

It is said that for every ten worries that run through our head, nine of them are meaningless.

Worry solves nothing; it just makes the initial problem appear worse.

Positive thought attracts good energy, which, in turn, if we learn to adopt it as a way of thinking will actually provide answers to our problems. Even without the intervention of our guides, if we see things in a positive light we are looking at potential problems more clearly and are more likely to get the answers we want.

Unfortunately we will not always get the answers we would like.

If a relationship's over it's over. If you have created financial problems there is no magic wand to erase them.

Positive thought will help you find a solution that will make the pill, however bitter, easier to swallow.

How do you tap into this endless well of positive energy?

Meditation. Which will also open the door to our dreams. Where lies the first secrets to the afterlife.

Chapter Nine: Death And Near Death.

The banging on the frosted window was insistent.
Bang bang bang bang bang.
A voice shouting out my name, urgency in the tone.
It was Uncle Bill, yet it couldn't be.
A passage, ginnel, separated the two properties. Half way down the passage were two small frosted glass windows. The other side of these windows were the pantries.
For the uninitiated, a pantry was a large room where food was stored. The surface was made of stone, and the room itself had no artificial light. These could be found in most homes before refrigerators made their way into our lives.
 Because this small window was situated in the passage it kept heat and light at bay.
It was also good for getting my attention. If the neighbours knew I was on my own, and needed an errand running, they would use a broom handle to bang on the little window to get me to call round.
As I'd gotten older I'd learnt to ignore the knocking, in which case it was followed by a voice shouting out my name, or in Betty's case a shrill scream. Keithyyyy!!
But this morning, I was getting ready for school, and it was Bill.
A shiver ran through me, desperate to push away the incessant calling. Ignoring these pleas not because I couldn't be bothered,

I'd have done anything for the old man, but because it was making me, once more, question my sanity.

It was the third morning in a row; a shame dad was on day shift and had gone off to work several hours ago. Although such events never happened unless, I was alone.

The pantry was set into the wall at the back of the living room.

In frustration, I threw open the door. The banging abruptly stopped.

Silence.

Closing the door, shaking, I sat back down on the sofa to finish my cereal.

After a brief pause the knocking returned, more urgent than ever.

Again, Bill, shouting out my name.

Only this time in the living room.

But no-one else was there.

It was easy to assume that Bill had come round to see why he was being ignored. The only thing was, he had been dead for several months.

Heavy footsteps could be heard on the floorboards upstairs. Someone getting out of bed, walking round the bedroom, opening the door.

Danny's old room.

I paused between mouthfuls of sugar puffs, the spoon hovering between the bowl and my chin. My mouth opening and closing like a goldfish. Balancing the cereal as footsteps began descending the stairs, which creaked and screeched in all the usual places.

Frozen with fear, the only way to begin to describe how I felt.

The inevitable moment when the door between the living room and the hall sprung open.

Another pause before a relief of sorts kicked in.

Again, no-one there.

Had to be all imagination. Despite the door, despite the creaking floorboards, forgetting the knocking, Bill's voice.

Imagination was the only answer.

I'd not felt quite right since that warm August night when Bill had come into the kitchen.

'Will you go and get your Aunty Betty for me, I'm not feeling well.'

Today we'd have just rung for an ambulance, then rang the club, or sent her a text. But this was 1973.

Betty had never really gone out socially with her husband for years, other than the infamous club trips when we all went.

At least we had done when mum was alive. Still they had to have been together for well over thirty years, if not longer.

More recently she had started to socialise with a new male friend. To this day I couldn't begin to tell you what that was all about, but Bill was aware of him and seemed unconcerned. This other man would come for tea on occasion whilst Bill was also at home.

Mum would have referred to him as her 'fancy man.'

Though he stayed in her life for years after Bill's passing.

On this night I'd seen them go out together, it was August Bank Holiday Monday, 1973.

Another great mystery never solved. There were more pubs and clubs than I could name, so why always the same club?
Even before I was old enough, I started drinking at fifteen, the few times I went into that club I never saw the allure. There was no attraction for me at all.
Though by the later Seventies my action was to be found in discotheques. Working men's clubs were definitely not on my agenda.
As fast as my legs would carry me, I set off into town to get Betty. It didn't matter how fast I ran; there was still the wait for the bus, but at thirteen your mind doesn't always carry that sense of rational thought.
Dad had been out afternoon drinking and was on the night shift. If I'd have woken him up would it have made any difference? I knew years later the answer would have been no, but it didn't stop the question being asked at the time, 'Why didn't you come and get me?'
'Because you're bloody useless and anyway you were pissed.'
Of course, this was never said. It didn't even enter my head then.
She was there in the club with her 'fancy man.' Bet there weren't strippers on that night. Organist, drummer and a bit of bingo. She left with me.
Her friend didn't follow which saved for small mercies.
Betty is in her sixties and back then, though it's become a bit of a cliché, people of sixty were much older than their counterparts today. This is because we tend to live better

lifestyles. Also we have evolved. Our personal energies have increased in vibration, which in turn alters our perceptions of life.

But she's sixty and not fast on her feet so once we get off the bus, I find myself running on ahead and tell him, she's on her way.

And that was how I found my first dead person.

I'd not been there at mum's passing. I had been at school when Danny died. So this was the first time I'd experienced death close up. He was laid out on the floor; his head tilted, resting on the edge of the sofa.

I couldn't bring myself to go too near, in fact it didn't really look like Bill at all, but some waxen image laid out to fool everyone. I remember looking around the room as if expecting him to be hiding in some nook or cranny, though there wasn't really anywhere to hide.

Betty arrived home.

I was willing her to make him wake up, or at least tell me that my suspicions were right, and this wasn't him at all.

I almost laughed out loud when she removed her coat and gloves, and then proceeded to fill the kettle and set it on the gas ring.

Almost casually she sauntered over and ran a hand over his forehead. 'He's gone love.'

Once I saw the tears running down her face I realised that this charade of normality was for my benefit.

Didn't want to upset me.

'Go and tell your Dad. Ask him to come round while I go to the phonebox. Ring the Doctor, let everyone know.'

I did as I was asked.

You soon sober up when you learn of someone's death and dad did his bit, missing work in the process.

I didn't go back into the house, the sun was still shining outside, but I went to bed none the less.

And now Bill's back and I think I'm going crazy.

Forgetting all of my previous experiences. Mum, Danny, well we suppress what we don't understand.

So this was a first, at least in my mind. The same sort of thing three days on the trot. The banging, the calling of my name, lasting for no more than five minutes.

The footsteps upstairs, that had been different though.

By the time I'd gotten to school the incidents were always relegated to the back of my mind.

Kids are good at doing that.

The same day. Dinner time, I've left the school grounds after lunch and gone for a walk. A random memory has taken over, and I can't shake it off. Something else that I'd cast aside, stored away in my subconscious. It was a day out in Scarborough, club trip, 1968.

I was eight years old and the afternoon had been spent on the beach. I've been told to go and wash the sand off of my feet so I could get dressed ready to go back to the coach, so I'm sitting on a large rock trying to get the water to lap at my feet. Only I can't quite reach, my legs trying to extend themselves but flaying around just above the surface of the water. So I push myself a little further forward but to no avail.

I give up. It's stupid anyway. Ok, I'll wash my feet, but they'll only get dirty again when I step back onto the beach.

Getting up, I slipped, falling backwards, Arms doing the flaying now, I crashed into the water.

First off, I can't swim and second; it seemed no-one's seen me fall. I can hear everyone on the packed beach, but that's about fifty metres away from the rock and did I say I can't swim!

The water drew me beneath the surface. Eyes firmly closed, body still, as if paralysed.

I wanted to shout out, panic was the order of the day, but surprisingly I did neither.

I felt calm, almost cocooned, at peace. It overwhelmed me to a point where I could have stayed there forever.

Not beneath the water but in a room. A room in which I was lying in a bed. The room, the bed, myself all bathed in the brightest of lights.

I didn't understand this, not at all, but the feeling was beautiful.

Then I was above the water and found something solid beneath my feet.

Reality returned and with it the tears.

Shaking like a leaf, I made my way back up the beach to where mum was waiting, oblivious to what had just happened.

Did I nearly die?

I wanted to tell her everything, but nothing would come out of my mouth. For once I was speechless.

I stood before her looking like an idiot, mouth slightly open, drool dripping from my bottom lip.

I got a resounding slap round the back of my head for my troubles. 'You'll stop like that if you're not careful. Now hurry up, get a move on, they'll all be waiting for us.'

It was never talked about because no-one knew. By the time we got home it was but a memory of something that probably didn't happen the way I imagined.

But today that particular memory had resurfaced for no apparent reason.

So I'd broken school rules and left the premises to clear my head. There were times when I felt I was one on my own, no-one would or could understand what I felt or experienced. They'd say I was troubled, had problems.

Better to say nothing.

It was an odd day though, and I suppose I did feel troubled.

I went home to an empty house.

A note on the side. 'Gone back on a double shift. Left some money for some chips. Dad.' No problem. Homework, chips, telly. Good night all round.

Only tonight it was my turn to die.

There were no voices in my head. No more footsteps overhead. No-one called out my name, in this world or the next.

I got on. Did my homework. Half an hour of French and a Geography project which I gave up on after ten minutes.

There was nothing of note on the television.

It's one saving grace was that it was colour.
Dad had swapped it after Danny died. No
colour television coming into the house whilst
he was alive I can tell you. But if all there was
to watch was the news, a game show and
Coronation Street, then whoop dee woo.
Should point out there were no video
recorders yet and certainly only three
channels to choose from. Although if you
played with the ariel you could get a grainy
version of Granada which sometimes showed
different programmes.

So I started to read a book, in fact lost myself
in it. A book of short stories from school. I
loved English and all the different facets
involved in the process.

At some point I changed into my pyjamas.
Made a sandwich, drank several mugs of
milk. Forever going back to this book.

By nine-thirty I'd finished, and that was the
first time I realised I was still hungry.

The local shops were seven, eight minutes
walk down the street. Instead of getting
dressed again, I put a white mackintosh coat
over my pyjamas and set off to the chippy. It
had been raining and one of my slippers was
leaking. I knew I should go back home and
change but I wanted to get fed before dad
got home. After all, I didn't want to have to
explain myself, or worse, share my supper.

I passed several people, grown ups who
ignored me.

Then John, last seen on the swings near ICI
wood came running by. If he noticed the
striped pyjama bottoms or slippers, well there
were many a stranger sight on that estate.

The younger boy looked flustered yet
excited. 'There's some lads from another
estate on the shops. Looks like there'll be a
fight.' Looking me up and down, 'Where you
going?'
'Chippy.'
Carried on walking. Trouble or not, I was
getting some chips.
John had to have been talking out of his
backside.
There was hardly anyone around. Two
women in the fish shop. A young lad walking
his dog. A police car could be seen parked
across the road; its lights off, quite normal for
this estate.
If there had been any trouble, that could be
why everyone had cleared off.
I bought sausage and chips, wrapped. Better
take no chances.
In fact I was back on the street off where I
lived before I saw them. Two youths, sixteen
or seventeen. One, smoking, stood in the
shadows whilst his friend approached me.
It was meant to be menacing. 'Gizz ten
pence and I'll let you go.'
For some reason I found myself laughing out
loud. This lad was older but no bigger.
As mother would say, 'If in doubt, give 'em a
clout.'
Then I remembered he wasn't alone. There
was no face to the other youth, but the
cigarette glow made him look dangerous.
So, head down, newspaper wrapping almost
pressed under my armpit; I walked on
ignoring my tormentor, hoping he'd leave
me alone.

A pain ran through my shoulder where I was punched.

Startled, I turned face on to the youth. A second blow sent me crumbling to the pavement, followed by a momentary burning pain in my upper abdomen.

Rational thought would suggest curling up in a ball ready for the kicking that was to come. But all that was in my head was...he's not having my sausage and chips.

John appeared from behind me. He was not alone.

'Who is he?'

A voice I didn't recognise.

'Here hold these and don't lose 'em.'

Someone was talking about my supper, but I didn't realise this.

A punch was thrown and my adversary fell to the floor.

I felt dazed, which was ridiculous because I hadn't been hit, not really.

In the brief commotion that followed, the Interlopers both took a good hiding before being allowed to run off into the night.

I got up, remembered feeling faint. Drawing in deep breaths, only finding this difficult.

John and three older youths from the estate looked concerned.

'There's blood on your coat.

'It'll be his.' an attempt at bravado, shouting out, 'Bastards.'

'There's loads of blood.'

I looked down at the red substance, seemingly taking on a life of its own.

Inspecting the blood more carefully, I realised it looked serious. I opened my coat; half a broken milk bottle was jutting from my midriff, the wound pumping out copious amounts of amber fluid.

I'm sure my last thoughts before I fainted had some bearing on where my chips would end up. Shock, I suppose.

That was the first time I officially died.

Chapter Ten: Meditation.

Communication with spiritual energy, mediumship.
The tag line could be; you don't need to be a medium to talk to the dead, but it helps.
They are talking to us all the time; it's just that we aren't listening. Not all that often anyway.
So how do I listen to my guides, you are asking?
How can I get them to help me when everything seems to be going wrong?
First of all, they might have certain advantages over us, but they cant breathe life into your failing business.
Nor can they make your ex-partner love you again.
That's life and nothing stays the same forever.
Changes occur because we grow. Our views and emotional connections evolve.
Couples outgrow each other, and if a business is unable to move with the times, well everything as to have a shift, even if it's a subtle one.
A friend has been pining for her ex-partner, who quite frankly has been a prat. All she wants to hear is that he's coming back. I told her from day one it might not work because he was very selfish and adverse to long term commitment. Words that were proven to be all too true.
So, he's been gone for six months and she's still not moving on. A circumstance that is now compounding on her own children.

She's so wrapped up in her own angst she is forgetting some of her responsibilities.
Suddenly you have to question just how selfish SHE has become.
I get a message telling me she's been sat in a darkened room, focusing on her mum and grandma, both dear departed.
She needs answers, but they don't seem to be there for her. So now she's even more distraught.
Well first off, she doesn't meditate properly or regularly. Once in a blue moon and only when she wants something.
Secondly, the relationship is over. Time to move on with life.
If her mother or grandmother pop in and tell her that, she'll either get more upset or won't believe it.
Meditation is a two way street.
Is it not wrong to ring a friend only when you want something?
Should you not first ask that friend how they are doing?
Now replace the concept of that person being a friend with a family member who has passed and you get the picture. They may be in a different dimension but surely the first thing to do is say hello and ask how they are doing.
We associate meditation with good news.
Life is not that straight forward.
It's not just about getting to hear what we want to hear. It's also about learning to deal better with those situations that don't work in our favour. Giving us the strength to move forward, open a new door.

It's the difference between saying 'The relationship is over, move on.' or saying 'The relationship is over, you need six months to get over the hurt; but then you will meet the true love of your life.'

It's the reassurance that whilst bad things happen to good people; life is in balance, and the good will come round again.

I should point out that it's not measured in years, but events.

One moment of bliss or compassion can replace five years of drudgery.

We have a subconscious trigger that helps us forget the rubbish once it's replaced with something better. Ok, the hurt remains in our subconscious, but the mechanism for dealing with that pain kicks in and we find the strength to move on.

We have to deal with reality.

Our guides will try and help us, but not with false hope and lies. Even if they, temporarily, make us feel better about the situation.

The idea of meditation is to enable our guides to pass on information that will empower our lives. Help us deal with problems that confront us and show us the best way to move forward with our personal development.

I'll let you into a little secret.

While sleeping we are all meditating, only on a much stronger level. Remember, whilst asleep our two minds come closer together enabling our guides to communicate with us. Many people worry that they will fall asleep after they put themselves into a meditation.

I say, stop worrying; it's all part of the process.

Whilst we may be unaware of communication taking place when sleeping, it can be because our guides are storing information into our subconscious.
Knowledge for another time.
I've had an awareness of an event to come in my life for the past eighteen months.
I tapped into this knowledge before it became relevant; it still isn't.
But the result is two fold.
First I believed the circumstances were meant to happen more quickly. As a knock on from that, I pushed the issue and messed things up.
From that, it makes getting on with life more difficult at times because I'm now waiting for the situation to right itself and everything to happen properly.
Information is good if we know every detail. If we can only see half the picture how can we know where we are meant to end up?
Meditating means different things to each of us.
Some have it down to an art form. I can flick a switch in my head and be there. Great for boring plane and train journeys. This takes time to master, but it's a brilliant tool.
Especially if you want to switch off from those annoying people who tend to inflict themselves on us during such commutes.
There are others who have to follow a process to achieve the state of mind that allows them to interact. They may even suggest that the way I meditate isn't the right way. That I cannot possibly be interacting properly. Well, it's each to their own, and

there are no hard and fast rules. I used to have to visualise to make a connection, but I have a direct line these days.

There are some very good teachers out there, but you have to find someone that's right for you. The methods that suit one person might not feel right to you, and if you don't feel at ease the process will not be so effective.

Meditation involves opening up the body's energy points to help make a connection with spirit. The process also helps to align us because each energy point opens us up to fixing any problems created within our energy.

There are many different forms of meditation and many good books specifically aimed at this area.

As we have so much ground to cover on this journey I'm going to talk you through the meditation I show people who want to learn. I find this to be very powerful and the results almost immediate.

It involves 'Chakra spinning.'

'Chakra' is a Sanskrit word meaning wheel or disc. Chakras are energy centers positioned through out the body, primarily from the base of your spine to the crown of your head; each point can be identified, in the mind, as circular discs, or wheels of light, spinning.

Purists will tell you there are seven energy points, and they each should be spun in certain directions to achieve the right results. I say to people; it doesn't matter which way they are turning, as long as they are running smoothly. They will spin in the direction that's relevant to you at any given time.

Again the purists would disagree, but if they spin clockwise then the issues in that area of your life are based more in the present and future. If they spin anti-clockwise, then you are dealing with issues that started some time ago, even if they are affecting you now.

As with the senses, five major but many more minor, there are major and minor chakras. We will focus on getting the seven major chakras spinning, but there are many more minor chakra networks running through our body.

For instance, if the first major chakra is set at the base of the spine does that suggest there are no connections to our lower extremities. Of course not.

Energy runs through our entire being; it helps bind the molecules together.

Imagine a network of energies, not just running through our main frame, but through each individual limb. We can break it down further and focus on a complex number of tiny energy points in each joint.

That's why aches and pains can focus on single joints or isolated areas of the body and not always your whole being. Though this can have a knock on effect and the whole chakra system can become affected.

For the purposes of the meditation we will stick to the basics, the seven primary chakras. Each energy point has its own unique properties and meaning. It is easy to focus on one point if necessary to rectify an area that might hold a problem for us. You'll soon find out because as you set your discs spinning, if there is a problem, you will find it more difficult to visualise that chakra moving properly.

As we picture something in our minds eye, we give it the energy to become real for the time its with us. Be it a person who has passed, a situation we would like to have resolved, or an energy center in your body. We start from the base and work our way up, opening each of the seven energy centers. Eventually, once we reach the crown chakra, we can allow spiritual energy to enter our minds to help us understand events currently affecting our lives. Equally we may just wish to invite energies in to pay a visit. It doesn't always have to be overly significant issues we focus on.

Just remember, at the end of the session to close your energy centers down again. Failure to do so can lead to your emotions being more sensitive as your energies remain enhanced. This can make dealing with everyday matters more difficult. Although if you meditate before going to sleep at night your energies close themselves down.

So, to begin, sit in a comfortable chair or lie down if preferred.

Focus for a moment on your breathing. Make sure your breaths are relaxed and even. The calmer your body, the better the experience you are going to have.

Now working from the base chakra up to the crown chakra we are going to set each energy disc spinning. Don't try and push them in any given direction, just let the discs spin in their own way.

Each energy point can be represented by a colour and is connected to a different energy centre.

Root Chakra.
Positioned at the base of the spine.
Colour: Red.
Element: Earth.
Once open, this chakra grounds us and connects us to the Earth. It gives us a sense of belonging.

Sacral Chakra.
Positioned in the lower abdomen, below the navel.
Colour: Orange.
Element: Water.
Focuses on our health, sexuality, and emotions.

Solar Plexus Chakra.
Positioned at the point of the solar plexus.
Colour: Yellow.
Element: Fire.
This area focuses on our personal sense of power. Our confidence, or lack of it.

Heart Chakra.
Positioned around the heart.
Colour: Green.
Element: Air.
This chakra creates balance. The ability to look at others with compassion, and give us the means to love ourselves.

Throat Chakra.

Positioned around the throat.
Colour: Light Blue.
Element: Sound.
This point is all about communication. The ability to express ourselves properly.

Third Eye Chakra.
Positioned on the forehead. A point between the eyebrows.
Colour: Violet.
Element: Light.
This opens us up to our inner eye.
Subconsciously, we have the answers to most of our situations and, used properly, this can allow us to access that information.

Crown Chakra.
Positioned on the top of the head, radiating upwards.
Colour: White.
Element: Thought.
When balanced, this chakra allows us to communicate with spirit.

So focus on each energy point individually, set them spinning, and once you get to turning on the top tap, well enjoy the ride.
Some of you will find that nothing much happens. This will be because one or more of your other energy points are not spinning properly.
You might not think that by visualising on something that such a problem could exist, but try it and see.
If one energy centre isn't working properly then quite simply you need to focus on that

point more. Picture it spinning for longer. Eventually it will get easier and with it so will any problems associated with that area.

You might not think there is an issue, but there will be somewhere, your energies are telling you.

As I have stated, don't worry about nodding off. It usually means you've attained a certain state of relaxation, and achieving that for some people can be a feat on its own.

Chapter Eleven: Stepping Out OF Time.

I find myself walking in a field.
I don't know how I arrived at this place, don't
particularly care.
I'm faced by the brightest green I have ever
seen. More like a painting and the artists
gone for vibrant colours over more subtle
tones. Only there's nothing ugly about this
scene, quite the opposite.
I am overcome with the serenity of where I
am. The beauty of this place, breathtaking.
The grass is long, tickling my legs as high up
as my knees.
Overhead the largest sun I've ever seen
beats down. So huge the sky is more orange
than blue. Cloudless too.
I'm too in awe to notice how temperate it is.
A sun that size and it should be very hot, but
it's comfortable.
I'm wearing shorts and a T-shirt, and I'm
barefoot, something that under normal
circumstances would bother me.
Get my feet dirty and I might have to wash
them somewhere. Dread starts to descend at
this thought.
The concern lifts, banished from my mind, to
be replaced by....Sunday dinner. Roast Beef,
Yorkshire pudding. The smell wafts up my
nostrils on the same slight breeze that
continues to allow the grass to tease me.
Looking around for the source of this delight is
pointless. All I can see in any direction is grass.
There is a probability that I'm lost but don't

feel none of the concern that comes with
this. The setting is too perfect to be anything
other than safe.
'Over here.' A girl's voice shouting to me,
calling out my name. No, a name yes, but
not mine.
'Christian'.
Not from one direction however, but
seemingly from everywhere at once.
'Hello. Where are you? I can't see you.'
'Over here, follow my voice.'
I find myself laughing. Something I don't do
all that often. In fact I couldn't remember the
last time I felt this way.
'I can't see you. Are you hiding?'
The girl's voice, almost musical. 'Of course
not, Silly Billy.'
Looking around, I could still see nothing but
grass, and the smell of my favourite dinner,
making me hungry.
'Where am I?'
No answer.
I found myself breaking into a run. I knew
nothing of the direction I went in, but instincts
had taken over.
As if someone's flicked a switch, I can
suddenly hear flowing water. Not a torrent,
but a tide ebbing and flowing.
I run faster, ignoring my lack of footwear.
Anyway, nothing's going to hurt me here.
I don't think I can stop laughing. I'm aware
I'm running faster than I've ever ran before
and I'm still not getting out of breath.
A surge of energy courses through my very
being raising me up to a point where I feel I
could fly.

Suddenly I step out onto a path and the field is no longer in vision, before me lies a beautiful stretch of golden beach.

In the distance I can hear seagulls but they, like the mysterious girl, are nowhere to be seen.

There is, however, a large group of people on the beach.

The tide seems to be coming in, but there is a mixture of young and older people playing in the water.

The younger children are paddling, ploughing the shallower depths.

In the deeper waters some adults are swimming, and further, in the distance, I can make out several boats.

Sailing boats with masts.

Though I recognise none of these people, a small group gathered around deckchairs become aware of my arrival and begin to wave.

'Behind you.' Teasing.

I turn around. If I'd been an Ice cream I would have instantly melted.

She is tall, slim built, raven haired, and the most beautiful girl I've ever seen. Well grown-up really, she had to be sixteen at least.

The simple beauty of her smile reduces me to tears.

Nothing could have held back the flood. This was seriously the most gorgeous woman ever created. There wasn't anyone I'd ever seen that came close, though I am still only thirteen.

The tears are tears of joy.

'You shouldn't be here Christian. You're not

meant....never mind, let's take a walk.'
With that she took my right hand, and I
allowed myself to be led as if I were a much
smaller child.
I wanted to correct her, tell her my real
name, but could only muster a thought, 'Who
are you?'
'My name's Hailey, and you are Christian.
There's the name given to you by your
mother and the name I know you by. You'll
always be Christian to me.'
I'd been called many things. Dad often
referred to me as 'lad.' There were
nicknames. Magnus, don't ask, and Winker.
To my knowledge no-one had ever referred
to me as Christian. Yet it sat well, gave me a
sense of completeness.
'Where are we going? How do you know
me?'
A hundred, no, a thousand questions.
'And where are we?'
Hailey's laughter was gentle. 'You're home
Christian. This is where you once lived, at least
until you chose to move on. And one day
you'll live here again.'
We turn onto a street that comes upon us
from nowhere, leading away from the path
and the fields and the sea.
A tree lined street. No cars. No visible sign of
houses, but I'm only noticing the right side of
the road. The side we are walking on with its
high wall barely visible through the green
leaves and branches.
Neither of us speaks. No words seem
necessary.
I'm too young to understand these strange

feelings that have a hold on me but anyone old enough to understand would explain to me that I'm in love.

This isn't a concept I can begin to grasp yet, so I'm oblivious to any feelings she may, or may not, have for me.

A wrought iron set of gates come into view. Taller than both of us and apparently locked.

'Oh.' Hailey is clearly surprised. 'We might have to go back.'

'Back? Back where?' trying not to sound panicked.

The real fear lay in leaving this girl and the way she made me feel.

Hailey stops still, like a statue.

She seems to be communicating to someone through thought, seemingly lost to me for a moment, all the while though holding my hand in a warm but vice like grip.

Whilst she does this, I begin to feel something familiar about this house. I know through the gates there will be a river that runs down the left side of the property.

She suddenly snaps out of her trance, looks down at me with a mixture of relief and regret. Yet the smile remains, more beautiful than ever. 'We'll meet again soon Christian, promise, sooner than soon if possible.'

'But...' I was about to protest when she let go her grip on my hand...

'Thought we'd lost him there.'

Pain burnt into my abdomen and I was shaking like a leaf. My head ached and leaning to the side I threw up onto the ambulance floor.

'Bloody hell lad.' The same paramedic.
I remember laughing through the pain, something tickled me but wasn't sure what it was. There was a memory, images already fading into my subconscious. Not gone but stored away for a rainy day.

I felt a needle going into my arm and was thankful when sleep took me back, hopefully to some better place.

As far as I'm aware there was nothing in the local newspaper.

If there had been the headline would probably have read, 'Youth stabbed in gang fight.'

An exaggeration in anyone's language, especially as the headline should have read 'Youth stabbed in gang fight, wearing pyjamas and slippers.'

Only I wasn't stabbed of course. I'd been knocked to the ground and impaled myself on a broken milk bottle. The youth was guilty of nothing more than pushing me over. It could have happened to anyone who happened to stumble and fall in that place. Sometimes the truth is just too stupid to print.

The police interviewed me several times over the ten days I was in hospital. Different policemen, same questions. Descriptions of the youths. Did I know them prior to the incident?

No, no, no, and bloody no. I just wanted to be left alone to suffer in peace.

Whilst the bottle hadn't cut me anywhere too serious, the wound to my abdomen had managed to become infected, and they were concerned about it enough to keep me on an observation ward. Also, whilst it was never talked about, and I never brought it up, I knew I had nearly died, the paramedics' words haunting me.' 'Thought we had lost him there.'

My heart had stopped beating for maybe a matter of seconds, the shock I suppose. Fortunately this occurred on the way to hospital and not whilst I was being watched over by a group of youths greedily tucking in to sausage and chips.

A woman had rung for an ambulance from a private number but didn't want to be further involved.

Dad, well he was just dad. Did just enough. Visited every day and brought comics and school books.

Great idea dad, but nah. Too ill to look at history books but Batman doesn't hurt my head too much.

To the hospital staff I was a nice lad, and they couldn't understand how I could get caught up in that sort of behaviour. Though someone, very verbally, suggested I'd one day end up face down in a gutter. Once a villain always a villain. Never to my face, but always within earshot.

'I was wearing my pyjamas for Christ's sake, what sort of villain does that make me?' though I never said it. That was one aspect of this I didn't want getting out.

And there was something else. Something that happened, but I couldn't quite remember. Not then anyway. It niggled me almost more than the ache from the wound. There was a shoulder injury as well, but this

was like a gnat bite in comparison.
Eventually I healed, went back to school.
There was a cursory curiosity, after all not
everyone got 'stabbed'. Well, who was I to
argue, but the event was soon forgotten.
Some kids would have milked it for all it was
worth, but not me, keep my head down and
get on.
All calmed down at home. No strange
footsteps. No banging on the pantry window,
or spirit voices shouting my name.
 I gave them very little thought, but was still
too young to understand that they had been
trying to warn me of impending danger.
Thinking about this, years later, I wonder if I'd
been aware of their presence, understood
how they worked, would it have made any
difference to the outcome?
I still carry a scar, a reminder of that night, but
feel that, in the bigger picture of my life, the
event was meant to happen. For no other
reason than it helped unlock another part of
my mind. A new experience to stand
alongside all the knocking, stomping and
window rattling. Only this was safely locked
away, at least for now.
Dad's reaction to all of this. 'Get dressed
before you go out.'
Good advice, and on this occasion I was
more than thankful I had a dad who didn't
overreact.
My 'attacker', to my knowledge was never
found. Though to call him that is probably
unfair, after all he was the one that got a
good hiding. I could have brushed shoulders
with him dozens of times afterwards but

wouldn't have known.

The youth, like many things at the time, was purged from my mind.

Life moves on. We remember the good, do our best to suppress the bad, but know as eggs is eggs that nothing stays the same. I almost died, almost. To my mind there was nothing beyond that.

What could be worse?

One difference, even dad noticed, was that I became more detached. My happy demeanour was replaced by something resembling anger. That, and frustration.

On the plus side I knuckled down at school, both feet in the real world, for once. The dark nights were drawing in and my disappearing for hours on end had stopped.

Dad never ever found out about my visits to ICI wood, not that it would have made a difference either way.

What really surprised dad though was my insistence on going to bed early. No later than nine, even on a weekend. Even when there was football commentary on the radio. I hadn't become lazy. Wasn't sickening for anything. I just felt content in my bed. Nothing could get to me; it was my safe place, and I slept so very well.

My dreams often left me waking in an excited state, but rested. Always rested. Rarely did I even remember these dreams, just a desire to go straight back to sleep, to return to them.

I never could, found the whole idea impossible.

I did remember snippets sometimes. The field,

the golden beach, the really big house like a
mansion. And sometimes there was
someone there with me. A woman, but not
mum. At least not as far as I could tell.
It's just that this was the most comforting
place anywhere in creation.
Of course, the early nights were just a phase,
and asking what could be worse than
death....

Chapter Twelve: Dreamstate.

While I touched on dreams earlier, and their importance once the spirit departs for pastures new, let's look more closely at this subject because to understand our sleep state brings us closer to helping make us emotionally more stable and ties into our meditation.

We have opened up our chakras and we have, hopefully, unlocked a door in our mind allowing us to visualise whatever our guides want to share with us.

Our guides do this when we sleep anyway, through our subconscious.

If nothing much is happening up there and you seem to be waiting forever, feel free to create a scenario in your mind's eye.

This serves to enhance the workings of the creative part of your brain to its optimum levels.

You could choose to visualise anything.

A sitting room. Only you choose the décor and the furnishings. You can make it as simple or as ostentatious as you like.

Remember though, you are preparing this room for your visitors, not yourself. Fill it with the things they would like, this encourages them to want to come forward.

It doesn't have to be a sitting room. It can be absolutely anything from that 'golden beach' to the top of the Eiffel tower.

Whatever draws in those you want to communicate with the best.

Use your imagination, even if you feel limited by what you create.

What you should not do though is introduce a cast of strangers to your scenario. By imagining people you don't know, you are simply inviting unwanted guests to gatecrash the party.

Whilst no-one's going to hurt you; it's a waste of time and energy sharing the space in your head with a load on nondescripts who will serve little more purpose than to try and gain your attention. They will talk about what they want to talk about, not you.

After all, you don't know each other.

These creations are easier to imagine as we head towards sleep state because the process becomes more natural.

Only instead of consciously creating scenes to help us play out these visits, we do the same thing subconsciously and the results are stronger and more stable.

Whilst half awake we can still be distracted. Once asleep everything plays out without conscious control, good or bad.

During meditation our guides, or visitors, may very well purposefully draw us towards sleep. Why?

Because they may want to impart information for later. Knowledge that is little or no use at that moment, but will be of immense relevance when the time is right.

So, you say, why tell us now, why not at the right time or nearer to the event.

The answer is preparation. Forewarned is forearmed as the saying goes.

I am certain that many people, particularly

the elderly, subconsciously know of their deaths up to two years before the event. This is not true of every one of course. Just those open enough to get the message. They make subtle preparations, unaware they are doing anything different. Putting their affairs in order, making peace with loved ones, even down to sorting out photographs and documents. Think back to loved ones you have lost and the steps they took leading up to the months before their deaths. You may be surprised on reflection.

Another reason for imparting information is because of fate.

Fate points will open up to us irrespective of whether we want them too, or not. Even if that point passes us by. It was still open to us, beckoning us in.

Free will, choice, allows us freedom to run our own lives between these points.

For fate to happen, we have to have the relevant information that will propel us to be in that significant place at the right time. Of course we believe, usually, we have made the decision based on our own thoughts.

We have less control of the path we take than we realise, particularly where fate is concerned.

Choice is a different ball game all together. The ability to say 'I will' or 'I wont.'

Only, even given a choice, we are guided by meditation and our guides try to keep us on the right track through dream state.

The problem is, if your guides were particularly objectionable in life, there could well be evidence of this in their traits whilst they try to help you.

Let's build a scenario to explain this.

You've met a fantastic new partner, to your mind anyway. You can't get them out of your head. You want to spend every waking minute with them.

You are ignoring the fact that he/she drinks a little too much, will become aggressive when drunk. Further more, you ignore the little put downs and their lack of responsibility.

For after all as the relationship develops they will start to see the error of their ways, and you'll mould them into the person you want them to be.

Sound familiar? It will happen to the majority of people at least once in a lifetime. Especially the younger generation.

Your emotional guide can see what is happening, where it's leading.

This isn't your life partner so you have a choice to be with them. But in six months you'll be a nervous wreck because they'll have stripped away most of your self confidence. Being with them won't be fun anymore. You'll just feel crushed and tired as they take your good energy to feed their negativity. That's not to mention the further potential for violence as the drinking gets worse. After all, they won't be happy with the way things are going either.

So your guide will be niggling away at you, trying to shout their warnings.

This will translate as heavy feelings in your abdomen, random thoughts passing through your mind, reminders of how good life can be.

Suspicions building in your head that something is wrong, but you just aren't sure what.

Your partner will accuse you of paranoia, and you believe them.

It's the only logical explanation because there can't possibly be someone inside of you, helping you along.

So they connect to you in the only way that is left open to them. Through your dreams.

You will have no knowledge of them the next day, not usually. When our loved ones visit us from spirit, we only remember the experience if it's been a pleasant one.

When they tell us off we follow the most common of human traits, we defend ourselves.

From their place in our subconscious they explain what we're letting ourselves in for, the pains and torments that will be inflicted.

For our part, metaphorically, we put our hands over our ears and go lalalalalala.

The two parts of our brain go into conflict. Further heightened by the fact that our guide might not have been one of the most tolerant of people in this world and may well be building a pyre to burn your new partner on as we speak.

So there are two scenarios playing out simultaneously. Both sides of the mind telling different tales, which translates into a dream of bizarre proportions.

This dream will not usually even involve your partner and certainly not your guide. After all, they are respectively the hero and villain of this particular piece.

The dream will usually leave you feeling uneasy and still tired since you have been working through a conflict.

And remember, as good or bad as they were in life, they aren't wrong. They may have been objectionable, but they can now see more than we can.

The more stressed you are about life; the stronger the dreams will be in all their surreal fullness.

Though a person doesn't have to feel stressed in order to have their dream state invaded by the cast of a horror film.

Subconscious stress; events we have blocked out of our mind, situations we feel we have confronted and moved on from, childhood memories stored in the archives of our personal library, these can create dreams that recur from time to time.

We play out, what we think, are identical scenarios, the same dream over and over. If your mind will allow, you will notice that there is always something slightly different about this 'same' dream. You see while it is going in some sort of loop; it is also moving forwards and backwards depending on where you are in the act of putting the scenario to rest.

These dreams can be resurrected months, even years later. Triggered by a present day event that will connect to whatever is stored in your mental filing cabinets.

These dreams are usually linked to fears. Changes in work status, relationship issues where the couple has been together a reasonable amount of time, health, and the thing we tend to worry about most, other people.

The simple fact is that people are born to worry and if there is nothing wrong, then we'll go looking for something, even if it revolves around others.

My advice is this, if you are stress free then be thankful.

Worrying about other people is not going to solve their issues for them.

Yes, of course I worry from time to time but I am fortunate in that I have little responsibility to anyone but myself. So if I'm doing fine, then the world around me is doing likewise. Aren't I the lucky one?

Our dreams, remembered or not, are not just intended to create conflict. They are also there to help us map out our lives.

Every night our body goes through a spiritual cleansing and some of our energy departs in order to make way for 'The Cleaners'. This happens, usually, between the hours of 2am and 3am.

That's why we feel grotty and out of sorts if we are constantly up at this time. Don't just blame that feeling on hangovers, spiritually you aren't getting the fix your body needs.

At this time your spirit goes up onto the astral plane.

Now you're all scratching your heads and saying what's an astral plane?

Imagine the different levels of existence beyond this world and we'll visualise them as different floors in a huge building. It would be realistically bigger than the universe and then some.

We are on the ground floor.
When we die we move up to the first floor,
then as we evolve we are meant to move
from floor to floor until we reach the top.
Those on the upper floors can come down to
visit us, but we can't move up to be with
them until we have ascended to match their
vibration.
However, each of these floors has a
reception area that we can enter.
Most people don't get beyond the reception
on the first floor, but that's ok.
This reception area is the astral plane.
So our physical form is getting spruced up.
This doesn't heal all illness, obviously not, but
it does help.
It is said in hospitals that more patients die
between two and three, three-thirty in the
morning than the rest of the day put
together.
Some hospitals have been known to refer to
this as the 'Death Hour'.
If it is that person's time to move on, then the
spirit doesn't return to its physical shell.
One day we visit the first floor reception only
to be shown to our new life. It will come to us
all eventually.
The purpose of visiting this place isn't just to
clock out, it is also about cosmic ordering.
Many of you will have heard of this but
maybe not know what it entails.
There are those that meditate in order to ask
for certain things to be provided or events to
take place.
If you've earned it, or something is necessary
to help you along the way, then your guides

will help provide.

How?

Well imagine the biggest machine ever. So large it would drive you mad trying to understand how it operates.

Not millions or billions, but trillions of interconnecting cogs all turning continuously. Each cog represents a person, physical or spirit, and each turn of that cog represents an event in our lives.

Each click of our wheel will impact on those intertwined with us, a knock on effect if you like. But our cog will also change direction and connect with a whole new set of cogs from time to time.

We are working our way through a labyrinth that has no end. Searching for other cogs to rest alongside us that can most enrich our lives.

First of all, there's no point asking for the impossible.

You have to have the ability to make something happen.

It's unlikely we'll become Kings and Queens, in a literal sense anyway.

Likewise, if you are trapped in a loveless relationship it's pointless asking for someone new to come along until you've sorted out your current predicament.

Perhaps you are single and looking for life's one true love.

Maybe you are punching below your weight at work.

If something is within reach, then your cog will start to turn in the direction that will best get you where you want to be.

Remember though, ask for too much at one time, and your cog won't know what direction it's meant to turn first. Prioritise in your mind. What's more important, the new job, or the new relationship. Who knows, one may lead to the other.

This is part of what we do every night. It's just that we neither have a recollection of doing this nor are aware we have a list to work from.

But of course we do.

Our desires and dreams are on the list. it's just that it's very hard sometimes for those things to become a reality.

Be aware also that it's your wish list, not your partners, or parents, or siblings.

You can only ask for things for yourself, not others.

At least in this sense.

Absent healing and projecting are quite different, and we'll talk about this shortly.

If you've split with a partner or fallen out with someone, cosmic ordering won't necessarily put it right.

Their wish list might not include you or your feelings at all.

Neither can you use this as a way of getting back at people. It's not black magic or voodoo, which again I discourage anyone from getting into.

There isn't some spiritual hitman out there wreaking revenge because your wish list wants someone to 'suffer plagues, pestilence, and ultimately death.'

This is about you, your development, and helping you find balance to your existence.

And if they can throw you together with the right partner in the meantime, or help you get that dream job, then they will.

They also try to provide materially for us, particularly financially, but it isn't there fault if we overspend or have unhealthy addictions that eat up all of our money.

So we visit the astral plane, sending out our wishes, wills, and want messages.

Our guides pass them along to the various departments engaged with providing the services we desire or require.

If the goods are in stock, or close to hand, results can be very quick. If those goods have to be ordered from higher up, then the process takes longer.

Things can get lost on the way, just as with any transaction.

What if you send out a message, 'I want a partner to share my life with.' Then you lose your job. So you put in a separate order; 'I need a new job.'

The new job takes priority and the original order for a new partner, whilst not getting forgotten, goes to the back of the queue. In the meantime you actually meet your new partner but don't make the connection because it's no longer the right time for you to be settling down.

So after you get your new job you have to reorder. You will still be with the love of your life, but the timing's had to change. They've since met someone else, but it won't work. It's just the length of time it takes for the situation to come around again.

There is a way you can help things along.

It involves visualization and a statement of intent.

Take a blank sheet of paper.

Think about the things that could most enrich your life.

The targets have to be realistic, though everyone's sense of realism is different.

If you believe you can scale the highest mountain, then it is within your grasp. If your reality takes you no further than round the block, then that will be your world.

Now write down, in priority order, a list of events you would like to happen for yourself. Again, remember to keep it real. Try not to make anything complicated and it has to be entirely about you.

Asking for your ex to come back will only work if they want the same thing.

Also let's not have a hundred different wishes. The fewer, the more chance of getting everything you want. Try to say limit yourself to three wishes, just like the storybooks. You can always make a new list once this is completed.

Whilst it's wise not to put a time limit on this, spirits senses of timing are different to ours, twelve months is a fair measure.

Three wishes a year isn't being too greedy, and if we multiply that by everyone in the world, then someone's going to be very busy moving cogs around.

So you've written your list, your statement of intent. Now put it somewhere safe, but away from prying eyes. This is for you and not to be shared. After all others may try and manipulate you away from your wishes.

As long as you don't forget it and you look at it from time to time, that's it, simple as that. I've even known people put their wish list in an envelope and place it beneath their pillow.

By writing down these things you've created an energy that will set the path to your wishes in motion, if there is a path that can be followed. Asking for the lottery isn't a path that's going to present itself, unless it's your fate to win it.

So your trips onto the astral plane take on greater purpose because those energies their to help you, now know exactly what you want from them.

And don't be shy in asking for anything. Just as a receptionist gives out information, or an electrician does your rewiring, or a waitress takes your food order, your guides have a job to do on your behalf.

As well as giving out advice, they are there to provide, to help nurture our needs.

Only they can't help if we don't ask, or have the where for all to communicate with them in the first place.

Occasionally, we have reality dreams. My visits to the field, the beach, and the big house being one such example, though to this point I was still a child and this was way beyond my comprehension.

We often remember reality dreams, because we are meant too.

A loved one comes to us in a dream they are paying a visit.

If the dream isn't particularly pleasant, it's usually because we are introducing other unrelated elements, situations that are causing us to be stressed or worried.

We are hoping our visitor can help find a solution to the problem, which isn't usually the intended nature of these dreams.

Think, those of you that do remember reality dreams, of the times you wake and wish to go straight back to sleep because your dream is so lovely. Only to find that once back in even half consciousness you can't recreate the experience.

Well this is something akin to what death will feel like. Only multiply the experience a hundred fold and you will be getting close to how beautiful the afterlife can be.

And if you've ever woken up shaking; it can be the body, but particularly it is felt in the head, as long as it isn't a symptom of illness, you have probably had an out of body experience.

You may have stayed, for whatever reason, on the astral plain for too long. The sensation relates to your energy re-entering your body but not being bedded back in properly.

It won't have happened to many of you, but if it as, don't be too perturbed.

It can suggest that your vibration is altering slightly. That you are opening up to spirit and becoming more 'aware.'

It can also be the first signs of the body being prepared or physical mediumship.

Chapter Thirteen: Now, Then, And There.

Now...
I've ran a bath.
Taken clean towels out of the airing cupboard, which, considering what I intend to do, seems a little bit stupid.
I'm drinking tea and staring at a blank piece of full scrap, torn from my English book. Less likely to be told off by my English teacher. Another stupid thought under the circumstances.
I didn't know what to write; the words were not there.
No, there were words were in my head; plenty of them, just not the right ones.
'If in doubt say nowt' rivalled 'If in doubt give 'em a clout' but the former saying gave me an answer. I screwed up the piece of paper and threw it across the room.
I supposed I'd hoped for some divine intervention, but it didn't come. No words to soothe me, just a darkness that had taken a hold, enveloping me in its icy grip.
I undressed; letting my clothes drop onto the floor by the fire, which I had on all three bars. A way of getting at dad, bloody make him pay.
Yet, in my note I had wanted to apologize. Say sorry for what I'd put him through. I felt guilty for so many things, still only thirteen.
It had been a busy few months since Bill had died.
The first time I cut my arms; no more than ten

days before this evening's events unfolded; I had gone into shock.

Taking a razor blade. I cut both of my lower arms at least thirty times. I can't have meant to kill myself because I left my wrists well alone.

There was a blank. Then the next thing I recall was standing in the street, being consoled by a concerned school friend who took me to his home to get help.

I knew why I'd done this but was too upset to say. The lie I told was just as unforgivable, but it saved me from the truth.

I told them I'd been attacked by two boys, memories of the earlier confrontation maybe. The police were called; dad finished work early, and there were questions and more questions. In the end I admitted my own actions.

Embarrassment for me.

Embarrassment for my dad who clearly didn't know how to deal with this. There was the threat of a children's home, and the question 'Why?' asked a dozen times in quick succession.

As for the family whom I had inflicted my troubles on, I don't think they ever forgot. There was certainly no forgiveness for my actions, and who could blame them?

It was still easier than the truth, slightly.

I didn't know why at first, but I went into the kitchen and got a small hammer which dad kept under the kitchen sink. I left the light off, hiding my nakedness; the bright light would have reflected outside.

Sitting back down on the settee; I held the

hammer by the handle and allowed it to hover above my right foot by about eighteen inches.
Closing my eyes, I let the hammer drop.

Then...
She was called Moira and I hated her with a passion. Not because she was taking all of dad's attention, but because she was a chain smoking alcoholic who's every other word began with 'f' or 'c' and she swore openly in front of me and dad did nothing about it.
Bloody and bugger might have been used commonly in our house; mum had been the biggest culprit, but nothing much stronger than that. Not ever.
I knew all the words, quite liked some of them, though their was a jokey context and there was this.
She had taken to being there when I got home from school, and I was scared she would move in. To make matters worse, she had half a dozen kids of her own, and they were always in trouble.
None of them ever came to our house though. Small mercies.

Now...
The hammer hit my foot but hardly hurt. So I repeated the process, this time holding the hammer higher.

Then...
'Why don't you go out for a few hours, get some fresh air? Me and your dad need some

time.'
Looking to dad for support. No response, no help.
Eyes glued to the television, 'I'm watching this and then I have homework to do.'
Dad would have known this to be a lie, but he remained impassive.
I can hear his excuse rolling off the tongue, 'But I get lonely.'
How many times did I hear it as a child?
I may have been more respectful had I been told that this was his choice, that I would have to accept it, not some whiny excuse that wouldn't cut the ice with anyone.

Now...
This time there was some modicum of pain. A twinge but little more, the toes looked redder.
I attacked my left foot in the same way.

Then...
This game went on for weeks.
Moira looking for ways to get me to go out, whilst I remained unmoved. Dad sitting on the sidelines giving nothing away.
Then eventually she'd give up, going off to whatever rock she'd crawled from under.
Leaving me with a sense of relief, until next time.
She never stayed over, and they never slept together when I was there, which he had started doing with his one night stands.
That was until THAT Saturday night.
Unusual for two reasons. Dad was off out and yet was on six til two, starting the next

morning.

Also, 'Did I have a mate's house I wanted to visit, maybe stay overnight'?

Sensing something was up, not that I ever did sleep over anywhere, I did little more than shrug my shoulders and get on watching television.

The early to bed routine had come and gone as most things did. Probably lasted no more than a fortnight. Fads and fancies to torment and delight in equal measures.

I occasional got an ache, a reminder of what had happened. Less than six weeks had passed since the incident with the milk bottle, but the memory was already fading, locked away with the rest of what couldn't be fully understood.

And this night there was a Dracula movie on starting at half past eleven.

So, dad coming home drunk didn't faze me in the slightest. In fact in light of recent events involving a certain woman, dad's behaviour actually hadn't been that bad at all.

Why was I surprised when she came back with him?

My stomach muscles tensed before they even got down the path.

Her laugh was like a witches cackle. Come to think of it, she looked a bit witchy. Dead skinny with lank dark hair.

They came into the living room through the front door.

Dad seemed happy enough, but then he was drunk.

She was happy until she saw me lying on the sofa in my pyjamas; eyes locked on the

television.
'I thought you'd be in bed.' dad sounding hopeful.
'Watching this film. It's good.
Moira removed her coat; fish and chips wrapped in newspaper nestled beneath.
Dad went into the kitchen, put the kettle on.
Moira sat in the chair next to the settee and started eating her supper.
Danny's chair, the bitch. I remember thinking this, but where else was she going to sit?
Dad, 'Don't you want a plate for those. Knife, fork?'
'Cup of tea will do.' Turning to the boy, 'And you can fuck off to bed.' She was breaking off bits of fish and feeding her face using her fingers.
I ignored her. Shut the words out as if she wasn't there.
Suddenly a piece of cod landed on my face.
'There, if that's what you're waiting for, now fuck off to bed.'
Sitting up, removing the batter from my pyjama top, staring at the food, unsure what to do.
Suddenly wishing dad wasn't skulking in the kitchen. To which he'd closed the door at some point so hadn't seen this interaction.
Carefully I reached across and replaced the fish back in the wrapping.
'Sorry.' Stupid thing to say.
I looked at her closely. Blood shot rheumy eyes, eating chips through greasy fingers, staring back at me like an opponent in some weird game of dare. The prize. This bloke who had shut himself off in the kitchen. Probably

not a prize worth falling out over.
'Keep looking at me like that and I'll knock
you out.'
Food flew from her lips mixed with spittle.
'I'll fucking stab you, only do a better job
than the last lot.'

There...
Then nothing.
Darkness overtakes, a serene darkness.
Calm, alert, safe.
Many different emotions bound together in
my mind. Cocooned in a place no-one else
can enter.
Yet there is someone stood there sharing the
darkness with me.
A young woman. I feel I know her..
Urgency in her voice, 'No Christian, no!'

Then...
'NO! WHAT ARE YOU DOIN' LAD? NO!'
Dad's voice, and further more, hands pulling
me away from Moira.
She is still sitting in the armchair, but she now
looks to have red sauce on her supper, which
she is mostly wearing on her cardigan and
across her face.
Breathing heavily, I'm busy staring at my
knuckles. Scraped, bleeding.
Back to Moira, split lip, bloodied nose,
suddenly sober.
And I've done this to her but really don't
grasp what has happened, not fully.
I'm sorry, the guilt washing over me.
She suddenly looks pitiful, sat there staring
back.

Again I say sorry, only this time with good reason.

Now...
The toes on both feet were red and would bruise.
Enough, I thought, enough.
Leaving the hammer where I dropped it, I went to the bathroom.

Then...
I'd cleaned myself up and gone to bed.
Dad would deal with me tomorrow, whatever that meant.
I hardly dared look in her direction when I came back into the room.
'Little bastard,' Moira's good night call.
I listened to their voices downstairs, waited for her to leave.
Some time passed before I drifted off to sleep. Occasionally she would raise her voice; I caught the odd, nasty, word.
At some point, I thought I heard her crying quietly but couldn't be sure.
There was also an over riding niggle.
Something I felt I should remember, yet it was so far away. A memory maybe?
Sleep finally came, dreams I would not remember later.

Now...
The bath water had become little more than lukewarm. Too much time spent pondering, hesitation perhaps.
I'd removed the razor from the bathroom cabinet and held it in my right hand. It felt

heavy, cumbersome. I'd never really noticed before. Unscrewing the top of the razor, I removed the blade.

Tossing the razor onto the bathroom rug, a sense of nothingness came over me as I ran the blade over my arm. A small cut, clean, no pain.

I lay back, allowing my head to rest on the back of the bath tub, closed my eyes and began to search for the peace that was hidden away just out of reach.

Tears ran down my face; I desperately wanted my mum.

Then...

I heard the front door slam closed, unusual because dad was normally so quiet in a morning.

Then the night's drama returned, and I realised dad must be really mad.

Then I heard the bed creaking in the next room. He hadn't gone to work; then that must have been her leaving. Noisy cow.

I quickly returned to sleep.

Sometime later, not sure of the time. Daylight creeps through the curtains casting a shadow across the back wall.

A figure sitting on my bed making me sit up, alarmed.

Moira.

She's wearing dad's pyjama top and nothing else.

Confronted by this sight, I began to tremble. Fear of the unknown.

Ok, I'm thirteen, but still innocent to the ways of the world. This is more than a few steps

beyond a crafty snog here and there.
There'd not been much of that either, a few dares maybe.
'What do you want?' No bravado in my voice. Not this time.
She took my hand and placed it on her right breast beneath the pyjama top.
I pulled away in horror. Oh, I knew what I was touching alright, but this wasn't pleasant. She stank of cigarettes, booze, a fading waft of perfume, and something more pungent I couldn't make out.
And quite frankly, she made my skin crawl.
So the horror was completed when she removed the top altogether and got into bed with me.
There were no pleasantries, but thankfully she didn't force me to have full sex. Maybe because I wouldn't have had a clue and I was petrified.
I tried, partly succeeded, in closing my mind off. Ignored her hands as they worked their way down my body.
There was nothing romantic, no sense of fulfillment or satisfaction, just plain disgust and confusion.
The former because of who it was, the latter because I'd not felt able to fight her off.
After all, I'd done a pretty good job the night before.
But no-one had touched me there before and whilst she certainly disgusted me, the confusion came from the way I'd sexually responded to her.
She got out of bed, wiped her hands on Dad's pyjama top and headed out of the

room.

'Next time, I'll tell your dad what you've done to me, and then he will have you sent away. Dirty little bastard.'

She left the room, leaving me alone to my fear and confusion.

Shortly afterwards I heard the front door slam for the second time that morning.

I know I've done nothing wrong, know she's, I barely can think of the words never mind say them. But equally I realise how little I know my own father. Who would he believe?

Even if he believed me, well as dad's favourite saying goes, 'I get lonely.'

Then I have to try and understand what Moira meant by, 'I'll tell your Dad what you've done to me.'

What exactly had I, could I, have done? After all, I'd switched myself off to what SHE was doing, but there was a strong sense of guilt.

Something bad had happened, yes, but something even worse was starting to take root.

For a moment, I'd been excited. I'd been aroused but had no perception of what this meant. Just how could this vilest of women excite me in anyway?

Now...

And three weeks have gone by.

Dad has barely spoken to me. Other than cursory comments, there's been no reaction to anything. I assume this is because of my antics involving the police.

I waited, with dread, for Moira to turn up, but

she never did.

I didn't know it then, but I would never see her again.

Though the damage was done and the guilt had settled with heavy hands onto my shoulders. No longer was there any doubt in my mind, whatever I did to Moira was wrong. Dad must never know, no-one must ever find out, the only people who could help me were all gone, and I felt very isolated, alone. So now you know why I'm lying in a bath full of cold water bringing an end to a life, notable for, well nothing really.

I'd been little more than everybody's burden.

There...

And I must be in heaven because I can hear music playing quietly.

Anthony Newley, 'If she should come to you.' I haven't heard this song since my mum last sang it to me.

It must be night because everything is pitch black. Yet I feel oh so calm, soothed by the music.

A voice, female. She may have been singing the words. 'Let the music leads you, go with the music.'

Now...

I open my eyes.

Still alive, very cold, still feeling lousy, a headache for my troubles.

I have hold of the razorblade; my only wound the single cut to my left forearm.

The first rule of suicide as to be.... don't fall asleep in the bath.

Of course it was never going to happen. But there was a place I had arrived at, a place called despair that a youngster should never have to visit.

But a place I would come back from.

I even managed to clean up all signs of the nights events before dad came home.

And as for Moira, I heard that she was taken by cancer a few years after the events of that weekend.

Chapter Fourteen: Physical Mediumship.

Every aspect of mediumship takes on a physical form requiring the basic senses to interact.
Clairaudience, for instance, relates to the medium's ability to physically hear a spirit.
Clairsentience is the most common form of communication and is done through a sense of smell. Usually flowers, tobacco, or perfume. Something that could easily be associated with the spirit when alive.
And a Clairvoyant, meaning 'all seeing.' is top of the pile.
Using every sense to communicate with spirit and not just relying on one.
In physical mediumship there are also different forms of communication.
Transfiguration, direct voice, trance, apports. Whilst there are many who will be thinking, I know about this, heard it all before, equally there will be as many, if not more, who are scratching their heads in puzzlement.
So those of you who are familiar with this subject, or think you are, please be patient.
There just might be something here you don't yet know.
Physical medium ship, today, is a rare phenomena.
Yet from the 1880' onwards up to the early 1950's, physical circles thrived throughout the world.
People would sit in psychic circles for years, developing, in the hope that they might go

all the way and become physical mediums. However, a lot like smoking, physical mediumship could damage your health and the mediums didn't realise this.

Most physical mediums suffered illness and many died.

They weren't able to keep up with the punishing constraints this practice put on the body.

Eventually, usually too late, we learn not to indulge in those experiences not good for us.

So you may be surprised to hear that, despite everything I've just written, one of my aims is to perform full physical mediumship on stage. I'm sure there are many who doubt it can be done publicly in this manner, but despite certain constraints I believe it is more than possible.

There are a small handful of people out there claiming to be full physical mediums.

So why has no-one reproduced this phenomena for the world to see?

You'd have thought that with today's technology that one display of physical proof could send such a positive message out to the world.

And if the medium made the sacrifice of their life, well we're going to a better place and no-one has a better knowledge of that.

I know it all sounds a bit melodramatic, and I'm not really suggesting anyone fall on their sword, I'm actually questioning the validity of their claims.

One simple act of affirmation and most of the skeptics are out of business.

Those sat on the fence become believers

and only the most hardcore nonebelievers
are left to find some slight of hand to explain
their ignorance.

I haven't experienced this phenomena in
others, though I am a bit of a dab hand at
transfiguration, even though I say so myself.
That's making my face change into someone
else's for the uninitiated.

Most physical mediums sit in closed circles.
Working with a group of familiar faces who
help the medium develop. The belief is that
they have to sit with the same people in the
same place for a number of years to create
the right atmosphere.

Which explains why this form of mediumship
has become rare.

In a world of television, computers, ever
changing relationships, and more open
social opportunities, we don't all want to be
sat in a development circle. Especially one
which is really serving to develop someone
other than ourselves.

There is one man in this country who offers
the service for small groups at £100 pound
per time. He works in a pitch black
environment. No-one can see what's
happening in the room, and he won't allow
anyone to repeat the experience.

So the 'show' might be genuine, it might not,
but don't hide your light under a bushel my
friend. You'd fill a stadium with people
wanting to share that experience.

His argument is that this sort of work has to be
carried out in a properly controlled
environment, with the correct supervision and
safeguards.

This is to ensure the mediums safety primarily, but as for the environment, surely the essence of a thousand people's energy would make a more powerful generator than a handful. Yes, there will be a mixture of positive and negative energies in such a big crowd, but that small group you sit with still won't be very pleasant if everyone's had a bad day.

As for the health of the medium, let's remember that fifty years ago people were less healthy and their life expectancy lower. Today we live better, have healthier diets, keep fitter, and are aware of any restraints that may affect our bodies. Forearmed is forewarned; we can prepare ourselves better, so the chances of becoming ill are reduced.

Spiritual energy wants to communicate with us. Otherwise I wouldn't be sat here writing this book.

Why, when they've gone on to a better place do they want to come back here? Our loved ones, as I've said, will retain much of their earthly personality. So common sense dictates that they will want to look in on us from time to time.

Also, they are trying to make the world a better place. It doesn't serve their purpose to see us killing each other or sit back and watch us destroy our planet.

One of the purposes in this life is to create. Until we have something we can use in this realm, Sprits don't get access to it over there. So if the world goes bang, in theory anyway, their ability to evolve through accessing our creativity is destroyed with it.

This leads us into the heady realms of parallel universes and alternate realities, and we certainly aren't there yet.

A word of warning before we move forward. Ouija Boards are very popular with some people and represent another form of physical mediumship. Well it's a bit like playing with fireworks. Unless you have a responsible adult to supervise proceedings, don't even open the box. By responsible adult, I mean someone attuned to spirit who at the very least knows when to close the circle down.

Not all spirits have good intentions. If they weren't nice in this world chances are they suddenly haven't found sainthood over there.

That can only come through ascension. People who haven't a clue what they are doing will tend to attract lower end energies. Mediums have strong guides who should be able to keep the rubbish out.

Here are the most favoured forms of medium ship, in the physical sense, practiced today.

Materialisation.
This is not to be confused with ghosts. Ghosts are an essence of spiritual energy disconnected from its host.

Usually attached to a building or an area where it will travel in a loop. Sometimes being seen in the physical when the energy appertaining to that area is at its strongest. Materialisations, on the other hand, will use the energy that has built up in a room to appear.

They can be seen, sometimes as shadows or reflections occasionally taking on full form. There are occasions when you may not see a figure but instead hear a voice. This is usually no more than a few words, rarely a sentence, though if the energy was really strong I don't believe a conversation would be impossible. In its purest form we would ideally be aiming at an apparition forming in the room and having a conversation.

People claim to have had this experience but where's the proof?

Sorry, again, to sound skeptical but the proof is in what we can see.

Many experiences have happened to me that I have no proof of, so whilst I would not doubt someone's word on anything that as happened to them, share that event with the world.

We have to be able to reach out and show everyone where we're coming from.

One other aspect of materialization refers to lighting.

Many mediums work with red lights, sometimes blue. There is a belief that spirit is attracted to these colours and drawn away from white light.

Well each to their own. When working I like the room to be as bright and white as possible. Not too much glare though, we don't want blinding. This works well for me. However, and I can only speak for transfiguration, I get the best results from subdued lighting, trying to recreate that half light ambience we get around dusk. When

the suns setting and the lighting effects
become more subtle.
Which leads me on to....

Transfiguration.
Around about the time I moved to
Harrogate, so 2001, I started with my early
experiences of transfiguration.
I was sat at a ladies home in Doncaster; it
was her first reading with me and we hadn't
met before that day. I was aware of nothing
out of the ordinary before she jumped out of
her chair.
First she said my faced seemed to vanish and
was then replaced by the image of her
Grandfather overlying the space where my
own features had been.
My comment at the time was' I don't mind as
long as he was good looking.'
I think she was too freaked out to get the
joke.
My first thought was, she's got problems and
she's imagining things.
Later that same evening another friend
claimed to see my face become that of her
Mother's and I realised something was
happening.
So what is transfiguration?
Well, quite simply the image of a spirit
overlays on the mediums face creating the
illusion that their face is changing into that of
the spirit.
Taking this to another level, what quite often
happens is that this face will interchange with
other faces, so you have a group of people
taking it in turns to appear before you.

My inquisitive mind asked the obvious question, to me anyway, where exactly are you coming in from?

The answer was unexpected, made no apparent sense.

Two degrees to the right of my third eye..
I pondered on this for months as if the very fabric of creation hinged on the answer.
Of course, it's simple.

Look in a mirror. That point between your eyebrows where your third eye sits. Change your focus, move over slightly to above your right eyebrow, got it?

No, I know you can't see anything, but if you move your third eye in that direction things begin to happen.

It's all about refocusing this third eye.
Look ahead, but visualise your third eye moving off to your right. If you do this correctly, everything in the room will take on the feeling of going out of focus. If you hold it for too long you'll probably start with a headache. It takes a certain amount of practice and takes time adjusting too.

Eventually not only will the room go out of focus it will start to disappear. You'll be aware of yourself sitting in the same spot, but the rest of the room, including everyone else sat with you, will begin to vanish.

Of course they haven't, but you are refocusing your mind to the point where our energy jumps the moment we die.

Physically our energy leaps to a point two degrees to the right of our third eye.

That's the step off point, the beginning of the afterlife.

By switching our third eye over to sit in this place, we allow spiritual energy to connect with us and overlay their energy onto our face.

The results are much stronger, though can take time to develop. But then that's the name of the game, and development takes time.

That's from the medium's perspective. Who ever is sat watching the change can also enhance their experience, or even use this as a way of linking in if they are struggling.

Remember those 'magic eye' pictures that were so popular a few years ago?

The faces vibrate anyway because that's what energy does. The images will appear to come forward and move backwards to a rhythm.

Try it out. Two people can take it in turns being the medium and the viewer. With practice, it will eventually start to work if you really want it too.

Direct Voice Medium ship.

I've never witnessed this, and it would be one of those 'don't be daft' moments had I not spoken to rational people who had the experience.

Picture a conical shaped object with holes at either end.

Not too surprisingly it is known as a 'trumpet' because I imagine the earliest trumpets were more likely associated with conical shaped seashells.

The 'Trumpet' is placed in the centre of the circle of people sat in the room.

Using the energies present in the room, the device is said to rise into the air and communicate, the trumpet serving as an artificial voice box.
Note to self. Must put it on my 'to do' list.

Trance Mediumship.
I have done this, but with mixed results.
My desire to have control over my environment initially makes anything physical difficult to achieve.
The spirit takes control of the medium's body, controlling the voice box primarily, but can also control certain physical functions,
moving the arms and legs like a marionette.
A bit like a temporary possession if you like.
Well my thoughts are very strong on this subject, it's my body so you can all bugger off.
For the medium, it's a little like being on auto pilot. You are aware of your environment, and the spirit around you.
Yet you are giving them permission to use you to communicate without the interference of your own thought.
I suppose on the plus side you could get away with blue murder and blame it on the spirit entity, but seriously though, a medium needs to be very trusting to allow someone they don't know to use them in this way.
Tried it a few times, not for me.

Full Physical Mediumship.
As I've said, rare because of the physical stresses this can put on the body.
The spirit forms using ectoplasm which exit's

the medium's body through any available orifice, but usually the mouth, nose, or navel. The medium is usually placed in a cabinet, which in turn as a curtain in front of it. The experience of initially seeing the ectoplasm leaving the body is said to be distressing for some.

So these precautions are taken to protect the audience.

The medium is sometimes bound to their seat to prove nothing underhand can be occurring to create an illusion.

Personally I would come with a government health warning and want people to experience everything I was going through.

Again it is said that red light energizes the spirit and white light inhibits. However, this is not true.

The nature of the light predetermines the nature of the spirit you want to bring forward. The higher elements react better to brighter light whilst lower energies find the brightest lights too strong for them.

The spirits themselves will appear just as they did in this life. If they had a glass eye and a wood leg then so be it. They will clone themselves in every detail right down to their fingerprints.

They can walk amongst the audience, be touched, materialize and dematerialize before your very eyes. They can walk through walls, sing, dance, and play a musical instrument if they so choose.

Advances in understanding allow for a form of physical medium ship that is less reactive on the body than it was fifty years ago. It is down to the medium to attain the relevant vibration level to perform this task.

There needs to be a reasonable fitness level and a highly developed vibration for this to work properly, but I'm told that spiritual energy can appear using the energy created by a medium's aura, performing all the same tasks it could whilst using ectoplasm.

Once this has been proven it will open the door for mediums, of a certain calibre, to perform full physical medium ship with no real danger to themselves.

It's not. 'If we eventually get there.'' It's when.'

The solution isn't far away.

Chapter Fifteen: Not Just For Christmas.

I know I've been here before; I'm just not sure when.

I'm in a field of long grass, intent on tickling my bare knees.

A slight breeze envelops me keeping the warmth of the sun at bay.

I follow a path I recognise, but from where?

I know up ahead is a beach where there will be people sunbathing or playing in the water.

There's a big house somewhere, and a young woman. I use that term loosely because she's a little older than me.

Memories I cannot quite reach.

The field comes to an end and I find myself on the small road opposite the beach.

Music begins to fill my head. 'American Pie' by Don Mclean.

Imagine using your I pod or MP3, slowly increasing the volume until it feels comfortable to the ears. Well this was my experience; only such gadgetry hadn't yet been invented, and there was no radio or record player to be seen.

My head was the player, picking tunes from a selection stored in my memory.

Roast chicken, I could smell the meat, and this teased my senses to the point where I found myself salivating.

But from where?

The music, yes that was in my head, but the smell seemed to come from...well everywhere.

Making my way to the point where the sand begins, I looked down onto the beach.

There were caravans running from the middle of the beach all the way to the waters edge. At least thirty of them, probably more.

The tide had to be going out, but was lapping so gently I couldn't be sure.

 These weren't holiday type caravans. They were far more magical, almost surreal in appearance. You might see them in old picture books, as a representation of gypsy homes.

My mother used to allow Gypsies into the house from time to time when no-one else was around.

Yet she would always tell me to stay away from them, though she told me to stay away from everyone.

Likewise, Ledger week, she would always visit a 'fortune teller' at the race course. Not to have her fortune told, 'just to visit', she would explain.

Ledger week culminated in a big horse race, The St Ledger Classic. This was run on a Saturday. The racing would last for four days, but the fair was there for about a week.

I loved the fair and would sneak off to go there on my own, although dad wouldn't give a monkeys where I went anyway.

There was never any problems though, keep yourself to yourself. Her words would ring in my head forever.

I used to sit in the 'Fortune Teller's' cramped little caravan. Told not to speak unless I was spoken too. I didn't want to speak; she looked through me, made me nervous.

Only once, and I never was allowed in again. Where it came from I never knew. Only a few months before mum died, the words spilling out without thinking.

'If you can see the future, why haven't you got a bigger caravan?'

My head rang for a week from the thick ear I got.

The gypsy's camped out on the beach were from a different era. Their homes were horse drawn and by the look of them made the racecourse gypsy's van look palatial, in terms of size at any rate.

Where the horses that would pull these vehicles could be found, I had no idea. They were nowhere to be seen.

The gypsies were sat around in small groups. Some played musical instruments. Others listened whilst smoking and drinking.

Another group looked to be playing cards, whilst closer to the waters edge were the camps children. They sat in a circle being entertained by someone who had their undivided attention. A dark haired lady telling them a story. There was no story book, but I knew what she was doing all the same, her hand movements very expressive.

The desire to join them overwhelmed me, to hear their story, but I remained rooted to the spot.

What I believed to be my own thoughts filled my head again, only the words cut into the song, 'You won't be walking on the beach, not today anyway.'

A female voice. A name, Hailey. The young

woman telling the story.

I continued to watch the children but a few moments later she got up and gave me a wave.

Her summer dress hung on her in a way only the finest of artists could capture. Something even I couldn't fail to notice, even if my full appreciation was somewhat stunted by youth.

My stomach started to roll in a flip-flop motion and I was suddenly overwhelmed with happiness. Not just happiness, this was stronger, emotions that I have rarely experienced in the physical world.

She ran towards me and the children behind her began to disperse.

Laughter filled the air.

A few of the gypsies turned to look in my direction, seemingly curious, though none troubled enough to cast me more than a furtive glance.

Hailey, however, seemed overjoyed.

She covered the distance between us in no time, threw her arms around me, treat me to the biggest hug of my life so far.

Even barefoot she was a good five inches taller than me. Five inches for five years, I thought randomly.

Taking me by the hand, we moved away from the beach. This time, however, in the opposite direction from where she'd led me before.

'You've been a silly arse, Christian, but then you don't need me to tell you that.'

That name again. Not the name given to me by my mother, but the name she knew me by.

'What do you mean?'

'You know, that old razor blade thing. Wanting to run away from your life. You were a silly arse.'

I felt I should argue, put up some form of defence, but was captivated by her voice. For the first time I realised the music in my head had stopped.

Anyway there was no room for anyone but her.

I allowed myself to be led away.

We didn't speak for what seemed an age. Though the scenery didn't change much, grass, grass, and more grass on one side. The sea on the other. Somewhere the beach had receded so the water ran alongside where we walked. I hadn't noticed this change, had no clue how far we had come.

Time did not matter. The concept seemed to have a different meaning here. Moving more quickly on one hand but each second seemed to last as long as I wanted it too. Like fast forwarding to the good bits which you can then slow down to completely savor.

The tone to her voice welcomed me back from my thoughts. 'One day you'll grow into a fine young man. One day soon. No more daft thoughts about checking out early now.'

I realised her accent was Irish. Subtle but there was a certain lilt.

'You're very special, Christian. But being special can carry a great responsibility. You will have a job to do and a lot of people will benefit from what you will come to know. One day it will become your job to try to make them listen.'

There is urgency in her words.

'Who?, When?'

Smiling, Hailey puts a finger to my lips. 'Hush now. No-one's going to take you seriously for a long time. After all who listens to children? Who listens to what's different? Who listens to what they don't want to hear?' The smile saddens. 'Life's path isn't always easy, it's mapped out with obstacles, hurdles you will have to overcome.' Another momentary silence, 'But then surely the same can be said of everyone's life I suppose?

I did not have a clue to what she was on about, but I could listen to her all day. The best I could muster was to move my head much like the proverbial 'nodding dog.'

It's just that each life path is different, and yours will be different from most. There's a reason you find yourself alone. A purpose in what is to come for you. Everybody has to grow up, to mature.

I'm always going to be around, but we can only be friends, nothing more. Not in your lifetime anyway.'

Now I noticed she looked really sad, tears forming in the corners of her eyes.

Sensing my alarm she looked away. 'You have a life to live, love. We will help along the way, but it's your life to build.'

Breaking away from me, Hailey runs off, and laughter replacing the sadness. She turns, in full flight, shouting out, 'Come and catch me you silly arse.'

My immediate thought, too mature for a thirteen year old, how can you catch an angel?

The answer was....easy. Especially when that particular angel wanted to be caught.

The path came to an end, a five-bar gate blocking our path. 'Well, this is my way home.'

'Do you live on a farm.'

More laughter filled the air. If she was making fun of my comment, she hid it well. 'I move around, as if you don't know, now get away with you.' Sadness again, 'Of course you don't know. How could you?'

Confused, 'Oh. You're one of them. You're a Gypo.' Wanting to stuff the words back into my mouth, not wanting to upset her.

Over the years I would come to learn that speaking one's mind was very healthy if not always apt.

'Black, white, yellow, green with pink dots, what's it matter who, or what, I am? Ahh, you're still but a lad, you'll learn.'

I realise now that my witty reposts were no more than puerile childhood comebacks. There was no way anything I said to her would have sounded less than pathetic.

She continued to smile. 'Do you remember what day it is Christian?'

The nodding dog impression returned though I knew not why.

Hailey then did something extraordinary. Well she did little more than sit on the top bar of the gate, but it was the manner in which she got there.

Imagine one of those epics set in Ancient China where the heroine flies through the air in slow motion taking down three villains with her ritual sword?

She doesn't so much fly as hover.

Hailey, facing me with her back to the gate, levitated. Rose up, as if a pocket of air was depositing her onto the rickety make shift seat.

Seeing my bemusement, her laughter returned. 'Well, a ladies got to have her dignity.' Patting the space beside her, 'Come on.'

No hidden gust of wind came to my aid, and I had to mount the gate in the conventional way.

She took my hand once more, squeezing it tighter than ever. Leaning over, she whispered into my ear. 'Merry Christmas love.'

Then placing her hand on the nape of my neck she leaned across and kissed me. Not just a peck. This was a full blooded, 'remember who really loves you' kiss.

I found himself responding, becoming aroused, heightened further when her tongue found mine. Wrong maybe, considering my young years, but not dirty. Compared to everything in my life, good and bad, this was the nearest to heaven I could get.

The kiss became more urgent, her grip on my hand tighter.

I woke up.

A tingling tremor started to consume my body, no, more than that. Emotional heroin taking me to places I'd yet to venture in the 'real' world.

The love washed over me, holding me with

the memory of what had just happened.
Only these images were not fading like the others, if anything the tingling was increasing, taking root in the core of my soul.
It was some time before I drifted back to sleep.
The next day was Christmas day, 1973.
I didn't open a present before Boxing Day.
Though there were only three and I'd bought and wrapped two of them for myself.
Dad showed real concern when he realised I was probably going to spend the whole day laid on the settee in my pyjamas.
I tried to assure him that I was alright which seemed enough to placate him.
After all what could I say?
How could I explain something I didn't comprehend myself. Not yet anyway.
Other than a heightened sense of right and wrong, and certain dreams that seemed too real for comfort, I would have no further significant experiences for the next fifteen years.

Chapter Sixteen: Healing And Possession/Obsession.

At first I wondered why I was compelled to write about these two subjects together.
Then it became obvious.
After all possession is a form of illness and the healing process involves replacing bad energy with good energy in order to replenish the body.

Healing.

I do not profess to be a healer.
A healer usually works with their hands and produces a heat that is passed on to the subject.
This heat is meant to contain the positive energy that helps aid recovery.
Now there will be people better placed than me who, again, will have written books on the subject shouting out that healing is much more complex than this.
Probably right, but I am keeping to the basics here.
And whilst I fully support the concept of healing, well we never pick up a newspaper and read about miracles having happened as an everyday occurrence.
Not yet anyway.
All forms of healing have a place in society, but they should go hand in hand with conventional medicine.
It is said that medically we only understand six percent of the workings of the mind and body.

That leaves ninety-four percent to go at, so
surely we need all the help we can get.
Not really related, at this point anyhow, but
scientists are said only to understand six
percent of the universe.
What is it with six percent?
The truth is that, irrespective of what we
know, or don't, a person can only be healed
if they believe in the treatment they are
receiving, conventional or otherwise.
If you have belief, then the positive energy
you create will   give you a greater ability to
fight the illness.
Whereas if you believe in nothing, your
cynical mind will create negative energy,
which is likely to further complicate the
problem you already have.
One thing is for sure though, irrespective of
anything, if it's your time to pass, no amount
of healing is going to halt the process.
Being positive will just make the experience
easier to come to terms with.
There are many forms of healing based
around spiritual beliefs.
Some of these principals are believed to be
over a thousand years old, usually associated
with Eastern techniques but pre- dating
modern medicine by many generations.
Reiki Healing is the form that is probably most
well known in modern times, but consider
other sources.
Acupuncture, Reflexology, to name but two
of the practices that are even recognised by
many hospitals.
All of these practices have one common
theme, and that is they all focus on the area

of the body that requires healing.

Sounds really obvious, I know, and you'll think, well that's what's meant to happen, but... how many times do people go their GP and complain about some minor ailment, failing to mention that there's something more serious going on as well?

There's no point telling your Doctor about your Bunions if there's an abscess about to burst.

Our greatest fear is the unknown, so by ignoring the problem we hope it will go away.

Think about family members and how many actually refuse to see a Doctor and you'll understand where I'm coming from.

When I'm sat with people I often pick up on ailments they themselves are not yet aware of.

I've even diagnosed problems before the medical profession.

Simple. Your guides will know the answers. They are there to protect every aspect of your well being, health being top of the list.

Any good healer will get a sense of where your ailments really are irrespective of what you claim to be the issue.

However, there are reasons why Spiritual Healing doesn't work as a permanent solution at the moment. The healer replaces the damaged energy with good energy, often at their own expense. Healers can become very drained.

Very good healers can take on the symptoms of their subject for a brief period of time.

But everything radiates from the Chakra

system and that's what we really need to focus on. Not just each chakra singularly, but the whole system collectively.

To which everyone will be screaming that we only have one pair of hands!

Think of four wooden wheels on a cart.

Each wheel represents a chakra.

Three of the wheels are damaged and one is new.

The owner couldn't afford four new wheels so he just changed one. The strains put on the cart by the three damaged wheels will eventually put undue stresses on the new wheel, and eventually we'll end up back where we started.

So, ideally, we need to repair all the damaged wheels to be sure we've no further problems.

When a person's ill the entire Chakra system will become affected, the severity depending on the seriousness of the problem.

So focusing on one area of the body will not help the rest of the system and eventually the problem will return.

However, if we could work on the entire system at the same time, perhaps then we can go some way to beginning a true healing process.

It is possible if the healer attunes sufficiently. Which can be achieved by refocusing the mind before beginning the healing process.

I've done this, and it can work, both on a physical and emotional level.

I liken it to having a 'Spiritual Sunbed.'

Instead of focusing on an area of the body

that needs to feel those healing properties, then why not 'blast' the whole body with positive energy?

This is done using a process I spoke of earlier when I talked about physical medium ship. Recalibrating the third eye two degrees off centre towards the right area of the brain. When I do this, often transfiguration takes place, but that's good, it means the two realms are overlapping; we're parting the 'veil' so to speak.

What it also does is recharge the room itself, releasing a powerful stream of positive energy.

Clients often comment on the feeling they get when entering the room and how relaxed they feel.

Then by sitting and connecting with the patient and focusing you can replace their bad energy with good.

Where does this bad energy go?

Well let's just say I can feel rough afterwards. Have been known to sleep for hours and be good for nothing the next day.

The physical recovery can take a day or two if the patient has a serious condition, even be terminal. You can't cure a terminal illness, but you can ease the pain and even help that person deal with what's to come.

Several years ago I sat with a gentleman who had terminal cancer. He had never believed in spirits, never mind an afterlife.

During our sessions, my face would change into people he knew who had already passed over and they gave me messages to prove it was them.

Sadly he passed some time ago, but I like to believe I gave him a sense of belief he never had before.

When working with people with emotional problems the recovery rate can be different in that the cause of those emotional problems can hang around to torment the individual.

Many mental health issues have a root and are created through negative spiritual energy.

And for those scholars out there who have years of experience on the subject, I apologise before I start. But just ask yourself, as with much in this book, does what I'm saying make sense?

Possession.
Most of you will have heard of the term 'Possession.' Just as you will have heard the term 'Obsession.' Putting the two together, however, might come as a surprise.

Possession is thought of in terms of Demons making us do bad things.

We may think immediately of the film 'The Exorcist.'

Well bring your expectation down quite a lot and you'll get nearer to the truth.

Certain spirits, for different reasons, choose to remain closer to our realm than their own.

They cannot stay here for too long though, because their vibration will not slow down sufficiently.

So they move in to some, unsuspecting, individuals subconscious. Melding their energy with their hosts to allow them to stay

in this dimension for a longer time.
They will start to impose their will on their subject who is unlikely to be even aware of their existence.
This will translate into unexplained mood swings, at the very least, leading to addictions and depression further up the scale.
I am not saying that this is responsible for everyone who has a mental illness or an addiction.
I'm stating that this is one possible factor.
As I've already mentioned, people can get on a downer walking down the street if they come into contact with enough negative people, and they aren't all possessed.
Unwanted spirits can take up residence and make your life hell. Especially if you are vulnerable and open to suggestions from outside influences.
In its severest form, this can become multiple personality disorder, or schizophrenia.
Your unwanted spirit in residence is having a great time messing with you, so much so he invites some of his friends to come and join in.
Eventually these different personalities become stronger than the host, and they totally take over, and that person's body becomes little more than a vessel for their shenanigans.
The host is still in there; it's just that he/she's not as dominant as those running rampant in their subconscious.
Remember that the conscious mind only takes up 5.75 percent of the brain, so the squatters have most of the rooms at their

control.

It is possible, to remove these unwanted spirits, one at a time, piece by piece.

Consider this.

The brain is a sophisticated computer. All computers need hardware to function. Let's allow 8 percent for this. That leaves 92 percent.

92 divided by 5.75 equals 16.

Remove the 5.75 percent that takes up our conscious mind and that leaves space for up to 15 other personalities to move in.

And consider this further. What if several personalities shared one space?

Not trying to scare monger, but facts are facts.

However, as with most things, the process for removing unwanted guests should be simple. If we remove something, be it good, bad, or indifferent, we have to replace it. Otherwise there will be a void that will leave us feeling empty.

So if we remove one personality, or energy, we have to put something else in its place.

So replace something negative with something positive.

Get rid of the spirit with homicidal tendencies and replace it with a loved one who you were close too. Like a parent, if you've lost one, or a grandparent or close relative.

They love you so they don't want to possess you, and once you feel comfortable they'll gradually vacate the space, leaving you to get on with your life.

The only problem is that if you don't get to the bottom of what caused your issues in the first place there's no guarantee it wont happen again.

Replacing one spirit for another can be done by a very good medium, prepared to put themselves through the process.

Get the patient to visualise on the loved one they want around them. This gives the spirit the energy to come forward.

The medium then makes the unwanted spirit an offer it can't refuse.

Sanctuary in their own subconscious. A holiday if you like. With the option to move on if they get bored.

If the spirit refuses, then the medium visualises on the situation later.

Remember, think of someone who's died and you create an energy that draws them to you. So whilst the medium thinks of the unwanted spirit, the patient thinks of their loved one.

It only takes a moment for the unwanted spirit to leave the room and for your loved one to move in.

With nowhere to go the spirit takes up the mediums invitation only to be greeted by an army of helpers who assist the spirit in moving on.

Obsession.

We know, strictly s/peaking what an obsession is.

The uncontrollable persistence of an idea, or emotion, in the mind.

In spiritual terms it takes on a whole new meaning.

External possession.

Spirits can take control of an area, like a room, or a bigger space, a whole house, workplace, meeting place, i.e.: pub or restaurant. Though they won't be there all the time, because their vibration won't allow for this.

At night when the vibration between the two realms is at its closest they will be do their dirty work.

A bit like an animal marking its territory, they will leave an essence of themselves, which can then affect a person's personality.

Again, a little like passing someone in the street only greatly enhanced because the energy signature is in your home or a building where you spend much of your time.

Imagine waking up to an irresistible urge to kick the first person you meet. Well chances are that thought's only there because some mischievous spirit's left that feeling behind after a visit.

Most of us would resist the urge, but not everyone's mind is strong, and the odd one or two would enjoy giving a total stranger a good kick, beggar the consequences.

Knowing they can control our actions, the spirit will then up the ante, personality traits becoming more bizarre and out of character.

Governed by almost uncontrollable energy signatures left in the places you eat sleep, shower, work, and entertain.

Sometimes the spirits are trying to pass on a message.

They might have lived there before you and don't like what you've done with the place.

It could be the Mother-in-Law who never quite trusted you.

You might have ruined their lives and they want some form of retribution.

Or you just might be in the wrong place at the wrong time. A random event.

If you are strong enough to dismiss them, most people will, they may resort to other tactics. Who's seen 'Poltergeist'?

One important factor I haven't mentioned, those most affected by this phenomena are not the true believers out there.

If you know what's happening, you can do something about it.

No, those that these spirits take advantage of the none believers who are unaware of what's occurring around them.

Again, the way to handle this is simple.

If you feel you have unwanted activity in your home, then get it cleansed. The entire house/building to be certain.

Any medium worth their salt should be able to carry this out for you.

And remember if someone wants to charge you for these services make sure they are the real deal first.

He/She who charges the most isn't necessarily the best by any means. There are excellent mediums out there, but the really good ones are few and far between.

Chapter Seventeen: A Story Of Possession/Obsession, The Monkey Boy.

There are some events that can be recalled a lot easier than others.

Everyone does this, but my library contains material the rest of you would probably overload on.

Don't worry we'll go back to my early years and further look at what made me the man I've become, but this bears relevance now, so we jump ahead to 2001/02 when these experiences occurred.

My development has become my religion.

There isn't a church I go to; I'd fallen out with the spiritualist lot ages ago.

Swearing in church.

Does 'Bloody' count?

Bugger might, but if the spirit says it, surely we can repeat it.

I wouldn't really swear in any church.

The woman that ran this particular branch in Doncaster claimed that Spirits do not swear; they have ascended beyond swearing and obscenities.

Bollocks. You should hear some of things they whisper in my ear.

I'd gone to Sheffield to see some clients.

I don't like doing too many readings in one go, but times are hard and the rent needs paying.

I'd just moved back up North from London and no-one really knew of my reputation and anyway I'd not done sittings for awhile, so

getting back into it was hard work.
So I went to this house at the top of a hill,
always remember the hill, went on forever.
The house, however, isn't important.
Neither is the owner, nor all bar one of the
clients.
She was, thankfully, the last of the day.
The room they'd put me in was a throwback
to the days when the best china was put on
show in glass cabinets. In fact, everything
had a cabinet. Stereo, television, drinks. Nice
room though, comfortable chairs, leather.
Smell of polish, where the dark wood had
been brought up to a pristine shine.
If they'd done this for my benefit, the effort
had been wasted,
I would never say anything though. They
were lovely people who made me most
welcome.
And then she walked in the room.
Seventy years old or there abouts, but with
an air of arrogance, well something beyond
self assurance at least. Her face was heavily
lined; a walking stick to help her walk.
 Though she dressed as a much younger
woman would, and did seem to carry this off
very well.
Other than her age, I noticed none of this at
that moment.
A sense of oppression had entered the room
with her. Along with a, now familiar, icy blast
that enveloped me.
I felt overwhelmed and knew I wasn't going
to be reading this woman for love nor
money.
She sat facing me; her smile took on a

strange, surreal quality.
Like a child who's about to admit to
something really bad, but isn't going to give
a damn about the consequences.
I found myself sweating, trying to stay calm, 'I
might have a problem linking into you.'
To this day I can't recall her name, but I'll
never forget her words, 'I have a little Demon
who stays with me.'
No shit Sherlock.
'Two years ago we had nothing, and now
we're millionaires. We moved into a new
house and he was there.'
Now, despite my way of life, I was skeptical.
If this woman believed someone was around
her, then she would be empowering some
energy to do just that, but a Demon was a bit
of a stretch.
I tried to smile, couldn't muster anything
close.
'He doesn't like you, says he's not going to let
you in.' She seemed delighted by this.
I moved deeper into the chair,
uncomfortable, starting to sweat even more
profusely, though the room temperature had
dipped dramatically.
'Who is he?'
'He doesn't have a name. He's a monkey-
boy. He's stood right next to you.'
I did smile now, couldn't help it.
Back then, my beliefs were somewhat
different from today. Learning is an ongoing
process that has no end. Perceptions change
as we gather knowledge and if my
understanding could have fast forwarded to
the present, well I might not have suddenly

decided she was a 'fruit-loop.

'Spirits usually don't take on the shapes of both people and animals at the same time.'

'This is a Demon; I've already told you.' She was adamant.

I wanted her gone, out of the house but was also intrigued. Who wouldn't be?

'And this, er Demon was in the house when you arrived?'

'We moved to start a business and two years later we have everything. I knew he was there I just summoned him,' She laughed.

There was a glass of water on a table at the side of my chair. It fell to the floor, spilling the water in its wake.

Oh please, come on, I thought.

Any minute now her head would start spinning emitting projectile vomit in all directions. I was trying to remain professional, but this woman could not be for real.

Although if she had done any of the aforementioned actions I would have been out of there.

'Why have you booked in to see me?'

'I'd heard you were very good and wanted to see for myself.'

'My friend says you're not as good as you think. He's going to teach you a lesson.'

There was no menace, just a matter of fact statement.

Five minutes later she was gone. A man was waiting for her, her son I assumed.

The house owners could tell she'd left me troubled. I'd begun to shake at some stage during proceedings, and this hadn't abated. They explained her story, which did nothing to lift my mood.

The woman's companion was in fact her husband. It had been his idea to send her to me, as the Doctors seemed to have given up.

She was only forty, younger than me.

Two years ago they'd moved into this house and up to that time she had been fine.

Her husband's business was thriving, manufacturing garden gates or something of that nature.

She, however, had a different take on this. Within months, she was becoming more reclusive and taken to pushing her nearest and dearest away.

The business was flourishing, not through graft and hard work, but because she had found a new friend who was manipulating events and people.

This new friend being 'The Monkey Boy.'

Her husband was horrified as this was totally out of character for her. Admittedly it did appear that everything he touched seemed to turn to gold at the moment, but he didn't believe in such twaddle as demons.

The more she became obsessed with this new 'friend' the more she shut herself off and the more she began to age.

He forced her to see a doctor who in turn could give no answers.

Then an event occurred that frightened him beyond belief.

They were out walking when a woman on a horse almost knocked them over. There was an exchange of words and threats passed between the two women.

She told her husband she'd sort her out next time the moon was full.

The husband was ready for giving up on her. Then a few weeks later on a Saturday night the horse owner heard a screaming noise coming from the stables. She had three horses so went out to check a wild animal wasn't trying to get in to their enclosure. Two of the horses were bedded down for the night; the third wasn't in his stable, yet the door was firmly locked.

She found the horse in a nearby field. It had been eviscerated. The same horse she'd been riding a few weeks earlier.

The shock of what she saw when she found the animal was what they blamed for the stroke she had two days later.

All of this happened around the time of the next full moon.

All I could think was' Revenge of the Monkey Boy.'

I left the house, and thus far have never returned to Sheffield, couldn't tell you what happened to the woman and her husband. You see life is like that. Not everything is all wrapped up in a ribbon. People do disappear never to be seen again. We get half a tale but don't always get to find a resolution.

But this was nowhere near the end of the 'Monkey Boy' story.

It had been a full day and I was back in Harrogate for eleven thirty in the evening. There was still a ten minute walk from the railway station to my home.

There was hardly a soul about, not unusual for

a weekday night in the gate. Walking up my street is very pleasant, even in winter. Whilst on one side we have three/four storey Edwardian terraced houses. Only a few can still bear the title 'house.' They are mainly broken up into flats, the odd guest house, and even a few restaurants.

Imposing looking properties, most of them. On the opposite side of the road we have the Valley Gardens. A public park, gardens, pine woods. One of the most beautiful natural places anywhere.

So I hardly notice the small child hanging around outside the house. A child crouching in the darkness so as not to be seen.

I stopped in my tracks, feeling the November cold for the first time.

It's was too late for a kid to be out on his own, especially in Harrogate.

Doncaster and my childhood were polar opposites to where I lived now. Anyway that was thirty years ago.

'What you doing there. Where do you live? There was no strength to my voice; the words half whispered. Bloody hell it was only a little lad, stop it.

I moved forward purposefully and the child ran off down the road.

Only this was definitely not a child. Naked but covered in hair. A long tail whipped out behind him as he/it headed off down the street away from me.

It let out a cry like I had never heard before. Like a monotone chattering sound slowly rising in crescendo until it became like a scream. A noise that continued to resound in my head long after the image had disappeared into the night.

Imagination. At it's most extreme, the subconscious can kid the conscious mind into believing something's happened that would otherwise be irrational.

That had to be the answer.

I knew I'd just been a victim of this. After all, there could be no other explanation.

'Monkey-Boys' were not real, had no basis or foundation in real life.

It was still a good few hours before I could get to sleep.

I had a close friend in Doncaster, more like family really at the time.

Amy. A beautiful, if some what troubled soul. At her best she could draw people to her and would do anything to help anyone. The other side of Amy was her mood swings and change in personality that could transform her into someone else.

She had a boy, Richard. Eight years old, bright, bubbly, a real credit to his mum.

There was a boyfriend at the time, but he was going to go the same way as all the others, eventually.

She was in my life for about four years in all and as with most things, ran its course.

Would I have liked it to be more?

At the time, perhaps yes.

But once we start to see things from a different angle, and there is distance between two people, well that's when we truly find out how we feel. I cared but did not love Amy. At that time I was looking for a place to belong.

Emotionally, the truth is best seen from a distance because our energies disconnect once we are apart and only the strongest of emotions, good or bad, remain to remind us of what we had.

We spoke most days, much to the chagrin of her current boyfriend. Though for her to ring at seven in the morning was unusual.

'Richard woke up crying twice in the night and he wet the bed.'

Now Amy could edge towards the melodramatic but not where her son was concerned. 'He kept dreaming he was being chased by a monkey that wanted to hurt him.'

I went cold. All thought of sleep replaced by an urgent need to be with my friend.

Years later I realised I could have probably dealt with this best in my own little room. Everyone has a place, usually in their home, where they find some peace and quiet. For a practicing medium it becomes their work space and is generally protected from unwanted elements by the medium's spirit guides.

So packing a bag and heading off to Amy's, whilst seemingly the only solution at the time, well it was playing into 'The Monkey Boy's hands somewhat.

Of course, Richard's in school, the boyfriend's at work and I get to spend the day with Amy. All thoughts of unwanted guests put on the back burner.

After school the little boy seemed fine so, again, this put any idea of saving the day into perspective.

We have experiences, bad dreams, those 'There's nobody really there' feelings. Because they are outside our everyday understanding of events we tend to quickly push them into our subconscious.

Richard neither wanted to talk or think about his dreams. What frightened him was the uncertainty of whether he was being chased by some small orangutan or another child. Now think about this. How could a malevolent energy jump from one person it hardly knows to another connected to them, and so quickly?

I had only been aware of this energy for a few hours yet it already had my home address and had the means to find my closest friends.

Once that energy connects to you it gets into your mind. Can go into your filing cabinet and see everything in there. Past, present, and future. There is no easy way to hide information especially when you aren't expecting someone to gain access in the first place.

Anyway this was the first time this had happened and, at that moment, was way beyond anything I had previously experienced.

By bedtime, Richard had become all the more nervous. You could see his demeanour begin to become more agitated.

I found myself asking for help, in my head. Amy knew everything that had happened and there was no point in keeping it back from her. The idea that something was using her son to get at me didn't go down too well, but then it wouldn't.

I read Richard a bedtime story, and that's when the idea came to me.

Putting the book down, I asked Richard to close his eyes.

I described a young lady. Someone whom, if he went to sleep thinking of her, would protect him from anything he didn't want in his dreams.

She had raven black hair that ran beyond her shoulders, a constant smile, was wearing a white dress and summer sandals, leather. For effect, I added a white horse and a light sabre, which she would be expertly practiced in using.

If we take the trimmings away I was, of course describing the angel that was Hailey.

When I stayed over at Amy's, my bed was a mattress on the lounge floor. My back would cry out in horror these days.

But it was fine back then and, anyway, it was all about 'Demons' and protecting children.

Now, I'm sorry to disappoint you, would love to describe some great battle where good triumphed over evil and I saved the day, but real life isn't like that.

Yes, I had a bad nights sleep, and yes, I endured hell. That was mainly because Amy and the boyfriend were going at it until God knows what time, and I couldn't settle.

The boyfriend would do this in order to show me who the real daddy was. Though he never had the bottle to push me away all together.

Richard slept like a champion. Unlike yesterday he was happy to talk about his

dream, or what he could remember.
About a field that led to a beach where
there were other children playing in the sand.
He was riding a white horse but sharing the
horse with a girl.
The dream was fragmented but made me
think. Maybe he had made it up, something
to say maybe.
But how could he know about the field and
the beach?
 The 'Monkey Boy' either lost interest or found
another target very quickly.
Going home on the train next day, thinking
about Amy and Richard, what it would be
like to have a family of my own.
And a voice in my subconscious putting me
firmly in my place, 'You're a silly arse
Christian, you are that.'

Chapter Eighteen: Reincarnation, The Stories.

Reincarnation does exist.
It's just that it isn't a common occurrence
and doesn't happen in the way that many
people would like to believe.
For years I was convinced I'd been here
several times.
After all the origins of where we came from
are as important as where we are going.
The idea of constantly moving from body to
body, life to life, niggled away at me
somewhat.
Surely there had to be more, that's what I'd
always told myself.
In 1993, I underwent a series of regression
exercises.
To begin with, we focused on the times in my
life when certain traumatic events had
occurred.
Events I have already described to you.
The lady who worked with me also managed
to unlock the compartment in my brain
where my subconscious travels had taken
me.
Other than my dream on Christmas Eve,
almost twenty years earlier, the other
experiences had been buried, out of reach.
Without these sessions I wouldn't have been
able to write about my travels to this magical
place.
At the time, I was still unsure of whether there
was anything to validate this place has being
somewhere real.

What was certain though, was that my mind had led me to a safe haven. Somewhere to help me cope with the momentary trauma I was locked into on the earth plain.

Then I was taken to a time before I was born.

March 2000.

My head was banging and I'd been locked in the boot of a car.

It was the early hours, probably about three. I'd had something slipped into my drink and was being dragged off to God knows where. I'd gotten involved in the search for a missing person and travelled to a Greek Island with a member of the child's family.

One week to look around, see what I could come up with, see if I could find something everyone else, including the police, had missed.

Before I'd undertaken this task I'd conjured up maybe twenty pages of information, which I had channelled. Lack of experience or not, all this information related to two very different situations. They could have been connected, but they weren't. In fact for months I was sure there was a tie in.

Sometimes it can take awhile for the truth to sink in.

You noticed I said, 'months' not the week I originally allowed for this venture.

I'd written down the details, describing a house Could see the trees outside, two big, very different dogs.

My original instinct was that this house was connected to the missing child....and I found the house after three days of searching.

Working purely on instinct and where ever my guides were leading me.

The trip was being financed by a literary agent who was representing the family.

Through a greater sense of purpose for the better good, or the pound signs rolling before his eyes, he sent back up.

Well, a security team to be precise.

So I was talked into staying, and one week would become five months.

They'd been watching this house from a half built property which was on land next door.

The owners were Dutch and owned travel companies through out Europe.

My sense was that children had/were being kept in the house against there will.

So the house was watched for several weeks but to no avail.

Then the building was scanned with an infrared camera and they found no evidence of there being any children inside.

The team was ready for stringing me up, and all I could do was remain adamant. I knew what I'd been told.

Two ex-army guys decided to have a look at the back of the house. It was a big property and behind the house were about two miles of fields leading to the sea.

The first thing that caught them by surprise was a large look out built on top of the wall of the back garden. It was wooden and could easily house a full grown man for days if necessary. It had a roof against the wind and rain and would probably have given a good view of anyone coming in from the sea.

Thankfully no-one was there.

They put the dogs to sleep, humanely and temporarily of course, and went to work with their infra red cameras.

There were rooms below ground level, as though the basement had been altered and the windows were covered over with a tape that stopped unwanted eyes from seeing in. Including infra red cameras.

So we have the respectable front of house and much more dubious rear, and once more the game was afoot.

So, through a contact I had made, there was an invite to dinner in a restaurant with the Dutch couple and some English people who lived on the Island.

The idea was to try to read everyone at the table, of course they wouldn't know, and see what more could be gleaned from them.

The security people were watching me, and all was well with the world. Only once they saw what a great time I was seemingly having they left me too it and went off to find their own entertainment.

The car pulled up.

In my fugue I could hear the sea nearby, bloody choppy tonight. My first thought of real fear, I can't swim.

Images of a day long ago in Scarborough. How the hell did I get to this point?

Well the night becomes a blur after a while. The Dutch were the first to leave and I couldn't help but like them.

Awhile later several Greek guys joined our company and the next thing I remember is being in a small bar with them, and the original group have all gone off to 'who knows where'.

No knowledge beyond that until I regained consciousness.

The boot opened and I found myself being dragged out of the car.

It was unsurprisingly cold and I immediately began shivering.

After all, I hadn't dressed for a late night.

Though together with the headache, I thought I might very well be coming down with something.

Why did I always come up with stupid irrational thoughts in life threatening situations?

One of the Greeks pushed me to the floor.

The second pulled a gun from his waistband.

Pointed it at me. Moved closer, pushed the muzzle against my face.

And this almost familiar sense of calm washed over me.

If this is the moment so be it.

I should have been wetting myself, wanting to throw up.

Only later would I reflect on how scary my actions made me feel.

I grabbed hold of the barrel of the gun. And guided his hand so it was pressed against the space between my eyes.

Smiled.

Ardglass. 1916.

The boy is no more than seventeen.

They live on a farm, and what he does know is that his dad has been hiding rifles in one of the barns.

Fight the good fight and all that.

And they've questioned his dad for hours have the Brits, and now it's his turn.

He only knows about the guns because he's a watchful little Bastard and not much passes him by.

And anyway, if Dad says don't go rooting in there, what do you do?

However, the boy keeps his mouth shut, even when they start with their hob nailed boots and their sticks. They beat him black and blue the Bastards, but he didn't give anything away.

So the army truck takes him back home, after all he can hardly walk.

His ma fills the bath tub, and he doesn't have the strength to stop her from bathing him in front of his younger siblings. Two brothers and a sister, who keeps bringing jugs of hot water from God knows where.

His Dad sat at the table, quiet, having a seemingly silent conversation with his hands. The thumbs turning, in constant motion.

Then he's in his bed trying to find sleep. Something about his dad niggling away at him, his dad who couldn't even look in his direction, his dad who....

The bedroom door is flung open and four people crowd into his room.

In the hall he can hear is mother's voice shouting, one of the little 'uns crying in fright. He is manhandled from his bed, out of the house, into the night.

If he knows his abductors then he doesn't recognise them as they are wearing hessian bags on their heads. Holes cut out in the

appropriate places for their eyes and mouth.
If this wasn't so serious they would look
hilarious.
He's dragged into one of the barns and sat
on a wooden chair.
He can hear is mother screaming somewhere
off in the background.
'What have I done, what's going on'?
The pain inflicted by the soldiers has passed,
replaced by sheer terror. Morbid dread and
panic.
He urinates down his trouser leg, leaving a
puddle around his ankles.
One of the men produces a revolver, cocks
it.
'This is what happens to fucking traitors boy!'
Another voice, 'No, wait!'
Redemption?
One of the men removes their hoods.
He feels he should recognise him but doesn't.
This man, looking deeply remorseful, places
his hood over the boys head.
He wants to shout out but the words are stuck
in his throat.
He realizes they couldn't stand to see his
tears.
His last thought before they shoot him in the
head goes back to his father.
Why didn't he have a mark on him?

February 2000.
You see I believed I'd been here before.
Not once but twice.
Aardglass 1916.
A dream I had as a fifteen year old, that had
stayed with me and then resurfaced again

through regression.

How did I know it was Ardglass?

Well how did 'The Monkey Boy' know where I lived, or about the little boy, Richard? Something's we just know!

I got to my feet, unsteady, disorientated, all the while the gun remained pointed at my head.

I stumbled, fell again.

Words were shared in Greek. They laughed. Somehow I carried on smiling, maybe waiting to wake up.

The laughter turned to a snarl, and the man raised the gun intending to use it as a club. The other man spoke in a raised voice and the gun was lowered, then the muzzle pushed back into my face.

Paris. 1944.

She is in some basement of unknown origin. There are about a dozen men in the room but only two have her attention. One holds her whilst the other shaves her head.

Though she is tied to the chair, bound firmly by thick twine.

She is French and they call her a collaborator.

A charge which she denies but to no avail. Was she sleeping with the German officer? Yes.

Was she sharing secrets that put her fellow countryman at risk?

Absolutely not.

Anyway her man was a gentle soul and they were in love.

Not all Germans were evil. There was good

and bad in all people.

Her love was in France because he was stationed there. They met by chance in a café where she was a waitress.

If love at first sight can be quantified, well this was it.

They talked of running away together, planned for a life after the war. Naively she was open in her feelings for him and him for her. He was responsible for transport and supplies. An office worker really. He'd, as yet, never killed anyone. Only fired a gun during basic training. There was no harm in him.

But she had to choose and she chose him and her family were forced to disown her. Her sister and mother, who claimed to have been torn in two by her daughter's actions. There was no father. He'd died of influenza in '37.

Then one day her love was gone.

They had pulled out during the night, the allies closing in on Paris from all sides.

A letter had been pushed under the door of the small apartment they shared.

She suffered in silence, no-one to share her loss with. Shut herself off, only her tears for company, until they came for her three days later.

Breaking down the door in the early hours and dragging her away. Not even allowing her to dress properly, only a night gown hiding her modesty.

She was shocked; there must be some mistake.

But she grasped her situation as the kicks and punches started raining down on her

accompanied with one word. 'Traitor.'
Her mind was as shocked as her body. What was the greater pain?
The physical abuse that she could do nothing to stop or the betrayal.
Nothing but a letter. A promise to return but no indication of when.
Why hadn't he taken her with him?
Why no goodbyes?
Of course, much of her thought was irrational, but she was grasping for answers.
And now she was God knows where, her hair gone along with her dignity.
She became conscious of her nakedness, her night dress having been torn away at some point.
The men stood watching her for some considerable time, waiting for some sign of what to do next.
She began to tremble with the cold of the cellar, trying to be brave, keep her tears to herself.
After awhile she sensed the worst was over.
She thought she may be very well be back home by morning.
One of the men comes up behind her.
The last thing she heard was an audible click before he pulled the trigger and ended her time in this world.

This was my last regression session.
For several weeks later I had a German man talking to me during my meditations. The man turned up on three occasions.
It was the first time anyone had spoken another language in my head. Unfortunately,

I can't speak German so was unable to translate what was said.
The lady who had regressed me said she was told, by a spirit, that I'd died in a similar way once before the incident described and should understand what she meant.
Ireland 1916 and Paris 1944.
Once as a man, once as a woman. Yes, who's to say if we keep coming back that we can't/don't change sex?

February 2000.
I had held on to the idea of having been shot to death twice, potentially in previous lives, and here I was in the present with a gun to my head.
It did nothing to explain my strange sense of calm though.
The simple fact is it wasn't my time to die and in my subconscious I knew this.
'You stick your nose in business that doesn't concern you and you see what happens.'
This was the unarmed Greek guy who seemed to be in charge.
I'd like to say I followed up with some witty repost, but I said nothing.
'Maybe it would be best if you went home tomorrow, or maybe we make you disappear.
There was a thought now. I wondered what they'd say if they knew what I did for a living? I think it would been lost on them.
'Next time we see you it will be different, now go home, there's nothing for you here.'
They got in their car and sat watching me.
As they seemingly weren't going to offer me

a lift, I began to walk.

Keeping the sea to my left I saw as my best bet as, unless I had no sense of direction at all, this would get me back to the hotel.

After a while, the street lights became less frequent.

I was still aware of the car idling behind me. They were certainly dawdling, not wanting to overtake, maybe see what I did or maybe they'd been on the phone to get instructions from whoever had put them up to this.

Perhaps they were saving their bullets for someone more deserving. Maybe they intended to run me over instead, which to my mind was worse.

A bullet, well it's over. Knock me down and they might have to reverse over me to make sure the job was done.

This thought frightened me a lot more than facing the gun.

I tried jogging, as if I could outrun a car for God's sake.

Common sense said the car couldn't get me on the beach, but that door was firmly closed as the tide was in so I continued on down the road.

The game of cat and mouse continued for perhaps an hour, and I seemed to be going nowhere. Up ahead was still little more than a straight road leading nowhere, to my left the sea, to my right, fields.

Behind, the car continued to tease me.

Then another vehicle came into view from the other direction.

I decided I was going to stop this car even if I had to throw myself in front of it.

There was no need.
It was a police car, and it stopped. The officers, near perfect English, offered assistance.
The other car sped away as I was getting in.
I said nothing, was dropped off at my hotel, another crazy drunken Englishman.
I let my 'minders' know what genius' they were by bursting into their room at 5:30 in the morning.
For awhile the experience made me wonder if I'd survived something more than death.
The idea being that I may have been shot twice in previous lives and then beaten the odds on this occasion.
This stayed with me until my perception, once more changed. The reality is something much more complex than just jumping from body to body.
I had one more experience relating to reincarnation, or talk of it. Much later though, 2008.
My studio apartment is functional. There's everything in one big room, great for watching television in bed.
Separate bathroom and kitchen.
Though the kettle and fridge are actually in the studio, not the kitchen, and there are stainless steel sinks in both rooms.
I'd arrived in 2001, taking three months out to write a book, being told I wouldn't be leaving here until it was complete.
For each year that passed there was a stop/start process.
Every year I would start, and then quickly stop. Like facing a high wall, knowing that the

only way is over but it seems insurmountable.
And anyway there were other distractions.
My health wasn't great, didn't feel balanced.
I just did enough to live, nothing more nor
less.
My abdomen would shake inside as if
someone had put a phone in there and left it
on vibrate.
Again it was a question of perception. I didn't
know what was happening.
At this time 2004/05 I had no inclination that
spirit might exist on such diverse different
levels. Remember, lower end spiritual energy
vibrates at least 2000 faster than we can
blink, so try and imagine how fast the higher
energies can move.
When doing a reading the energies are in the
room with you, which isn't so obtrusive.
But when writing, those same energies would
connect through the subconscious; they are
literally inside of you.
There vibration cannot match with your own
so you get the shakes, internally.
The higher the energy, the more the effect
on your body. Your stomach feels knotted,
but as though that knot is moving inside of
you.
The brain starts to go numb after awhile,
though the left side starts to throb like a pulse.
At that time I had difficulty coping with this.
Didn't understand what was happening.
So I was drifting along, doing just enough.
It was a Sunday night.
I'm awoken by something falling and to a
pale blue light bathing the room.
Looking around I saw the kettle had fallen

into the sink. Impossible?

Someone would have physically had to have done that.

And why was there a blue light in the room in the middle of the night?

The sink was off to the right hand side of the room.

In the top left hand corner of the room was a blue ball of light. It was about a foot long in diameter and seemed to be revolving like a disco ball.

Describing the ball of light as blue isn't enough. There was every shade of blue imaginable pulsing in the sphere. The darker colours running through it, throbbing like blood vessels, tendrils reaching out, trying to expand the ball.

There was also an aura of white light that expanded the ball by another foot or so.

It was simply the biggest spirit orb I'd ever seen.

Now being an experienced medium, I leapt out of bed to confront the intruder, reaching for my handily placed crucifix as my only means of protection.

Of course I didn't.

That's what you might expect from me, but instead I pulled the duvet over my head shutting out the image.

After all if I can't see it, well it can't be there can it?

Would my actions be the same today, probably not?

Even then I'd dealt with scarier situations than this, living and not. The images of that 'Monkey Boy' just wouldn't go away.

This was different. This really did scare me. Whether this was said out loud or in my head, I couldn't be sure. 'Who are you, what do you want?'

A male voice replied, loud and clear in the room. 'God.'

Silence for a few minutes.

I very slowly pulled back the quilt.

The room was still bathed in blue light, though now it had settled down and was pulsating slowly, as if to a rhythm.

The voice again, matter of fact, 'If you don't carry out the task you were put here to do, then you will only have to come back and do it all again.'

The blue light vanished within a millisecond, and the room returned to darkness.

I was left to my thoughts.

It could have been a threat but wasn't.

It was a very clear message.

A cold hard fact.

Chapter Nineteen: Reincarnation, The Truth.

In the column that is 'for' the idea that we are reborn, well my experiences could be pretty conclusive.

Though I have never checked the validity of these events they felt real at the time. As real as my Christmas dream as a child, as real as the dozen or so 'other world' experiences I have yet to write about.

The 'God' experience put me well and truly on the back foot at the time.

But God never used the word reincarnation. He stated, simply, that I would have to come back and do it all again.

There was no explanation of how and when to accompany the statement.

I have learnt since what he meant and the answer, when we get there will be mind blowing.

In the 'against' column there is a simple fact that I now understand to be true.

When we pass over, generally speaking, we continue on with our journey, and that does not include an immediate return ticket to the earth plain.

There are exceptions.

Highly evolved spiritual energy can return if there is a purpose to be served in doing so.

Also, when we cross over, an essence, or percentage of our energy, can remain earth bound if we haven't fulfilled our purpose.

Generally speaking, you won't initially be aware of this occurrence.

You will simply feel that you have passed to the next level.

Those lower end energies that exist around level two, the very same energies that can torment so many people, taking up room in their subconscious. Well if they prefer this realm to their own, why don't they reincarnate?

Well they would if they could, wouldn't they? Usually only if someone has been doing a family tree, can I get links that are several hundred years old, but I get them all the same.

Remember if you think of someone that has died you then give them the energy to come forward. Irrespective of the amount of time passed, or whether you knew them or not.

If they want to be recognised, or have something to say then they'll put in an appearance.

Once we pass to the other side we do not return, but whilst not wishing to repeat myself, there are possible scenarios where a portion of our energy can remain on this plain to be reused later.

This plain of existence, as we know all too well, exists in time.

Sprit sense of timing is all different from ours. There is no past, present or future as we have here.

Instead, they live their lives as a series of events, many of which they will experience more than once, jumping from scenario to scenario.

Each person they interact with will be experiencing their own events in their own time bubble.

You go to visit your Grandma and Grandad, and you are a new arrival.

You sit and have afternoon tea. Chat about old times.

The tea is for your benefit because that's what you remember of them.

In spirit eating and drinking is not a necessity. It's your physical body that craved those things, not your spiritual energy. Eventual you'll come to realise this but maybe not straight away.

Your Grandma and Grandad will, most likely, take on the appearance of how you remember them.

Again for your benefit.

Their energy can take on the appearance of any age they choose too. They can look younger than you if they want.

Whilst your spiritual energies are running low after one visit, your grandparents may very well be tripping the light fantastic for some considerable amount of time.

They have more energy than you so will be able to function longer and do more in their 'waking' time.

So for you, the visit feels like it has lasted for several hours, and for them a much shorter period.

But each person's time in spirit is individual to them, where as time here is the same for everyone, in a physical sense.

This is because of vibration.

The more energy we collect the faster it vibrates.

Though this energy can slow down for a short

amount of time, it cannot be slowed indeterminably.

In order to be reincarnated from spirit we would have to slow back down, and that just isn't possible.

What about the moment we die, however? That short journey from the shell we have left and into the light that beckons us.

Sometimes, though certainly not as often as you may think, a portion of our energy remains behind to be reborn at a later time.

Throughout eternity we will share energy, the centre, or core, being the main element that will always remain within us.

This core contains all our memories, the knowledge we've collected, experiences undertaken. It is our essence.

Like a computer mainframe holding the data of our lives.

Sometimes we come to the end of our time here but we haven't achieved our objectives.

Like a half read book, or a movie we haven't seen to the end. Everything in this world and the next, has a cycle, and these cycles have to be completed.

We get as much help as possible to complete our circle of life but what the circle encompasses and the purpose, individually, may never be clear.

It could be as simple as learning a lesson about yourself as a person. Maybe to save a life more relevant than your own. It could even be to save the world. Anything.

Not everyone will identify their path, but if you get to a point, probably later in life,

where you feel content and fulfilled, then
you'll more than likely have achieved what
you were put here to do.
So, how much energy is left behind?
Let's look at the brain.
Imagine, to simplify matters, that we pass
over taking 94.25% of the mind with us and
leave 5.75% behind. The percentage taken
up by our consciousness.
Probably the minimum amount we can leave
behind.
So we are going into the light, that last
millisecond when time exists to us as it is now,
and it is ordained from on high that our job
here is not complete.
That small portion of our energy breaks away
with the intention of being reborn.
Now it isn't a case of coming back within
hours, weeks, months of passing.
Usually the waiting time is years.
The first job of that energy is to replenish, to
grow, and it does so by working as an
element.
What dictates this is your birth sign.
For instance, if like me you are a water sign,
and then you become part of the workings of
water and everything connected to it.
Earth signs become part of the growth of the
earth, not just soil but trees, plants, flowers.
Air signs will work in the atmosphere.
Fire signs at the earths core.
These energies can become animals, or part
of the essence.
Don't imagine for one minute that you'll be a
great white rhino rampaging around
because you can't have your old life back.

There'll be no such memories of a human life, but all the while that energy is growing and at the right time will go into the right person where your rebirth will take place.

No conscious memory of your past, a blank slate. Your mission is to complete what you were originally put here to accomplish.

You still won't know what it is, but the person you become will be better placed perhaps to achieve your goals.

The truth is we may have had a hundred goals to achieve and only managed a percentage of them.

There, again, are exceptions.

On occasion, particularly if the energy whilst on the earth plain suffered physical or emotional trauma, instead of departing into the ether and becoming an element, the energy returns to familiar territory.

A place where there are strong energy connections, particularly old buildings or close to ley lines.

The energy will take root seeking safety in familiar surroundings.

These are more commonly referred too as ghosts.

Trapped energy that goes around in a loop. Playing out the same scenario over and over for evermore.

They are not a spirit; just an essence of the spirit left behind.

Meanwhile In spirit, you are busy ascending unaware of the outcome of what happened to that part you left behind.

At some point you will become complete again, more whole than you can imagine at this time but to begin with you'll have enough on your plate evolving, learning how to improve yourself.

What if your failings on the earth plain were to be measured by some future calamity? An event of some magnitude that could affect hundreds, maybe even thousands of lives.

And that small part of you left behind is working as an element. Obliviously swimming around in a goldfish bowl or being admired for your beauty at a flower show.

Well this cannot be allowed to happen. So more energy is held back at the time of passing and rebirth can then happen more quickly.

What it means for your spiritual welfare, on the other side, is that you will evolve more slowly to begin with.

You'll have to work at collecting that lost energy before you can properly begin your spiritual ascension.

And then there are 'Walk-Ins.'

You or I could be a 'Walk-In' and you'd likely as not never even know.

No, it's not some deadly decease. Neither is it some anti-social stigma that drives people away.

It is full energy reincarnation.

At the moment of passing over you don't go into the light at all but almost immediately are reborn into another body.

What is the reason for this, what is their purpose?

Well they are like a sleeper cell.

Ancient knowledge from a time when the

path to heaven was closer, long since lost or forgotten.

Imagine individuals who together can explain the meaning of life.

Each privy to a separate part of a huge puzzle.

Individually they make little sense but together can build an elaborate tapestry that explains our purpose and history, and hold the keys to the secret worlds that exist beside our own.

These individuals can also be broken up into subsections.

The easiest example is to look at the four cornerstones of religion.

We have Buddhism, whose earliest links were to Taoism.

The Muslim religion, Islam. Christianity, and the oldest of all Hinduism.

Forgive my ignorance if I have any of this wrong, I have no desire to insult anyone here. These are the four cornerstones of religion because all other recognised religious groups have their foundations based around one or more of these doctrines.

We can go back to the Greek and Norse Gods in a sense.

They may have had different names these Gods, but they were just the same.

Their places were in the heavens and in a likewise manner we can change the names of those gods in to the names of Angels.

All one and the same.

I'm no expert on Gods but imagine the Norse god Thor, is known to the Greeks as Jupiter, would be known to Christians as the Angel

Michael.
All the same just under different names.
Now there is only one god.
He/ She is a universal energy that
encompasses and is part of us all.
It is not lost on me that the god that spoke to
me was male in the manner he/she spoke.
Though I'm sure the tones would have been
more dulcet and invitingly female had the
carrot been more relevant than the stick.
Back to religion. No-one religion is whole or
complete.
There is truth in all the scripts, but we are truly
meant to put the four quarters together to
find our truth path.
It's just that the true word as gotten lost in
translation over the centuries and that is why
there are different interpretations for each
message and much is open to abuse.
For sure, we are not meant to go out there
destroying one another.
We have always killed since Cain took a rock
to Abel's head. But that doesn't mean we
are meant too.
Most of us have primeval urges to protect
those we love but not many have it in them
to kill.
And perhaps those that do have it in them
quite possibly could literally have been an
animal for a short while at some point in time.
Remember for every rebirth there will be a
part of your subconscious where your history
is stored.
We are all part of one another or were at
some point in history.
Through rebirth, through our parents, our

ancestors, through one of the many realities out there.

If we inflict pain on others, whatever the form, we are inflicting that pain onto ourselves somewhere else.

God knew his plans would be abused.

Nothing is without flaws, and there are those forces that oppose the plan.

The Devil is not God's advisory, far from it, that particular energy is part of God. One of the many angels out there, given the role of keeping balance.

Without the temptation of bad we can never appreciate good.

Whilst we ascend in a certain direction in the heavens, relevant to our birth sign, those lower end energies take comfort under the devil's cloak.

Whilst lower end energies can manipulate and play with weak minded souls, the real evil that man inflicts on his own kind is just that. Man made.

It goes back to our instincts, not just to survive, but also to thrive.

Imagine a world without war.

A place of peace, tranquility.

Would that be heaven?

God has a blueprint for such a place and so as not to corrupt his master plan, he broke it up into four pieces and the ethos of religion was created.

When the Dali Llama dies it is said that his spirit passes directly into another chosen one, only not a new born but someone already here.

It is possible.

After all, he's only taking up one of the
portions of the subconscious available to him.
Though I'd be more convinced if the energy
chose a woman from time to time. After all
we are all God's children.
Everyone is meant to be equal, irrespective
of faith. The scriptures were written by men
for men and they are all outdated.
But the followers of Buddhism are correct.
Their spiritual leader, at the moment of death,
passes into another, preserving the age old
information that makes up there quarter of
the whole picture.
If this cornerstone is reincarnated as a whole,
then the other three cornerstones do likewise.
Now I'm not suggesting that Jesus or any
other religious figure has been reborn and is
walking amongst us, not at all.
I will suggest that someone who lived over
two thousand years ago has been
reincarnated through the ages, a figure who
started life as an observer at introduction of
Christianity and carries his or her quarter of
the puzzle.
For each cornerstone there is a walk-in, an
observer who subconsciously collates and
collects information, storing it away safely for
some time much later.
A time when the four cornerstones will come
together and eventually all religion will
become as one.
Not in this life time or any time in the next
thousand years, I hear you say.
Well who knows?
They co-exist in all the realms of all the worlds
in this universe and beyond.

No-one knows who these people are; they will be unaware themselves, will have been through out time. They could be the local village drunk, a nun working hard under some vow of silence; they could be in prison for unspeakable crimes, or a baby born just yesterday.

What matters is that, if the world survives to this point, they will eventually reawaken and come together with secrets to the universe way beyond this narrative.

Chapter Twenty: Energy Connections and Anomalies.

I've talked about those imaginary energy
meters and how they can cause and effect
any numbers of emotions on a personal level.
Energy links, singularly or on a dual level, as in
relationships of every kind, are what we deal
with every day.
There are other energy connections we
make, just as important in stature.
These links are collective.
Be it a group of friends, or a team of some
description. On a larger scale, we can look at
a platoon of soldiers, a workforce, and an
affiliation.
Even higher up the scale we can direct our
examples towards religious beliefs and
political alliances.
Irrespective of size, any group will dictate the
way we feel for the time we are connected
to the energy they are creating as a group.
Some groupings are pleasurable. If we are all
on the same page and in agreement, then
we'll feel pretty satisfied, safe even. If a
thousand people agree with each other,
they can usually assume that they are going
to share common ground, even if their
objectives aren't right.
You go to support your football team, and if
there are twenty odd thousand people there
cheering them on, then you can be sure that
the emotion in the crowd will be shared
whatever happens.
That collective energy can wash over to the

team and help them win. That's why sometime's a crowd can been seen as an extra man.

Alternatively, let's briefly look at politics. You choose a party to support. This isn't based on who can do the best for the country; it's who can do the best for you and the place you live.

We ask the question, how will this affect me and my way of life?

There's nothing wrong with this; self preservation is the most natural of instinct. And if we can't look after ourselves, then how can we look after those that matter most?

As a boy in Doncaster if anyone on our estate put a Conservative leaflet in their window, I feared for their well being. No-one actually got tarred and feathered, but I'm sure people were shunned publicly if their alliance wasn't red.

Red being the colour of the labour party posters.

Though, unlike football, political alliances can quickly change.

How often do we find we get most down over some political decision that detracts from our everyday lives?

Politicians are meant to represent us. Not treat us like children and tell us what we can and cannot do.

In fairness, the western world, for the best part, is very lucky. We don't have dictatorships or murdering despots to enslave us.

It seems that it's every man for himself; you

only have to look at certain political scandals for the proof, and most nations have their priorities all wrong.

We can't afford the money to repair schools and educate our children properly, yet we can send our monarch on a State visit that costs the same amount per annum.

The Government would say it's a different budget, and I would say, it's the wrong priority.

Let's put our money into getting the basics right, so we can build for our future.

Luxuries can come when everyone prospers again.

That's me off the New Years honours list anytime soon....bugger.

You see, thinking about politics as got a response from me and I'm not that passionate on the subject. Or I wasn't until two minutes ago.

So we step in and out of our groups. They will always tap into our emotion, always incite responses.

There is a way of creating balance in groups. A method that creates more emotion, as an everyday occurrence, than any other singular experience.

Music.

I'm constantly listening to music; whilst I write. It inspires me, encourages me to keep going when I'd sooner be doing something else.

Music as been with us since, well since time began.

Who doesn't listen to music?

Who doesn't feel inspired, impassioned, calmed, by certain songs?

Music can trigger any number of emotions depending on our mood and the particular sound you're listening to at that moment. Every ones tastes are slightly different, just as all of our personalities slightly differ.

Music is inspired by spirit. Our guides encourage us to write, compose, and perform.

Every piece of music, every song, is a shared collaboration between the composer and spirit guide.

Many song writers out there won't agree. They won't believe in anything other than what exists in this world.

Equally there will be many who understand exactly where I'm coming from.

This concept is also relevant to artists, whatever medium they may choose to work in.

Everyone who creates is inspired by spiritual energy.

The purpose, to pass on their creation to help the listener, or viewer, to achieve whatever the art form invokes in them.

So if we all take it on ourselves to listen to the right style of music at the relevant moment, we'll be more relaxed, and more focused.

So if all those politicians out there take ten minutes out to listen to a few of their favourite tunes before entering The House of Commons, then they might get more done.

Though don't' listen to Gangster Rap if you're a Jazz man, or vice versa.

I should say some songs are more inspired by spirit than others.

Be it The 1812 Overture, Handel's Water

music, Queen's Bohemian Rhapsody, or one of the great classics of Timmy Mallett, they are all sent to inspire us in some way.
It's just that some pieces are more inspirational than others.
Music is just one example of energy manipulation. An aid to help put us on the right footing.
There are other, less obvious examples.
For instance, superstition, numbers, and the base elements, air earth, wind, and fire.
These examples are usually tapped into by people whose own energy's, let's say, are a little different in form to many of their peers.
We see these people all the time; I may very well be one of them, perfectly lovely to be with, but somewhere between quirky and eccentric on the energy scale.
Nine hundred and ninety nine people saying Yes.
One voice saying No. Though that one voice maybe a little different from the rest, he/she is there to make you think, what if?
Just because no-one gets it, it doesn't mean that the one in a hundred isn't right.
Never ignore that lone, different voice. They can get things wrong, but rarely when it really matters.
I'm not talking about people who try to be different for effect. That's more about ego and being noticed.
This group is alike in many ways but do not even tend to interact with each other. They will be reclusive and party loving animals in equal measures. Free spirits who feel trapped. Tethered by everyone else's

concerns for them.

Some can become superstitious, smashed mirrors and walking under ladders definite no-nos.

They have a subconscious knowledge of not fitting in but not knowing why. They are drawn to a more aged way of thinking, searching for something, but not sure what. This type of person usually has a fundamental part of them that's somewhere else. A different place, or time maybe.

There's a search for truth that leads them to be drawn to other elements. Earth energies being the most common.

How many of us are drawn to water but have no cast iron theory as to why?

It's not about being a lover of nature, enjoy walking and know the name of every type of tree ever created.

This goes much deeper.

Actually seeing Earth energy in living form. Fairies, elfs, mythical creatures we only envisage existing in story books.

I've not had any such experience and don't expect too, though who knows?

People claim to have seen such entities, and I have no doubt that they are out there somewhere.

Remember, think of something and you give it the power to exist. So why not put your faith in the 'little folk.'

Likewise, think about Father Christmas. My ideal Santa has a long white beard and favours red as a colour.

The one I wrote letters too as a child, the one I visited in the shopping centre. Little knowing

that he was a bit like Doctor Who and had
taken many forms in his time, this one
courtesy of Coca Cola in the early twenties.
I can hear you saying there is no Father
Christmas, don't be stupid!
Millions of children, and a few of us adults
think about Father Christmas every year. You
see a child's face on Christmas morning, feel
that charge of energy, feel the love in the
room, then tell me he doesn't exist.
Not as a person maybe, but as an energy.
It's a day like any other, yet for a whole year
there isn't another day like it.
I'm aware it might be a bad time for some.
Losing loved one's is never good, but it is
more poignant at this time of year BECAUSE
of how good everyone else is usually feeling.
Elemental energy is as old as the universe
and holds more secrets than religion can
muster.
People worshipped the land and the sea
long before Christianity, and for a longer
length of time too.
So why is it wrong to still hold alliances with
the very nature of the planet we share? The
solstices, the change of seasons, the rituals of
a time long ago.
After all worshipping the elements is surely just
another way of worshipping God who
created it all in the first place.
I know nothing about numerology and little
about the power of numbers.
What I do know is that numbers explain the
workings of the universe through
mathematical equations and can prove
everything I'm writing in this book.

Mathematics is like any other language, only it is universal, intended to be understood by one and all.

A shame then, that I am so poor at the subject.

But each single number from zero to nine holds a power of their own.

Let's take the number four. The only number, at this point, I can talk about with any confidence.

Consider our everyday lives and how the number four connects to it.

There are four seasons. Winter, Spring, Summer, and Autumn.

Four base elements, Air, Earth, Wind, and Fire.

Four points on a compass, North, South, East, and West.

The four corner stones of religion, of which we've already spoken.

There were four prime colours, Red, Blue, Green, and Yellow.

Though yellow has now been removed and the list reduced to three. My house team at school was yellow, and we never did very well. Now I know why.

Four in a deck of tarot cards represents home and family and the four corners of a house.

Think about it, the majority of buildings and rooms within buildings are four sided, or square.

The number four is relevant for so many reasons.

I'm sure you could take any single number and make a similar list.

There are people who live their lives by the relevance of numbers and their meanings

when they come across them.
The simplest one that most people know of is
the counting of magpies.
One for sorrow, two for joy, three for a girl,
four for a boy, five for silver, six for gold, seven
for a secret never to be told.
There are variations on this and every other
numerical rhyme, but some people take
great stock in the interpretation.
More about those of us who may have a
quirkier side very soon.

Chapter Twenty One: That Was Then, This Is Now.

From the time of my Christmas dream to my full reaquaintance with Spirit, well fifteen years past.

There is little of relevance, at least from the perspective of this story moving forward. You could say it was my normal time.

I left home at the earliest opportunity; fell in with some unusual people, as most of us do. Positive and negative influences alike.

Worked for British Coal for a good fifteen years, briefly working underground before finding my way behind a desk.

Got married. A good woman, well I wouldn't have married her otherwise. It ran it's course and we parted amicably. I'd like to think so anyway.

There were no children, were never meant to be I realise now.

I desperately wanted to be a dad, but children would have altered my path and I very much doubt I would be sat here writing this right now.

I would probably have continued with a 'normal job' and continued living around my family, whilst they grew up at least.

Yes, being a father was important to me once upon a time. Like most of us who have difficult upbringings there seems to be a desire to prove that we can do the job better than those that helped mess up our own lives.

One point of small relevance. My Mother-In-Law, must have been gone seventeen years herself now, was a card reader. She was very good for a while as well. A lot of people swore by Ethel.

She was a typical Scorpio who liked to tell you what she thought but couldn't stand to be told back. A nice person though.

Both Ethel and the father-in-law, Ted, are in my head occasionally. Ted passed not long after his wife.

They come to me in dream state from time to time. Or it is as if I visit them? Who can really tell?

In my dreams they have a little house, and when you step outside you are on a beach. Neither of these things can be associated with them to my mind, but we occasionally went on holiday as a family when I was married. Good memories.

It was a Saturday night sometime over the summer of 1988.

I know because I worked six days a week and I was off the next day.

This was the first of many dreams over a six year period where I found myself in an amphitheatre.

I got so adept at finding this place that I could close my eyes anywhere and transport myself there.

Imagine a stone circle with seats that appeared to have been calved from the rock itself.

Each time I visited there were always people sat around the circle. Maybe a dozen, sometimes more. Some alone, others huddled together in small groups.

I found out later that they were displaced

spirits who, for one reason or another, had not passed properly.

They were waiting to be helped to cross over. The circle running through the centre of this gathering place was flat. Too small to be a bull ring.

If not for it's spiritual implications there would have been something gladiatorial about the space.

In the middle of this arena was a wooden door.

It stood freely. No frame work, no hinges. The door hung in the air like some prop in a magic trick left behind by a Magician.

This is my first time here.

I, as yet, haven't a clue who these other people are, or what I'm meant to be doing.

It was just another dream, or so it felt at the time.

If I was to have the same experience today, with what I know now, I would have taken so much more notice of what was going on around me.

Anyhow the door opened outwards and two ladies passed through.

The first person was my mother, just as I remembered her, right down to the purple pinafore she used to wear for work, and the old slippers that I used to think were welded to her feet.

A younger woman followed her through, thick lustrous raven hair halfway down her back, summer dress, and sandals.

She was clearly a woman now, but there was no mistaking Hailey.

Why they would come through together I

wasn't sure. Though they did have one thing
in common, me.

I can't remember Hailey saying a word on
this occasion; mum did all the talking.

It was the first time she'd come forward like
this since she had passed.

Much was said, but very little can be
remembered.

The basis of the message was that my
marriage was coming to an end.

It wouldn't be anything I could be responsible
for. A parting of the ways was how she put it.
She further explained how things would end,
and why, and that it would be a positive
thing overall.

Waking the next morning, I told my wife. After
all, it was only a dream, nothing to be afraid
off.

I remember my wife's unease. I remember
her tears as well.

Eighteen months later everything my mother
prophesied had come true.

December 1990, one week before our tenth
wedding anniversary, we split up. The divorce
took no more than a few months.

Who would have thought twenty years later
that I wouldn't have settled down again?

My wife did, and she has a son.

I hope she found what she was searching for,
and hope she is well.

I saw her, respectively, at her parent's
funerals. A few times afterwards socially,
though not for about fifteen years.

There have been partners, but not for a good
while.

Very few whom I could say I really wanted to

be with, and them with me.

I met a lady in 1992 who I fell in love with, but she was with someone else at the time.

Much of the mid nineties I was on self destruct so when there was a chance for us to be together, well nothing was right, and her family didn't take to me at all.

I still think of her fondly. I believe she's remarried, living in Lincolnshire.

The best hairdresser never to cut my hair. There are quite a few women I have fond memories of. Fortunately I haven't had bad dealings with the opposite sex, maybe because I try to be honest and upfront.

Anyway I'm older now. It can't be said that people always become more mature with age, but in my case my perceptions have grown.

I left British coal in 1993 and lost all sense of direction and balance. I wasted money hand over fist and ended up on benefits.

Spiritually my development had begun, but it did little more than cause confusion within me.

The idea of becoming a practicing medium didn't enter into things. There were people out there miles ahead of me. But all journeys have to start somewhere.

I developed for awhile in a Spiritualist church, but soon outgrew it.

Hailey was absent, but mum was often in my dreams. As if the meeting in the amphitheatre had uncorked some mythical bottle.

The amphitheatre became like a spiritual home. I would meditate and place myself there with ease. Always someone would be waiting. Never the same people twice, however, and the numbers would sometimes be greater than others.

The oddity was that this place didn't seem restricted by time. From people's attire it seemed that some may have lived several hundred years ago.

Spirit is not governed by a time line, so anything is possible.

Many people I communicated with I couldn't understand, not English obviously.

They never entered the arena, and I never again saw the door open whilst I was there.

Placing myself here gave me comfort, a sense of purpose where in life I seemed to have none.

I had some good friends at the time.

People tried to help me, but I simply wouldn't be told. Always had to learn the hard way.

I sold my home, moved away, had adventures that most people would only read about in books, and eventually found myself in Harrogate.

There, I've just encapsulated the most exciting time of my physical life into three lines.

All talk of adventures whilst relevant because they involve me using my abilities; well they aren't for this book. Whilst it involves searching for missing people and occasionally helping the police, it isn't going to explain how we get to heaven and would side track us far too much.

Anyway some of these 'events' have been ongoing for years, and I am not yet in a

position to write about them properly.
Let's return to the amphitheatre and its roots.
Remember my first meeting with Hailey?
The tree lined street and the house with the locked gate?
All the way back to my near death experience.
It was one of my last visits to the spiritualist church. Sitting in the private development circle, the Church President putting the group into a deep meditation.
I'm on that tree lined street. No sign of fields or beaches, nor Hailey.
The gates on this occasion are unlocked; in fact they are open for anyone to enter.
A pebbled path wound around close cropped lawns and a scattering of trees.
Up ahead there was a single wooden bench. Seated was a woman dressed head to toe in black complete with a veil covering her face.
Off to the right were tennis courts. I could see four women playing though their attire was more circa 1920s than modern tennis wear.
Beyond the courts, I didn't know, had never ventured beyond there.
To the left were high hedges hiding a short path that led down to a river and another path that went on indeterminably.
In future meditations I would sit by the riverbank with my mother and chat, watching different types of boats passing by.
I've seen everything from a motorboat attached to water skiers, to a gondolier. One man punting whilst a courting couple cuddled up.
But today I went into the house.

A large reception area greeted me.
Again, very much circa 1920s.
There was a staircase off to the left, the banister gleaming.
In the hallway upstairs I could see a number of closed doors.
There were twelve, but I didn't know how I knew this.
There were only three doors on the ground floor. One directly to my right, one at the back of the hall, I assumed this to be the kitchen but could have been wrong.
A third door was connected to the side of the stairs. I guessed it led to some lower level.
'You've been down there many times. You weren't meant too, but free will and desire go a long way.'
The door to the right had opened and a man stepped out, though I'd neither heard the door open, nor any footsteps.
'Come in, we have very little time.'
I followed the man into the room.
Now this man had a very distinctive look, not too far removed from the man who had brought me up.
Though I hadn't seen dad for ten years, I knew he was still alive. This was the only occasion I ever saw this man, never got a name, and wouldn't know if there was any family connection.
The conversation felt like it went on for hours though no more than twenty minutes past.
The man talked about two paths. The one I was meant to follow and the path I was on now.
Whilst the path wasn't marked with neon

lights, the basic message was that I was doing a fairly good impression of a waste of space, and it was time to grow up.

I eventually heeded that message, but it took another few years.

And that door that led below stairs, well that was where the amphitheatre existed.

And what's more, now I know where it is, that doors locked to me. Well and truly.

I've not been able to imagine myself down there in the last fifteen/sixteen years.

I moved to Harrogate, well because basically they told me to.

I'd spent time in London, then back in Doncaster, but nothing felt right.

I never became a clairvoyant with the intention of making my fortune. It was about learning, and managing to live whilst I learnt.

I did alright, could have done so much better had I put myself out there, and marketed myself. Web sites and advertising.

Simply, if you've heard of me then you know what I can do. If not then I could be any Joe Bloggs.

I know that will all change soon, but this were I've got to in my life.

I've evolved to a point where I have a fully formed perception of my purpose and the time of hiding my light under a bushel is almost over.

There is certainly a case to be made for my life taking on a more surreal feel now everything is laid out before me.

My dreams take on a whole new meaning because most of them hold a sense of reality.

As I have no memory of ever physically

experiencing an afterlife, obviously, and because I don't have the key to countless alternative realities, many of the stories from this point on will be based on dreams and meditations.

However, these tales are as real as if I had lived them.

Chapter Twenty Two. Alternative Realities.

This process is very different, but in the same way as reincarnation, intended to ensure we achieve our purpose here on Earth.

My original views on this subject was, well I dismissed the whole principal as rubbish.

Like most of my preconceptions, this too has altered radically.

Science fails to grasp the very basics with regards any form of afterlife, yet has proven the existence of at least fourteen time/space dimensions running parallel with our own.

They don't know what's in these dimensions, but it makes the probability of alternative realities very likely.

We've touched on how spiritual energy sees us, both in terms of present and future, but it is very apt in explaining this phenomena.

You are on the road that is your life and moving forward.

Anyone remember 'Highway to Heaven?'

The road is criss crossed with minor paths where you have made various choices.

Along the way you have your stop offs, or fate points.

After all a car has to stop to fill up with petrol, check the oil. The passengers will need rest breaks. So these points you will get to, irrespective of your life choices.

You may stop off at a place, but it doesn't necessarily mean you will purchase anything.

In other words, we will arrive at those points preordained for us, but we still might not fulfill

destiny for one reason or another.
Imagine you are eighteen years old. It's your
first time abroad, and you spend all week
making eyes at the gorgeous girl or boy you
see by the pool.
The holiday ends.
Tragically you are too shy to speak, go your
separate ways, never to meet again.
Well what if you were meant to spend the
rest of your lives together, what then?
You've blown it. There might be a hundred
partners who always fall short of your
expectations, or one whom you actually love
and spend your life with. Though your
perception of love might have lower
expectations attached than the average
person.
The fact is, you were supposed to spend your
life with that holiday fantasy you were too
afraid to say hello too.
Fifty years, three children, a comfortable
existence, never happened because you
missed your fate point.
Or did you?
What if you could exist in more than one
place at the same time?
What if there were five versions of you in five
different places, all interlinked
subconsciously?
Living similar lives, having similar experiences,
and if one of you misses a fate point the
other four will pick up on it. Then later on one
of them may miss a fate point that you can
pick upon.
Eventually, through fate achieved and
missed, you may all end up living totally

different lives but will still be interconnected.
Those times we feel down for no explicable
reason. We have extreme mood swings, feel
disconnected from everyone around us; it
could be because the other versions of you
are singing off a different hymn sheet. They
are in a similar place to each other and you
missed the boat somewhere.
You will not consciously be aware of the
others but will feel somehow that something is
missing.
The answer, simply it's to get on with your life
and sort yourself out the best you can.
My original thoughts moved towards the
'sliding doors' scenario where in one time we
get together with our hearts desire and in
another time slot we don't.
But the truth runs much deeper than this.
Some people's lifes are much simpler than
others. If your purpose is to have a family and
be a great parent, or run a company that in
turn supports a thousand employees, then
when you were created you might have
been placed in two or three realities.
On the other hand if you were intended to
find a cure for cancer or save the world from
disaster then there may be a dozen versions
of you in a dozen different realities.
Then we change 'Saving the world from
disaster' to Saving Worlds from disaster.
Because where we succeed in one, then the
act is repeated in all of them.
How many places can we live at the same
time?
The answer is infinite.
Even then there is no guarantee of success

and a number of those energies may have to return to complete their purpose.

I imagine, for many of you; it's a lot to get your head around.

Trust me, mines spinning as I write this for the first time.

Imagine this.

You are brought into this life, simply to have a child. That child will go on to do great things but needs the nurturing and love only you and your partner can offer.

So five versions of you are born into five different worlds at the same time.

In three realities you get together with your partner and have the child as planned.

In reality four, you have the child but remain a single parent

Sadly child number five is still born and passes back into spirit.

The other four children begin to grow.

Child three's parents divorce and he becomes emotionally damaged by the constant string of partners passing through his mother's life. So much so, in turn he never settles down himself.

Children One, Two, and Four meet the same girl.

Child Two messes up by sleeping with her best friend and they go their separate ways.

Eventually Children One and Four, despite different upbringings marry the girl and in turn have their own child that represents so much for the future.

The two remaining energies will try and make the best lives they can.

They may all have the same profession, the

same accidents and illnesses, likes, dislikes. Their time to pass could be the same, though one may go prematurely, before the others. And as for the special child that's born into these worlds, well there are two versions we know of, but any number of versions of this child could be born to different pairings.

Chosen for the experiences their child will undergo during the early years, experiences that will enable the child to grow and fulfill their purpose.

So it isn't so much a case of 'Sliding Doors' where we split and go in two directions, but similar lives playing out in different worlds running in parallel lines.

However, there is usually more than one purpose to life.

Child Two may have messed up the main reason for being here, but there could be a whole list of minor, less important jobs to be undertaken. And because of his path, he may be better placed to carry out these tasks than the others.

If Child Two totally messes everything up, then he may very well have to give over a part of his energy to be reborn in order to fulfill part of that destiny.

This would not impact on the other three energies. Whilst they are all connected they still retain their individuality.

What does this mean for us in this world? Let's face it, this is the only world that matters at this point, to us anyway.

You've all heard the saying, 'You have to play the hand that you are dealt.'

In other words, live your lives the best you

can. Try not to give the idea that there may be other versions of you too much of a thought. Whilst they may have similarities to you, they can't live your life for you. Whilst there is a subconscious connection, there is little else.

No point trying to communicate they can't hear you. Even your Spirit guides won't be able to help.

If we stick to the principle of five people, each will eventually go into spirit. All five will retain their individuality and develop separately.

All five will come together, but much later. So simply, the path we our on in this world and the next, will be repeated by each version of us, in our own time frame based on how quickly we ascend once spirit side.

Those of you that feel generally in balance with life will share more with your other selves than those who are bereft of something vital. Be it physical or emotional.

You see if all of your 'others' are settled and you are not, then it will translate itself by you feeling that your friends and close acquaintances are more settled than you, even if it's not the case. Like something is missing but you cannot put your finger on it. This would magnify into a deeper manifestation if the 'others' had the same partner.

What this would do for you though, is propel your energy in a direction that will eventually bring the right partner to you. He/She might not be the same person the others have hooked up with, but someone who is better connected to you individually.

This doesn't, however, happen through spiritual intervention directly.

A different form of energy comes into play where alternative realities are concerned. Elemental energy.

Five versions of you. Five different families, five different sets of spirit guides.

So your guides, on the level they inhabit, won't be aware of the goings on with the other versions of you. That's the job of their spirit guides.

A spirit guide's job is to look after the individual, not the collective.

Whilst there is no obvious link to the 'others', other than a subconscious niggle, they are actually closer to hand than we can possibly imagine.

All the different worlds, there are thousands, but were hundreds of thousands, are connected by a network of veins that run through the very fabric of our planet.

Many moons ago I believe these veins led to doorways that people openly knew about. These, doorways, or portals, led to the worlds that run either side of our own.

The world of spirit is raised, above us, moving off into the cosmos.

The alternative realities run alongside our own world, in parallel.

Effectively, never mind looking out to the distant galaxies for other life forms, we are surrounded by them. We are in a bubble with neighbours we have no conscious knowledge of.

In England we have a name for this network

of veins. Centuries old lines of energy, which have been mapped out through the length and breadth of this Fair Isle.

Ley Lines.

Whilst they predominantly are thought to be unique to Britain, these energy lines run all they way round the world. Coursing across lands, beneath oceans, through mountains. The blood vessels of the planet, pumping its life energy throughout the world.

Of course, blood vessels are attached to organs and in his case the organs are a metaphor for portals.

Maybe Stonehenge was an ancient portal, long since closed down. You see these portals will move. The more they are used the faster the energy will drain, and then that source is transferred somewhere else.

So scattered throughout the world are hidden doorways to other realities. Fancy a trip to the Bermuda triangle anyone?

So, I hear you shout, why haven't people from other realities crossed over here and made themselves known?

Why isn't there an ongoing network of worlds opening their boundaries to one another sharing knowledge?

Because we aren't meant too and generally we cant.

These gateways represent a way of measuring the health of each world respectively and can be responsible for many of the natural disasters we encounter. Forget global warming. There's the old adage 'If a butterfly flaps its wings in Tokyo, then the brewery will run out of beer in

Leeds.'
What we should really be thinking is this. If our neighbours five doors away blow their house up, theirs likely to be damage to our home as well.

What happens then if the world that exists five realities further down from ours becomes extinct?

What will that ripple effect through the portals do to us?

Natural disasters, that's what!

Of course, we need to protect our own world.

Global warming, pollution, war and famine, they are but a few of the many threats we face.

But how one world impacts on another, well we can't really control that at the moment.

So let's condense the idea of different worlds interacting through ley lines, which is what ancient civilisations attempted.

Instead of trying to connect on such a big scale, let's look at individual interaction.

We get inspiration from our elemental signs.

Water signs get inspiration from being around the sea.

Air signs would best prosper working out their issues at the top of a mountain.

Fire signs, well a week in a very hot environment should sort you. Earth signs need the countryside.

Whilst our guides are constantly helping us achieve our goals, we are further helped and inspired by the properties of our signs.

It's still a spirit voice you listen too, but it becomes amplified by the pulsing effect created by elemental energy.

A word of warning to finish this section.

It doesn't matter in the slightest how many versions of you are out there. Be the person you are and know you can be. If you are honest and true to yourself, then chances are you will not just come to understand your purpose, but have the tools to complete your journey.

Spirits and alternative versions of you, maybe they can help, inspire, but they can't do it for you.

Anyway these alternative versions, they may not be quite what you expect. Some of these 'other worlds' are far far removed from our own.

One further thought.

Irrespective of how many of you there are, at the time of conception there's nothing to suggest you will all be the same sex.

You might be male. A six foot three rugby player with a liking for women's clothing and cuddly toys.

No wonder, if the other dozen or so version of you are women.

Just a thought.

Chapter Twenty Three: Aliens And Portals.

These events happened a good five years apart. There is no connection in any way other than they raised questions about time and space, and connect to the principle of alternative realities.

Mothers Day: 2004.

I had a noon appointment with a young lady who wanted her mother to sit in on the session.

I remember the reading was more about the mother than the daughter, but then you see older people will generally know more about those that have passed than their children.

First let me explain the lay out of my studio for the reading.

I was sat on my bed.

The young lady across from me, no more than three feet away, sat in a comfortable reclining chair. Behind her is a half length wall mirror, the top positioned just over six feet off the floor.

Her mum is sitting on a hard backed dining chair, a few feet to my right, a small table between us.

She is just in my peripheral vision but not so that her daughter will not be my main focus.

I remember little of the reading. I wouldn't share her life with you anyway. Sittings are confidential.

Be you a Saint or a Sinner, my studio is safer than a confessional.

Though the reading isn't relevant to what happened.

At the end of the session, the lady asked me to do 'My face thing' or Transfiguration to the more initiated.

I explained that the process didn't work with everyone, but we would have a go.

It's quite easy for me to refocus my mind but if my subject isn't open, or in most cases doesn't know how to tune in to me, then they might not see anything.

There is no hard and fast rule. I've known practicing mediums not be able to see anything and total none believers won over by the appearance of their dear departed Gran or Granddad's energy appearing where my face should be.

More than enough people have witnessed this phenomena for it not to be genuine.

Off course my face doesn't change at all. The energy around my face however becomes charged with the spirit's presence.

If a person struggles to see anything, then there is a method of enhancing the experience, not dissimilar to those 'Magic Eye' images you can get in books and magazines. You know the cluster of dots that, once focused on in a slightly different way will become the image of a recognisable object.

I mentioned this phenomena earlier for those that may have short term memories.

Personally I've never quite got the knack and haven't had the patience to try.

That aside, I get my client to refocus their line of vision, making my face the 'Magic Eye image'. Either getting them to focus on my right eye, or that imaginary third eye and try and look 'through' me.

Often this does work.

Once they are able to see the face, or faces, appear before them, they can often revert back to a more natural focus.

The energy vibrates, so the image appears to be like a signal strengthening and weakening in turn.

I can't perform this task for too long. The energy drains from me very quickly; after all they are feeding off me to come though.

Quite frankly, it can be bloody tiring.

This particular day, I knew I was going to be horizontal later. The energy was as strong as I'd ever known it.

A whole host of spirits stepped forward to be recognised.

The mother could see as well as her daughter, and I remember her explaining to her daughter who some of these faces represented.

What happens to me is that the room starts to turn to a whitey grey mist. The people in the room become a myriad of colours as the two worlds converge, spiritual energy becoming the dominant force.

And this particular day everything was happening.

The young lady looked like a rainbow of bright light; all I could see of her mother was an orange aura sneaking into my vision, but she wasn't my intended subject.

The mirror came into focus surrounded by mist. This had never happened before and hasn't since.

Within the mirror, my attention was drawn to a separate ball of light, another energy.

The mother.

Slowly this light began to take on form, become a solid entity.

All the while the remainder of the room seemed to swirl around in its mist like form, the young lady's light the centre piece.

The Mother took on a sold definition, not as she was sat on the chair, but something else.

The word 'Alien' jumped out at me.

Think of the stereotypical image of an alien, tall hairless body, elongated face, and almond eyes. Then make it look less attractive.

These beings are drawn with smooth skin, pleasant features.

This alien face was out of proportion. The nose was too big, mouth too small, and I thought I could detect acne type spots.

The 'alien' blinked and I knew the mother was blinking at the same time. Because of course this is who it really was.

I brought the room back to normal as quickly as possible.

That was it for the day. In fact I never did any transfiguration for a good while afterwards.

The mother and daughter were highly delighted. The mother had been a bit of a skeptic before hand but could no longer have grounds for doubt.

If she'd seen what I'd seen she would have been put off her Mother's Day dinner.

Of course I didn't tell them of my experience. Something's are better left unsaid. Anyway if I couldn't get my head around it, what could I expect of these people who were just dipping their toes for a few hours.

They went to lunch and I went to the pub. As with all mysteries I asked my guides for an answer to the obvious question.

What had I seen?

She was a perfectly normal, nice lady. Her appearance bore little resemblance to the image in the mirror. Ok. Maybe the nose and mouth were the same shape, but she hadn't had almond eyes, and she had hair on her head.

I asked the question, but to begin with got no answer. None at all.

Are there aliens in spirit?

Well I suppose, if aliens exist, they have to go somewhere when they pass.

I hadn't had an opinion on the subject before now. I would have sat on the fence until the mother ship landed and then it would have been too late.

Now, however, my mind was running riot. It did for about a week and then, like most things; other wonderments took over and the incident was put in the 'unexplained' file, to be revisited later.

A month passed.

It was a Sunday night, a few years before God came calling to tell me off, but things tend to happen on a Sunday. I've thought about this and believe that Spiritual energy is at it's strongest on this day.

After all it is the day of worship, the day we think about God and heaven the most.

Again, think of someone or something and

we give it the power to be around.
Anyway I'm just in that place between the
two realms and the alien image returned.
This time there were half dozen of them, and
instead of appearing in the mirror, they were
in my minds eye.
Sitting up in bed, opening my eyes to block
them out.
Closed my eyes again.
Yes they were still there, as if hiding behind
my eyelids, and they weren't going
anywhere until they'd spoken.
I even wondered if this might be a prelude to
some weird abduction. They could bugger
off with their rectal probes that were for sure.
I gave in, settled back, and shut my eyes.
Best get it over with.
My thoughts must have been amusing to
them because most of the group seemed to
be laughing.
They were tapped into my thoughts, bugger.
Rectal probes, double bugger.
This group were very similar to the woman I'd
seen. Varying in heights and sizes.
By size, well there were no overweight aliens.
It's just that some were broader than others.
Whatever their diets, they seemed to have
obesity beaten.
I couldn't tell any difference in their sexuality.
No one was wearing make up, or clothes for
that matter.
'What do you want?' Not much of a
greeting, I know.
Why did I never have anything witty to offer
when confronted by other worldly
experiences?

Too busy being scared, I suppose.

One of the group stepped forward.

There was nothing that made him/her stand out.

They may have even telepathetically been saying, 'You talk to him.'

No. You do it.'

No, you're the eldest, you talk. Go on, you can have an extra celery stick to suck on later.'

The truth may have been that they were as much afraid of me as I was of them and came through mob handed, as there was safety in numbers.

'We aren't aliens.'

I'd like to have said, 'Have you looked in a mirror lately?'

Of course I didn't.

'We are part of you, just from a different time. A more advanced older version of you.'

Then they were gone.

Another anti-climax.

Maybe abduction might at least have made the journey worthwhile.

But I was, as usual, left with more questions than answers.

At the time I came to believe that they were time travelers come to pass on proof of who they really were.

Beings who's transport covered time and space through dimensions and not out there in the galaxy.

Some of my assumptions were right, but I realise now how little I really knew then.

You see; time travel isn't realistically possible, but side wards movement through portals is.

There are worlds much older and much younger than our own. Evolution is at different stages. So whilst we run alongside in the same time frame, the age of each world is different.

April 2009.

The Black Swan in York.

Over six hundred years old, and said to be one of the countries most haunted pubs. Well with that much history there's should be as many spirit's haunting the halls as spirits drank over the bar.

I'd stayed there a few times and never experienced anything.

There had to be something, as I've just explained, so I guessed they were avoiding me.

Remember Ghosts and Spirits are two very different energies.

Because I'm a medium and commune with spirit, well that's not to assume that I'll come across ghosts on a regular basis.

Well the landlord and landlady, Andy and Steph, had only just moved. They'd ran a pub in Harrogate and we'd become friends.

It was Andy's birthday.

The pub has three rooms downstairs. Bar, lounge, and dining room. Upstairs there are letting rooms and a function room.

The function room, like those downstairs, isn't huge. They didn't do huge in those days. Everything was...well, functional.

At this time the letting rooms hadn't been renovated, so the gang that went over from Harrogate, over twenty of us, all found somewhere to stay.

My room had a single bed, but the room next to mine had half a dozen mattress' for people to crash on.

There are two other sleeping areas in other parts of the pub.

All three rooms are located around the function room.

There was a buffet that people were making the most of.

One of the local lads from Harrogate, Rob, was performing. Brilliant guitarist, excellent performer, but can we get him to do American Pie?

The room was packed and some of us had to stand in the hallway to take in what was going on.

I was with a group of friends who were local. I'd met them recently when I'd visited their home to do a session. I did a three for one. A mother and her two daughters.

The mother Janette, had recently lost her husband, and the session was about getting him through for them.

This was very relevant for one of the daughters, Livvy, because her dad had been a musician, his speciality being the drums, and she sang with two bands.

Since then she has cut this down to one, Mostly Autumn, which her boyfriend formed. To begin with she was a backing singer with the band, but has since been promoted to lead vocals.

Anyway, they have joined me at the event and we're all sat in the hall.

The elder daughter, Rebecca, isn't there.

Don't know her too well, but not sure it's her scene. Not enough hunks in the room for her maybe.

The point is they are good people and not prone to flights of fancy, and Livvy whom I was stood with saw what I saw.

Sat at a table by the door was another friend of mine, Leslie.

I'd had my eye out for her because several men had been bothering her slightly, being single and in her own company so to speak.

Though no-one was really in their own company because we all knew and looked out for each other.

There were a couple of other people sat at the table, prominently another one of our crowd, Peter.

They were watching Rob perform.

Popping into the room I checked Leslie was ok.

She nodded in the affirmative.

I went back out into the hall and continued my conversation with Livvy and Jeanette.

There were a few other men sat there, Livvy's boyfriend, Bryan, was downstairs, presumably at the bar.

Peter suddenly appeared red faced, angry, pushed past Livvy and stormed off down stairs.

Moments later to be followed into the hall by Leslie, her own anger clear for all to see.

The only thing about her I hadn't noticed before was the white cardigan she wore over her dress and that she had her hair up in a bob.

She barged past Livvy and headed off

through a side door into the room where she was staying.

Poor Livvy being knocked around like a human pinball.

I was apologising for their behaviour, the manner in which they'd barged past as if she wasn't there, when Jeanette asked what was wrong.

We explained what had happened, was frankly surprised she hadn't seen what had gone off, though she had been talking.

She looked in to the function room. Then back towards me, surprised. 'Your friends are there.' Or words to that effect.

I went into the room.

Peter was still sitting watch Rob perform.

For her part, Leslie was in the middle of the room, taking photos of Rob, and just about anything, anybody that moved.

There were no angry, ashen glares to be seen.

Neither was there a white cardigan, and Leslie had her hair down.

So this isn't a story of ghostly goings on.

Quite the opposite. All the protagonists are very much alive in every sense.

Something, I believe, happened with the energy. We were at a party. Lots of frivolity, a mass of good energy. In a place with a history of the weird and unexplainable.

What if, for a moment, the two worlds overlapped.

I can't speak for the rest of us, but at least Peter and Leslie were at this alternative party and something had caused them both to storm off. They barged past Livvy as if she

weren't there. So maybe in the alternative it's
as simple as that. She wasn't there for them
to barge into.
I remember speaking to Leslie, asking what
was the matter, I remember her looking
through me as if I were a stranger.
Maybe in the alternative reality I was.
You see there are examples, if not conclusive
proof, of alternative existences.
It, at least raises questions.
Livvy bore witness to those latter events,
probably wore bruises as a consequence,
but she's certainly as sane and rational as
anyone of you.

Chapter Twenty Four: Parallel Universes.

Why would there be a need, in a spiritual sense, for parallel universes?
Well, like everything else, the answer is simple.
Remember, this plain of existence is necessary for creating and inventing. If we weren't able to do so in a physical sense, then spirit wouldn't be able to evolve.
So if our world came to an end, would that in turn mean and end to spiritual evolution?
Well no. Not as long as we have other worlds to fall back on, a base we can build from.
As long as there is a physical world out there in the cosmos spiritual energy will survive and be able to thrive.
Each of these thousands of worlds exist simultaneously, in the same time as far as minutes and hours go.
What differs is the length of time these worlds have been around.
At one end of the spectrum we may have a world that is in the final days of its existence and go all the way to the other end where a world is in its infancy, the wheel not yet invented and everyone running around naked living life by instinct.
For you doubters out there, still trying to get your head around the basics. Well God created the universe in which we exist. There are claims that he's all seeing, which is probably true, and all knowing, probably also correct. Though, in most people's eyes, he get's things wrong.

Either that or God's will can be pretty crap
sometimes.
So why create just one universe when he can
use the blueprint to create many more?
We need physical plains of existence, not just
for mankind, but also for spirit to continue.
God knows this, so he isn't just going to
create the one single version is he?
Originally there were many more worlds
because we didn't have the technology to
destroy ourselves.
Natural evolution ends in death, the cycle of
physical life come full circle, as it must with all
living things.
If we last that long, we believe the sun will
eventually burn up the planet. Though before
this event becomes a reality, we will have
been consumed by a black hole as part of a
natural progression.
Don't worry we will all have become extinct
by this point.
The timing is such that as this world dies
another will be created. All part of the
natural order.
Then there lies the problem, unnatural
progression.
Technology gives us the capability to do bad
things to ourselves, often in the name of a
better good.
So if worlds become extinct before their time,
the planets themselves remain but without
the ability to do the job for which they were
intended.
No more creating and evolving, because
everyone's either passed or devolved, living
a life that becomes about survival and not

growth.

We, on Earth, are developing physically and mentally at a faster rate than God originally intended.

Technology has overtaken spiritual growth for many of us.

Though there is still a divide. An out of kilter balance if you like.

Pockets of people with the ability to build, create, and grow. Then visit any third world country and we see those abilities become diluted because it becomes about survival over development.

At least we haven't started pressing the wrong buttons.

Not yet anyway.

We need to find a way to protect all worlds, not just are own.

Of course that appears beyond our reach so the best we can do is better learn to take care of our own environment.

CO_2 emissions are said to be responsible for much of the problems related to global warming.

My understanding of the truth is that it currently could only be responsible for a small percentage of the whole problem.

That's not to say that you can now go out and have an aerosol spraying party or get all your friends to do fly bys in their private jets.

Every little helps preserve what we have.

But evolution happens.

There was an ice age in the distant past. Now sometime before this event and then again afterwards, the world's climate must have altered dramatically.

Those radical changes are well documented,
but there weren't jet planes, fast cars and
deodorants to plague the planet.
Yet those changes were on a much grander
scale than anything happening today.
Also, if we are to believe everything we read,
there was that business with the ark and the
bloody great flood. Though reality would tell
a different story.
Yes, there was a flood, yes there was an ark,
maybe not on the grand scale described,
but it was real.
The writer of that particular parable had
probably just finished his third bottle of red
and was half way through his second doobie.
Seeing everything on a grander scale than it
really was.
Remember they would probably have
thought of the Earth in terms of being flat, so
the world to them would have been limited
to what they could see.
Noah's whole world may have only covered
twenty square miles.
So the great flood would likely have effected
an area, or region, not the whole world.
However, I'm getting away from the point.
Disasters happen on many different scales.
As with everything out there, scientists and
other relevant experts will still only understand
a small percentage of what's occurring and
why?
On the whole, most phenomena's are only
understood in part. The remainder clouded in
mystery. Left open to speculation and
debate.
What is clear though is that what ever

creates natural disasters has to be something on a huge scale. Something beyond our natural conception.

Picture an infinite time line.

Parallel to the time line are markers at regular intervals where it as been split into sections running alongside one another.

Each of these sections represents another universe.

So there we are all in a line, evolving.

Hopefully learning in the right way.

Old worlds breathing their last, new worlds being created.

Theoretically there is a universe created two thousand years before our own, existing four sections away from us to our left. That world has a war that decimates the population making the surface of the planet uninhabitable.

Something unnatural has happened to that world and the effect will ripple through the universes around it.

Remember Old Danny? He once told me, when I was little, that when the Germans bombed Sheffield during the Second World War, some of the windows where blown out in Doncaster. Twenty miles away, but that was the size of the shockwave.

So what would a nuclear war, albeit on another world, in spitting distance of our own planet do to us?

Well weather conditions would become less predictable, hurricanes and tornados sweeping the world.

The seas would destabilise. Floods would become more devastating.

There would be eruptions as the centre of the earth shook; long dormant volcanoes awakening from last time an event of this magnitude took place.

Well think about this for a moment. How many of these occurrences have happened since the turn of this century?

And ten years is no time.

Disasters of an unparalleled magnitude.

Events with little or no explanation.

Some things may have been predicted, but not the magnitude of damage or loss of life.

There will always be those of you that cannot take this seriously. But tell me this doesn't at least make some sense.

Remember this book is channelled and hard enough for me to get my head around, so I can understand disbelief in some quarters.

Essentially imagine over a thousand universes all in alignment, of which almost four hundred can no longer sustain life as we know it.

Furthermore, as many as another two hundred are in danger of extinction through old age or self harm.

These universes have lost their natural order and are dying out faster than new universes can be created.

Now imagine you are a brilliant scientist and have vast knowledge of time and space.

Your planet is dying. You can no longer inhabit the surface of your world and have taken to living a subterranean existence.

You do have the secret of travelling through time and space however, so you build a mothership to find a place where you can live on the surface of your world once more.

Unfortunately, despite countless films that tell us differently, time travel just doesn't work for us in the way we would like to think it does.
Yes, it is more than likely that this form of travel may one day be possible.
Let's take a trip back to our childhood, have a look in on ourselves.
What I wouldn't do to have another day with my mum!
Though I have eternity to visit her once my time here ends.
Anyway you get aboard your time machine and go back forty years. Nothing too greedy just a handful of years.
Even such a short journey would have consequences.
There's a small matter of vibration to consider.
Throughout our lives, our vibration increases as it does through out eternity. As does the vibration of the planet itself, and everything animate or inanimate that as an energy.
Forty years isn't that long in the bigger picture, but the planets vibration was slower then, as was everything on it.
So we turn up to find that the world back then cannot sustain us.
We would speak faster than the people of that time. They might not be able to see us as we may be vibrating so quickly we come across as a blur.
We simply wouldn't fit, not to begin with anyway.
Slowly we would devolve, our vibration slowing as we acclimatize to our new environment.

The damage would be irreparable. We would be affected mentally and physically. Let's go back even further in time, a hundred years.

People's diets were different, food richer, the gall bladder and tonsils still a necessary part of our anatomy.

But you no longer have either organ, because they are pretty much redundant, as we have evolved.

Also people adapt to their time, if the immune system's doing its job properly. Step out of time and your system would become more overloaded the further away it gets from its comfort zone.

Mentally we would suffer through an altering of our perceptions.

Imagine a standard size refrigerator full of produce. Then you are forced to replace that fridge for something half its original size. Well something has to give because the new appliance won't hold all that food.

Now replace that refrigerator with your brain. The slower the vibration, the less information the brain can equate, the faster we begin to lose a grasp of some of the information contained within.

Like anything appertaining to the time we've come from.

We may even forget how our time machine works and how we got there in the first place. So before you decide to go back to the time of your Great Grandfather, think twice. It will not be the experience you imagine.

Whilst it is easy to see why time travel might not be the best solution for our holiday needs,

well consider space travel as an alternative.
I'm not referring to a trip to the moon or a
Martian landing, this space travel is closer to
home.
Remember my experience with those
'Aliens'?
Only they claimed to be from another time.
They had connected telepathically to me,
which suggests forms of communication
between the realms can certainly take
place.
If we jump ahead who's to say how we
evolve.
Telepathy, in some forms, is possible now.
Cave Dwellers of several million years ago
looked more like apes than people, all part
of the evolutionary chain.
So what will we look like in another million
years?
Even less at the rate we are evolving.
The hotter the planet becomes the less body
hair we will need that's for sure.
Technology is advancing at a rate of knots
here so where could it be in a world way
older than our own?
We shouldn't take anything for granted
though; maybe events have occurred to
stunt their growth.
Anyway, less not make matters more difficult
than they need to be.
Instead of time travellers we have our
brothers and sisters from another galaxy
slipping through dimensional portals to pay us
a visit.
They can't stay too long because the same
vibrational rules apply. Each Universe will

have a unique signature, their own vibration different from ours.

So short visits, drop offs. Just enough time for the odd abduction or two to see how we are evolving in comparison to them.

We may not know where these doorways are, unless some government department has been hiding them from us all these years, but there are places throughout the world where the fabric of space is thinner and things can slip through.

Go back to ancient times.

The architects of the great pyramids and drawings of flying chariots said to be contained there in.

Think also of the Fabled underwater city of Atlantis.

Myth, fact, or somewhere between the two. We can do little more than speculate, but what if?

What if there was a space portal beneath the oceans and some sub group from another universe co-existed between the two worlds, creating Atlantis because it was close to the portal, so vibrational effects occurred more slowly?

What if some other group found a portal and gave technology to a group of people, simple in nature, to give them a leg up if you like. And built the great pyramids around the space portals in order to protect that place and stop these ignorant souls from accidentally journeying back the other way?

Just think about it and decide for yourself.

So why is portal travel done in such a clandestine way?

Well if they turned up mob handed we'd do our level best to destroy them. They might come with the best will in all the universes, but paranoia would surely kick in.

No more so than the major powers who seem to carry 'paranoia' with them wherever they may go.

So there we have it.

Minded boggling certainly, eye opening for me because, whilst there's little or no scientific basis, much resonates within.

Anyway, perhaps it not about me catching up with science, but science catching up with me.

Chapter Twenty-Five: Journeys Into The Unknown.

Over a three month period I had a number of
reality dreams that effected me both
physically and emotionally, and not always in
a good way.
After my 'Alien' experience I started to ask
more questions in my meditations about
these other worlds.
At first it felt like I may as well have been
talking to myself but, as with most things
spiritual and other worldly, they eventually
got round to helping me understand the
wonderment, and horrors of these other
places.
I knew the dreams were visits to alternate
realities, but at this stage I didn't know how
close to our own world some of these places
existed.

My very first experience happened some
years ago and I believe, at the time, I had
tapped into another version of me. Not so
sure now.
It was a midweek afternoon, would have
been around three, three-thirty.
I was meditating in my room, laid out on my
bed, aware that eventually sleep would
overtake me and I'd go somewhere deeper
into my subconscious.
Which is exactly what happened.
I awoke as a note was slipped under my
door.
Not the room of my studio however, but a

much larger space.

A hotel room.

The bed was king size, unlike the double bed in my reality.

There were other rooms leading off elsewhere, which suggested I was in a suite.

Music was playing, but nothing I recognised.

Everything was neutral in colour. Cream sheets and a beige duvet, which matched the drapes hanging around a big bay window.

Traffic outside, heavy traffic.

I knew I was in London.

I know the note read 'Dinner, 7:30' without even looking at it.

All the same I got up to go and get the piece of paper.

I had a sense that the note was from a woman. The thought excited me somewhat.

As I got up I returned to my studio.

No note had been slipped under the door.

There would be no night of passion with some alluring female.

The experience left me shaking, my stomach flip-flopping as if I'd just alighted from some dodgy fairground ride.

An example of different vibration, I learnt later.

These other 'dreams' took place years later.

After I'd asked to be shown examples of what these worlds would be like.

Were it not for those shaking feelings the following morning, I would suggest they were figments of my imagination.

The following scenarios, however, were as

real as I can remember.
In no particular order, and no idea how near
or far away these realities exist. Though I
sense the more normal experiences occur
closer to our own reality than not.

This was a more recent experience, is short,
but I believe, again, could have shown yet
another version of me.

I wake up.
I'm in my studio, and it's breakfast time.
I am aware this is a dream but get on with my
day as per normal.
Crawl out of bed. Kettle on, go to the
bathroom, quick rinse, 'A cat's lick', my
mother would have called it.
That was the first oddity, usually I jump in the
shower.
Back to the fridge. Milk was needed for my
tea and cereal.
Oddity number two. No milk.
In fact nothing in the bloody fridge at all.
Though not a total surprise, as I tend to shop
on a daily basis, not weekly. I'm more careful
about what I eat that way.
So I get dressed to go to the shop.
I slip out of the back door of the house and
set off, no more than a five minute walk.
I would be tucking in to my tea and muesli in
no time.
The first unsettling thing I noticed were the
cars.
Well not the vehicles themselves exactly, they
appeared pretty much the same.
The number plates were different.

At the time I remember thinking, everyone's started speaking Welsh. No disrespect to the Welsh mind.

These plates weren't just numbers and letters, but symbols as well.

They looked like Hieroglyphics, that ancient Egyptian language if you will.

I couldn't for the life of me spell anything I saw, or recite lines of script that could be broken down into a new language.

This just felt wrong and began to overload my mind with confused thoughts.

There were a couple of vans, the company name stencilled on the side, but no names that made any sense.

Several houses had name plates, but they may as well have been spelt in Mandarin Chinese for all they meant to me.

I turned onto the main road.

All the shops looked the same; just the names were different. Then I realised a few of the shop fronts had changed after all.

In my reality there's a bakery joined onto a farm food shop.

Here, there was the bakery joined onto what looked like a butcher's shop, selling meat, not the organic produce they specialised in.

The name plates had been replaced by signs that seemed to have been written in double Dutch.

There were consonants and vowels but mixed up in a way that made no sense.

Somewhere off, into the town, a siren sounded.

It was a work siren like they used to have at some coal mines.

Trust me, there's never been any mining in Harrogate.
But what about an alternative place?
Looks mostly the same but spelt in another language.
I couldn't wait to hear someone speak, would they understand me?
Again the anti-climax.
I woke up to that familiar shaking I'd now become accustomed too.
At least I knew I had some milk for breakfast.

I have mixed thoughts about writing this story. On one hand, it's happening out there in some space and time, so it's relevant. On the other, I have no desire to start some new, sick craze involving the drinking of blood.
I'm in, what I believe to be, Tokyo.
It's is certainly a Japanese city, though my companion is English speaking.
A beautiful blonde lady whose name I never find out.
It's raining heavily. My companion has an umbrella which she doesn't seem to want to share.
I'm soaked through to the skin in no time.
I'm shown into a waiting room filled with a cross section of people. Young and old, male and female. All Japanese in appearance. Every one of them was ill. All looked thin, some emancipated.
A young girl tried a smile, drawing my attention to her teeth.
The incisors were extended and protruded, making her look like a vampire.
'It's pandemic,' said the blonde woman.

'More people get hooked every day. It doesn't help that the food supplies are so scarce. Other countries have cut off aid altogether. Looking after themselves now you see; it's become every man, or country, for themselves. Charity begins at home. If there isn't enough to go around in the first place, then there isn't enough to share.'
After awhile my perceptions of these situations gain such clarity that I know what's happening, and why. As though I become part of the scenario I'm being shown.
Worldwide, there's a food shortage.
Problems created by a population explosion, half of the world uninhabitable as a result of nuclear war, and now we have vampires.
But not the demons of old, walking the earth as folklore would suggest.
This was worse.
A drug had been developed. Mixed with blood it put nutrients into the body to help make up for what was missing through little or no diet.
This narcotic had been messed with and had become as addictive as heroin.
And now three quarters of the population of this country had become addicted.
These extended incisors were false but carried the drug. Once the wearer bit into another's vein the drug and blood mixed together hitting the blood stream and creating a chemical high.
That's the best way I can describe it.
My companion told me that a grandmother had recently been arrested for kidnapping her two grandchildren and feeding off them

for over a month.

She, in turn, had taken to feeding the children with her own blood until they too were addicted.

A new problem had developed. Many were so far gone that they were no longer using the narcotic at all.

They were now simply addicted to the blood.

Contracting unspeakable diseases, neither realising nor caring just what dangers they were in.

Thank God we know better in our own reality.

These stories have no beginning, middle, or end.

They are just events, or part of events, meant to give me a flavour of what is occurring out there in the cosmos.

Across from my home, I've already mentioned this, is a public park called, The Valley Gardens.

It is arguably the best public gardens in England with regards to plant life, and the many different variety of trees to be found there.

So to see it as a bomb site came as quite a shock.

Let's take a step back.

The same street where I live today, in peace and tranquility, well there was nothing but mud and rubble in this world.

The are over one hundred houses on Valley Drive. Construction began at the town end around 1890 finishing twelve years later in 1902.

Many of the properties are four stories high,

and the interiors are a work of art.

But no longer in this reality. If they ever had been in the first place.

There were craters and smaller holes in the road.

Most of the properties had been reduced to rubble.

A few still remained, almost in defiance against the landscape, but even these had been badly damaged.

This time my companion was a man.

Again no name, why do I never ask for names?

I was led into the gardens or what was left of them.

'They threw everything they could at Menwith. We just happened to be in the way. Menwith Hill is a base near Harrogate mainly manned by American Servicemen. It's no secret that, amongst other things, it's a listening post or spy base.

So it existed in more than one reality and in this one it had been attacked, possibly even destroyed, by god knows who.

Though my understanding of Menwith Hill is that much of its infrastructure is actually underground to protect it from such threats.

There was nothing recognisable about the gardens as I knew them. Just miles and miles of trenches running of in all directions.

A scattering of buildings remained, but all had suffered some bomb damage.

'What happened to the people?' was what I said.

Have I died in this reality? Was what I was thinking.

My companion jumped into one of the trenches. No encouragement or invitation to follow, but I did anyway.

Mud, stones, bits of tree trunk, everything you would expect clogged the way, and we were quickly muddied to the knees.

We came to what looked like a metal cover fixed into the earth.

He tapped on the cover two or three times and waited.

There was an audible click and he pulled open the hatch.

I followed him down the hole, feeling oddly safe and at ease, but thinking of 'Alice in Wonderland' and the 'Mad March Hare.'

The tunnel led off to a network of other openings, which really did put me in mind of a rabbit warren.

There were thick pipes running through the tunnels pumping air in the uplet and out through the outlet; I worked out.

This place went on for miles and the further we walked, the deeper into the earth we travelled.

Up ahead the ground suddenly shook.

'The Bastards have started their bombing again,' he commented.

Whoever 'The Bastards' were.

We had started passing more metal doors, unevenly spread out, but painted different colours. Some had numbers painted on them, some symbols, others both.

We suddenly stopped at a lilac door. The number 240 stencilled in green.

'The wife. Said we had to make an effort.' explaining the design.

He opened the door and went inside.
Again, without an invite, I followed.
The space had been fashioned into a make
shift home. The walls had been shored up
with timber. There were only two rooms. One
for living, one for sleeping, I presumed.
There were two settees, though old and
worn.
Two children sat on one, reading books.
There were a few board games on a table.
Several pictures had been put on the wall,
Home from home.
I never saw the other room, but I knew there
were mattresses and several big chests which
would contain bedding and clothes.
Just like I knew there were make shift latrines,
wash rooms, and a communal room where
they shared out their meagre provisions.
You weren't going to find any dogs or cats
that was for sure.
They had served their purpose some time
ago.
These people were waiting for help, aid that
would probably never come.
This was one story that would probably never
end well and I was thankful for waking up.
That day I cancelled clients and went
walking.
Some nightmares make you thankful for what
you have.

I wanted to finish on a positive but put
yourself in a new environment, and well it
does take some getting used too.
And if it were all fluffy clouds and rainbows,
then there wouldn't be a great deal to report

back.

It would have been nice to know there was a world out there close to the utopia many of us dream of, but if there is, then it wasn't shown to me.

The message, I believe, is that the only Heaven on Earth we will find is by making the world we live in a better place for everyone. Not just a chosen few.

And to do that I repeat the mantra spoken many time already in this book.

Remove the frame that encapsulates your perceptions so you can begin to expand your mind.

Keep life simple.

Be positive and create good energy.

Share the love and light.

PART TWO: THINGS YOU NEED TO KNOW TO HELP GET TO HEAVEN.

Chapter Twenty-Six: The Journey's Only Just Begun.

Maybe, like me, you need time to come
back from alternative realities and parallel
dimensions.
Remember, as individuals, the world that
matters most is the sanctity of our own.
Everything physical in nature, already
created and still to come, exists alongside us.
Whilst Spiritual energy is all around us, as our
lives come to an end, that energy evolves on
the other side and we ascend upwards
towards the heavens.
Travelling in the direction, preordained at
birth through our astrology, into the heavens
and onto to the centre of the universe, where
we'll find heaven.
The home of the ultimate energy.
Again, we have portals, this time though they
represent our ascension through the world of
spirit.
Twelve doors that mark the route to heaven.
Most of us won't need to go through all of
them.
The more spiritually aware we become on
the Earth plain the more we are prepared
and able to bypass the lower levels.
I see them as doors, but they could be
anything that symbolises ascension.
These doors, or portals, could be as simple as
walking down a corridor, or consist of a trek
to far off horizons.
For these journeys are our own and will differ
depending on the manner we live this life

and ascend after passing over.

I've broken down the journey to heaven into simple sections in an attempt to make it easy for you to follow.

The reality, as with life, is that nothing is straightforward and the truth of this particular journey is that it's multi-layered and our sections could in reality be further split into a hundred, no thousands of pieces.

The truth of this book is that every answer will throw up many more questions and I'm only able to access the basics at this point.

I can already see the possibility of half a dozen other books that no-one else could begin to imagine, never mind write.

Not that I'm claiming to be all seeing.

I can only talk to you about the subjects that spirit chooses to share with me, and they could do that to anyone with an open mind and evolved to the right vibration.

You might think that everyone with a high vibration would have an open mind but not so.

We are all human and the time we spend in our conscious, our Earth time if you like, can and will effect our beliefs and the way our mind works.

Our likes, dislikes, desires, fears, victories and failures aren't necessarily going to change because we have access to a higher knowledge.

It's one thing to have that access, another thing quite separately to have the means to pass that knowledge on, and then a separate association altogether when it comes to teaching ourselves what we preach.

Just look at elements of the Church, their doctrines, and their very public failings, to understand where I'm coming from.

I always say the best place to start is the knowledge of what is right and what is wrong.

Stick to the right path and you will not go far wrong.

But this talk isn't getting us to heaven.

Imagine a wooden wheel, its size infinite.

Half shaded in light, half in dark.

The centre of the wheel is heaven.

In the light we can see thousands of spokes, each one representing a universe.

The shaded area is a black hole waiting to be filled with the light of new spokes, or universes.

One of those spokes is the universe we know.

The constellation, all the other planets, Earth, right down to us mere mortals.

Our place is close to the rim of the wheel, where the tyre would go if there was one.

The idea is to work our way up the spoke, to the centre of the wheel, through ascension.

First in life, then the afterlife.

And that's what we're going to do now, work our way gradually up that spoke.

Chapter Twenty-Seven: Meeting The Authors, And A Brief Encounter With Hailey.

On this occasion I planned to stay around Harrogate for three to six months to, as I said at the time, write a book and get fit.
Over nine years later I'm still writing, and people must be tired of me telling them how I'm going to lose my weight.
But then there's the other side of my life.
It's almost impossible to share my other worldly experiences because no-one can, first hand, relate to what's happening to me.
Going back to my childhood and the first part of this book, I felt it was important to write about my origins, and how my abilities became part of my everyday life.
I can't speak for anyone else's upbringing, but the life I led was split into sections.
There was the public face.
Being a little kid. Chasing. Being chased. Trying to be normal.
I used to tell white lies to big myself up during the time after my mum's death. Believing I had to do more to be accepted, to try and fit in, be 'one of the gang.'
Though that was just one face, the fitting in face.
They had no idea about Moira and unwanted bedroom experiences.
No-one got to hear about that until I was an adult.
What happened behind closed doors stayed behind closed doors, though I'll say again,

my dad did nothing wrong. In his case ignorance was certainly bliss.

Then there was the, 'this is my life deal with it' face.

No-one knew about my visits from Danny and Bill.

The dreams of visiting other worldly places, of a raven haired princess.

Who wouldn't think I was mad?

Stricken by the grief at losing my mother, unable to keep a hold on my grasp with reality. Lock him up, bit of electric shook therapy to see him right. Maybe a frontal lobotomy.

I'd seen plenty of films to know what would happen, so there was my 'I've got to appear sane' face.

It puts me in mind of a film on television at the time, something all us kids watched, 'The Many Faces of Foo Man Chu.'

I've often thought about those events November 1970 - December 1973. From the death of my mum to the Christmas Eve dream where, afterwards, a new chapter in my life began and I guess I slowly grew into a man.

A lot happened in a short time and this is the first time I've encapsulated it this way.

There were other factors.

In 1974, dad met a woman who stayed in our lives for awhile to give me some fun and stability. She was much younger than him and it didn't last, but she stayed in my life in one way or another throughout the remainder of my childhood.

I even stayed with her and her partner for

awhile.

I've sat and pondered that time.

Were they unusual events in a normal childhood?

Or were they normal events in an unusual childhood?

Anyhow instinct brought me back to Harrogate.

A friend saw an advert in the local paper and I found myself in the studio that has kept me safe from the outside world.

I'd been there about three months.

Hadn't done any real exercise and hadn't written a word. I was just about paying my way by doing readings. I remember having to borrow money to get through the Christmas, wondering how long I could get by.

Seems like a lifetime ago now.

Across the road, I was sat under a tree listening to my walkman disc player. It would have been something mellow, easy on the ears.

The park was quiet. It was mid week, children at school, the weather mild but overcast.

I can't even recall why I would have been sat where I was in the first place.

My eyes were closed and there appeared someone before me, smiling.

Mother.

I open my eyes to stare up at a grey sky through the branches of the tree.

The only thing that remained the same was the music playing in my ears.

I closed my eyes again and my mother was stood staring at me against the back drop of my eyelids. Odd things had been occurring for years, but each new event still created wonderment and awe for me.

I turned off the Walkman. Well we could hardly have a conversation otherwise; I thought.

'Someone wants to meet you.' she said.

Suddenly we were transported into a chamber of light.

That's the only way I can describe it.

Every shade of every bright colour greeted us, and a few I've not really become acquainted with.

'Now best behaviour, remember where you are.'

She sounded nervous.

I had the advantage of being able to open my eyes at will. I could make all this go away in a blink. Not that I tempted fate by doing so.

'And don't speak unless you're spoken too.'

I felt myself smile. Irrespective of my true age, I was still ten years old to her.

'I hope you know how lucky you are?'

The last time she said that I got a 'cowboy rifle' in Skegness.

I'd say a door opened, but it was more like the light parting down the middle.

Opening up to reveal....more light.

White light. Sunglasses bright white light.

I remember thinking I needed to open my eyes to get rid of the glare, which was absurd in so many ways if you think about it. Anyway I was not going to risk losing this connection, if in fact I could.

The whole scenario had me totally

enthralled.

We entered the second chamber, and there were four people waiting to greet us. Two of them were seated, two standing.

There was no floor, walls, or ceiling to speak off, just the light I was gradually becoming accustomed to.

It reminded me of a song, 'Floating on Air.' Though if they were floating then so were we even though I was standing on something solid.

In reality I was lying on my back under a tree, but by now I was so far into my subconscious they could have crated me up and packed me off to Madagascar and I would have been no wiser.

If there was a leader, it was a bald headed 'Buddha' character sitting at the top end of the chamber on a golden throne. You've all seen images of Buddha in pictures, trinkets, and statues. Well this could have been the real thing.

I thought of him as being in charge because he was the most imposing of characters and took his place at the head of the room.

There was one lady.

She appeared ageless, flawless skin like alabaster. A tall, slender woman standing off to the Buddha's right.

The other men were less assuming.

One was small, slim, swarthy looking.

The other, much taller, thick set.

Both of these men had dark features and sported large beards.

Everyone wore white robes, or what looked to be robes.

Quite where the robes ended and the mist began was anyone's guess.

The Buddha caught my eye and me his.

'So this is him.'

I think I was smiling, trying to get my head around the absurdity of my situation.

Mother spoke quietly, 'Don't you know where you are? Bloody behave.'

Now this did crack me up. For all I knew we could have been stood before the big man himself and my mum still managed to throw a 'bloody' into the mix.

I noticed her head was bowed, and she was gesturing with her hands madly.

I think she was trying to get me to do the same but realised I wasn't following suite.

Those in the room seemed to share my amusement, so thankfully there wasn't going to be a plague of locusts coming to Harrogate anytime soon.

And I didn't feel the need to bow down to these people.

Whilst I certainly couldn't claim to be anything close to an equal well they didn't offer any kind of threat, quite the opposite.

'You don't need to lower your head here Gladys. Your boy certainly won't pander to us, not yet anyway.'

I remember her looking at me, that 'wait til I get you home look' and I started crying.

Not at all because I believed she would hurt me but because I realised how much I missed her.

The one person that's ever truly loved me.

'There are those that want you to write your book. There are others who want nothing of the sort. We are the former and the latter are of little consequence. You are writing for us and for yourself. A joint effort if you like.'

Later I wrote all of this down, or as much as I could remember.

Then he said, 'Our substance and your endeavour,' which sounded like 'We provide the content and you do the graft.'

And that's more or less how it's worked out. Those elements that don't want me to write this book, lower end energies who for awhile could really get to me.

I would start writing every year only to stop after a few weeks. The content was still there, but the desire to write it down absent.

Distractions, other avenues to explore that enticed me but carried no real substance or meaning.

Relationships that never really got going. Work plans that I was never quite ready for.

And my worst trait of all. Laziness. The ability to do just enough to get by.

Which takes me back to the journeys we undertake and the length of time it takes for each person individually.

Could this book have been completed years earlier?

Or is the reality that it was only meant to be finished now?

I have since learnt that the answer is the latter but back to the chamber of light and the parting shot from my hosts.

From somewhere I found my voice. 'Are you God?'

I didn't know who I was addressing, but knew immediately the answer was no.

Just as I knew that all four characters were equals even though Buddha had the biggest throne.

The answer will stay with me forever. 'Would you go to a pond and waste your time having a conversation with a fish?'

That would definitely be a 'no' then, I thought as I opened my eyes.

Another anti-climax I know, but I won't embellish on what's not there.

They gave me no clue to their names, though I realise now it's not about who they are but what they represent.

The four base elements in physical form of which one will always be female, Mother Earth.

Their purpose, well that will become clear in what follows but let's not get too far ahead of ourselves.

That's where this book really started. The first thread if you like.

The stepping off point.

Over the next few nights I had recurring dreams where mum came visiting.

We were sat on a river bank having a picnic. We'd never done this in life as far as I can remember, but it was a pleasant experience. We didn't say much. Watched boats go by and chilled.

The relevance of this dream was that she was showing approval of what was to come.

Then there was the second dream. Beautiful, surreal and a little unsettling at the same time.

I was on a tube train.

It was busy; all the seats taken, others

standing.

The oddity was that no one seemed to be getting; off but a few more joined the train at each station we stopped at.

The carriage was clean. None of the empty cups, papers, or bags, common place on the London Underground.

Though I doubt this particular carriage is one many of us will be boarding anytime soon.

If the stations had names, I saw none.

The train pulled in and four more people got on.

Standing room only, everyone becoming compacted.

The newcomers two women and two men moved my way, stood nearby.

I had no idea where we were headed, when I was meant to get off. Just along for the ride I guessed.

The lead woman brushed against my leg.

'Sorry.' the word came out, though neither of us was guilty of any misdemeanor.

She smiled, pulled back startled. Looked away.

I took her in for the first time.

White overcoat, scarf. Matching white hat with a black band around the rim.

From a time gone by but still fitting in with the other fashions present. Nothing seeming out of place.

Though I once saw a man on the Northern Line wearing pyjamas and nobody batted an eye lid, I kid you not.

Her look was perfect. Dark eye shadow, thick lustrous lipstick. The first time I'd seen her made up, the first time as a mature woman.

Hailey all the same, more beautiful than ever.
Only one difference, beneath the hat, her
beautiful raven hair was now fair.
No-one else was on the carriage, just us, or so
it suddenly felt.
Her surprise was replaced by that wicked
smile, 'Always popping up where you're not
meant too, silly arse.'
This time I decided instantly, where she goes I
go, wherever.
Her smiled saddened. She knew my intention,
the futility of trying.
'You've grown up. We've grown up.' was all I
could muster.
'Is that how you see me now? All woman?'
'You're beautiful.'
'Well thank you. Look after yourself now.
I awoke to more questions than answers as
usual.
Where were we?
Time passed in this world.
Lots of questions waiting to be answered.
And as always, with patience comes the
solution. To some of the puzzles anyway.
When we see a person in spirit, they appear
to us in a way that fits the circumstances.
So if two people share a dream where they
were visited by a loved one, each dreamer
may see the spirit differently.
To one person they may be an older person,
to the other a child.
To everyone else on that train Hailey may
have appeared as a child but to me on this
occasion she was an adult.

Chapter Twenty-Eight: Level Two Energies.

I've realised that whilst I can clearly see what happens after death, the process that occurs at that moment we cast off our mortal coils is not so clear.

Let's go back to my trip in an ambulance all those years ago.

'Thought we'd lost him there.' and then, 'Bloody hell, lad' as I threw up all over the floor.

If, in fact, I had died for a few moments, well I was only later made aware of the dream. I have no memory of anyone beckoning me towards a bright light.

There's no recollection of any light what so ever.

Though spirit tell me that's because it wasn't my time and I hadn't in fact died at all.

There are twelve keys.

Each unlocks a door that leads to heaven.

The First Key is used the moment we are conceived, the door opened to allow our creation.

The Second Key unlocks the doorway to the world in which we live our physical life, and allows us to be born.

The Third Key represents passing from this physical life into spirit, death.

Forget the key as being the everyday item that unlocks doors.

This is no metal object or swipe card.

The key is the light.

We take our last breath. Our energy lifts from our physical shell and we are drawn towards an all consuming light.

Our energy is free, no longer trapped in the body, and able to speed up. A little like a spaceship hitting a button and going into overdrive, or warp speed.

There is a rush of energy as the light consumes us and then.... We find ourselves in a room.

A room of light.

There is definition. Floor, ceiling, walls, but no doors or windows.

Usually there will be familiar faces there to meet and greet, to help us settle in, but that's on Level Three.

This is Level Two.

A place between worlds where the journey will take us if we haven't sufficient energy to ascend properly.

Maybe we have taken our own lives, or not prepared ourselves for the transition.

And now you're thinking, 'transition', what does he mean?

Most people, subconsciously, know it's coming up to their time, sometimes up to two years before they actually pass.

They will start to do little things in preparation. Not necessarily the obvious tasks like organising wills and settling outstanding disputes with loved ones. The little things like putting personal effects together and visiting places that hold good memories.

Wills and disputes are governed by conscious actions.

Letters, photos, and visiting old friends, very

much in the subconscious.

It's not necessarily the atheists and 'I don't believe in anything' crowd that start at level two. What an individual voices publically and feels privately can be two very different things.

Level two spirits have suffered earthly trauma or have lived their lives really badly so haven't collected a sufficient amount of energy on order to ascend properly.

Then there are some that just simply refuse to move on, pining for their old lives, declining all offers of help to ascend.

But back to the room of light.

There may not be anyone there in a physical sense to help, but there is a voice. The voice of your primary Spirit guide.

You are energy, yes, but you still retain all your primary senses to begin with.

Memories of your old existence.

You are told to close eyes that are not really there and imagine yourself from a time that you were happy, in an environment that felt safe.

Open your eyes and that room of light will have taken on the form you imagine.

You could look eight or eighty years of age, finding yourself in a replica of the living room you lived in when you were thirty. The age you choose to be and the room you create don't have to be from the same era.

This is both your first spiritual form and your first home.

Close your eyes again.

Imagine the furnishings you want for your room, Furniture, carpets, curtains, television, stereo.

Open your eyes, some or all of these items will be there.

Close your eyes.

Give the room a window and a door.

Open your eyes. Hey presto.

There is a limit though. You are creating the room by using your own energy. If you try to create a mansion, you'll likely as not be disappointed. If you are able to build such a fine place, you'll quickly realise you don't have the energy to do anything else.

A little like walking around with a rucksack full of house bricks. It won't just slow you down and tire you out. It is also completely unnecessary.

In this world we budget our finances, well the more sensible amongst us do.

Well money isn't relevant in spirit, but we still need to make a budget.

This time for the energy we have at our disposal.

We take on the same principals as a rechargeable battery.

The more we create, or tasks we undertake, the faster our power drains and the sooner we have to put ourselves on charge to replenish our energy.

There is no hard and fast rule. The more energy at our disposal, the more we can build, the more we can achieve.

The other side of the coin is that the more energy we have the longer it takes to recharge.

I touched on this earlier, but this explains why no two spirits have quite the same sense of time.

At the lower end of the spectrum, where we are now, a spirit may use up their energy within a few hours of Earth time.

Until they learn to adapt, to budget and prioritize.

Whilst at the other end of the spectrum an energy may be seen to function for years and years before going into hibernation.

So we've taken a form and built a house, surrounding ourselves with objects that give comfort. Feeding off memories of a not too distant past.

No door is necessary to leave our room, just simple thought and will power.

Close our eyes, picture ourselves outside the room.

We are looking in on our room.

More importantly we are stood on a street like any other. We may as well still be Earth bound.

There are houses, shops, even pubs, restaurants, night clubs.

We won't be able to see them all at once of course, but they'll be out there somewhere.

There appears to be an atmosphere, but the sky is grey and this is a constant on level two.

There is no sense of day or night, no change, just a drab grey sky. Neither will we find rain, wind, or snow.

Unless we waste our own precious energy by creating it.

It really is as drab as it sounds.

We are not meant to stay here, and most will bypass the place altogether.

In spirit, there are no more illnesses, mental or

physical, but each individual has to learn this.
So if you are looking for a drink and drugs you
will create them, or seek them out, but you
are just wasting energy on a placebo that will
not give you that much needed high.
You will get clean, and then hopefully move
on to be with your loved ones.
You cannot hurt anyone else.
Go into an environment on any level where
you lose your temper or become violent and
you will have a 'Groundhog day.'
Forced to live the same day over and over
until you overcome the issue that created the
anger in the first place.
Likewise, if someone doesn't want you
sharing their space, they remove you by
breaking the connection they have to you.
A scenario may ensue where there are six
people in a room. You may, however, only
be aware of three other people being there
as the other two have no desire to
communicate with you. Or you with them.
We can choose who we wish to interact with.
No more having to put up with the mother- in
-law on a Sunday afternoon, no more ear
bashings from anyone unless you choose too.
The greater the problem you created on this
plain the longer it can take to move on
spiritually.
This does not include those that leave a
legacy of real evil on the world. Murderers
and those that govern regimes by hurting
others as an example. The list could be
endless.
Level two is still too good for them.
We're dealing with individuals who were

troubled in life. Not the mentally disturbed who have no knowledge of their actions but those that created their own downfall.

The brightest thing on all spiritual levels are animals.

Every type of creature imaginable is present. Though you are usually restricted, only coming into contact with creatures you would be familiar with.

They will show an interest because they are there to help us move on.

It's your choice; you can have as many pets as you would like. Eventually they will stop being your pets and actually become an extension of your spirit, once you have enough energy to provide for them.

Eventually most spirits settle on one animal to be around them, more than one could be a waste of resources.

But you might not like animals. Reject all of them.

They won't give up on you, and at the very least there will be birds hovering around your space.

Then there are those who choose to remain on level two for an eternity.

These are the individuals who find a way to take up residence in the minds of the living, simply refusing to evolve. Hiding away from higher level energies who are trying to help them move along.

Eventually these individuals come together and form groups.

Unable to sustain themselves for too long they steal living energy to feed on.

The more mischief they create, the greater

the stress inflicted on their victims in this world, the more energy those lower end spirits can consume.

The bigger the groups, the more damage that can be done. Some of these groups are the equivalent to the size of small countries. Their combined power can detect and keep higher end energies out.

There are leaders, just as in any group, but the minions can only be there by choice. They have the ability to leave, or begin to ascend at any time.

There is a word for this place. Purgatory.

Though it certainly isn't Hell.

Though the antics of some of these individuals would grant them the earthly title of 'Demon,' and their stealing earthly energy can be known as 'possession.'

I suppose you become accustomed to constant grey skies if that's all there is on offer.

Like any addiction, you get hooked and lose our touch with
reality.

In the same sense, spend too much time on level two and it becomes easy to forget that this is just the start of the journey and there are happier, sunnier climates to explore.

It's the principle of the group. Get too comfortable, feel apart of something, and we forget there's a whole wide world out there to explore. Not everything evolves around our own back yard.

Let's get back to those animals.

You had a favourite Labrador, and she's waiting for you.

An animals energy vibration is not as high as a human being. So whilst your nearest and dearest are vibrating too high for you to make contact with, a man's best friend can do the job just as well.

Whatever your issues, well eternity's a long time, and most individuals work through their problems quickly.

All the time their energy source increases as experiences becomes a more positive and bad is replaced by good.

You have your room, the comfort of your pet, ever obedient, always receptive.

Then your connection to the dog becomes complete. Part of your energy melds with the animal and the real work begins.

Your 'pet' can see with your eyes.

You can be in your room and out in the world at the same time looking through the eyes of your faithful friend.

Whets more, you can be busy recharging and this extension of you can still operate using its own energy.

The purpose is simple.

As you collect energy, start to move towards ascension, you will become aware of a light in the East.

Like a sunrise on the Eastern Horizon.

This light will not just get brighter and brighter; it will start to draw you in, beckoning you towards the beam.

Everything spiritual moves in a clockwise direction, or simply forward.

So we leave the home we've created and head east. Our companion will go on ahead marking out a path for us to follow.

Only those on the path to ascension will see the light.

As we head towards it we will continue to learn, and evolve.

This journey may take us through streets and houses, through towns and open spaces.

Another journey may take the traveller on trains and planes.

The same journey to another may be as simple as leaving one room and entering another.

Whatever the destination, it will always be east of us, and always shrouded in bright white light.

One thing is certain. However long, or short, the journey, it will result in a rush of energy as we are consumed by the light...and then we will be in a room.

As before, a room with definition and glaringly bright.

Unlocked by **The Fourth Key.**

Chapter Twenty-Nine: The Squatter And The Clean-Up Crew.

I have taken to having a great number of recurring dreams since the time of meeting whom I've grown to think of as my mentors. They show me enough to make me think but never reveal their hand until I've shown how thick I can be by missing the point completely.
I used to have dreams about my old job, usually at times when things were not going so well, or I had some work concerns.
The dream differed from real life in several ways.
In the dream I had a dozen or more people working for me, in real life I did not.
In the dream 'my staff' were systematically taken from me and given promotions. Put in positions that superceded mine whilst I was overlooked for everything.
In the end I always ended up alone, no staff, the only Indian amongst many chiefs.
On this occasion there was a change of direction to my dream.
I decide go to see the manager to find out what was going on, only he wasn't any colliery manager I remember has a boss.
I was going into the office to be greeted by my Buddha sitting on his throne. The others are also present but, again, he is the only one sitting.
They already know why I'm there of course, look unamused by the griping to come.

One of the others speak, not sure who, not a female voice though. 'Why are you so impatient, Keith? So afraid you are being left behind, worried that everyone else has something you want but can't have. There's a reason why they are moving on and you are still here. None of them can gain entry into this room and someone will need to take over when are gone. No-one else can truly manage them but you, when the time comes.'

That's when I tried to wake up, expecting the usual shaking in my head and abdomen to a point where I couldn't get back to sleep. An occurrence that followed most reality dreams Only this time the dream didn't end.

Instead I returned to my office.

Now devoid of furniture. The plaster on the walls removed so the brickwork was clear to see, rotting and crumbling. The electric sockets removed; bare wires exposed.

Just like someone had stripped it back to the bones whilst I was otherwise engaged.

Now in reality, the colliery had been gone for a good few years and the land had become a nature reserve as far as I'm aware.

I remember thinking, 'What's happening?'

A voice, the same man who'd spoken to me in the manager's office, 'You don't need to be here anymore. This place is redundant to your needs.'

For the first time I noticed the office window. Outside it had to be early evening. The sky was a grey pallette. It looked empty, devoid of life.

With that, I was outside, looking at the office

building or what remained of it.

It was literally falling in on itself. I would have been buried alive in the rubble had I remained a moment longer.

There were holes in the roof; bare beams exposed, the brickwork rotting before my eyes. Imagine a painting that has turpentine poured onto it. The picture will spoil, the colours running into one another leaving an almost garish backdrop. Well this was similar.

To the left, as I looked at the building, tendrils of pitch black nothingness began to consume the building. Where there had been a wall, was now just a black empty void.

The process was slow and could have crept up on me if I wasn't seeing the building being devoured before my very eyes.

Suddenly, I'm stood, literally, at a crossroads. One blink and the offices have gone from sight, instantly transporting me to a different destination.

I can't see what's behind me, nor to my left. My focus is on the terraced properties facing me and, what appears to be, an open fronted café to my right.

I've seen images from the Second World War where the Germans had bombed London. Half a street raised to the ground, many properties damaged but amongst the carnage, one house remaining untouched. Almost as though someone had put a protective shield in place, and the bombs were unable to penetrate that particular space.

Well this was the same.

A row of terraces had a hit one miss one look.

Several properties were in differing states of decay; then there would be a property that looked brand new, obviously occupied and well taken care of. Then more properties in need of knocking down and starting again. Every now and again there was a gap where a property had once stood. There was something wrong with this picture. The space had not just been cleared; there was a dark empty mass where the houses should have been. The same black entity that was eating up the colliery offices was present.

To my surprise a man appeared through the front door of one of the falling down houses; I caught his eye and he hurried back inside slamming the door.

The grey gloom didn't change. It got no darker as expected.

The terraced street went on until it lost itself in that inky black darkness.

Two things were absent. No street lights and no vehicles of any kind.

Though from the few houses that looked pristine, there was the glow of some form of light. Candles perhaps, lamps maybe. My mind trying to be rational. After all when we're dreaming, we don't realise its not real until we wake up.

Though since this particular event, not so long ago, I'm more aware of what happens when I sleep. I've also developed a strong ability to return to dreams if I'm woken prematurely.

I turned my attention to the café I'd seen close by. At least I assumed it was.

Approaching the building, I can see up to a dozen people sitting around chatting.

Again several oddities.

I said the café was open fronted; you know those doors that can be pulled back to let in light and warmth during the summer.

I was wrong, sort of. Clearly it was open fronted, but there was no door, nothing at all to close it off from the outside world, or the elements. Though this evening, despite the grey backcloth, seemed mild.

I haven't a clue as to what I was wearing, never gave it a thought, well we don't in dreams do we?

The second thing that was 'off', whilst most of the patrons sat at tables; two men sat separately at a long bar that ran the length of the building. There was a bartender as well. I remember him for his handle bar moustache and white apron covering his sizeable midriff.

But no-one was either eating or drinking. In fact there was no signs of plates, glasses, or bottles. Nothing you would associate with such an establishment.

That's when it dawned on me; they are all in spirit.

'Have I died?'

Well it is an obvious question under the circumstances.

That same voice, 'Don't be stupid, Keith.'

So I'm 'over there' staring down at a small group of people minding their own business, and I ask one of the great questions of our time...not.

'What year is it?'

Everyone looks at me quizzically.

'Alright then, keep it simple, what's the month?'

Why I asked these questions, I'm not sure. Perhaps I was looking for a dozen different answers. Proof that they were each from a different era. I don't know.

They ignored me, carrying on with their own muted conversations.

I stood staring like the kid who everybody ignores at school.

'You aren't meant to be here feller. Not now, not ever.'

It was the bartender, who seemed as though he may remain rooted to the same spot for eternity.

Once more I seem to blink and move.

I'm indoors. A house that appears to have many rooms. Has the feel of a bungalow but the rooms, as just about everything else I've come across is in decay.

There is movement off to my right and a man appears from between two marble pillars.

The same man I'd seen scurrying back into the terrace. Though this was too ostentatious to be any terrace I'd ever seen. Also, it was all on one level as far as I could tell.

'What do you want? A direct question from an uncertain voice.

I honestly didn't have an answer. 'This is a dream. I'm dreaming.'

'For you maybe.' There was the hint of a smile, 'Am I in your head?'

'Well yes, your in my dream.'

That wasn't what he meant, and I knew it, but what other answer was there?

'This isn't the house I saw you at is it?'
'Course it is.'
He went back through the pillars.
I followed.
There was a camp bed, blankets and pillows.
If he had anything else, I wasn't aware.
So what's this all about? In my mind to myself.
No voices this time, not immediately anyway.
Just images of a man. Not this individual in his
dishevelled state but the person who had
created this living space.
Arrogant, proud, materialistic, a bully who left
a trail of broken hearts and minds in his wake.
I couldn't see him but got a sense of the
character.
Of the wife who stood by his side despite a
lifetime of lies and betrayals. The daughter
who disowned him years ago, refusing to
bow to his control even though she can't
form a relationship of her own due to trust
issues. And the other daughter who he totally
controlled, emotionally abusing and loving in
equal measures. There are many more
people whose essence runs through this
dwelling, but they are the one's I feel.
No names, just as sense of who they are,
damaged people.
The creator of this hell as recently moved on.
Either he's gone into the light and ascended
having learnt the error of his ways, or he's
simply found a new place to exist. Joined a
larger group, spreading his bile elsewhere.
He's bad, but not evil. Though those he left
behind may hope he's in hell, or its
equivalent.
These dwellings aren't merely houses.

Created through the tenants own energy, these properties may look uniformed in appearance from the outside, but once inside they can be as modest or vast as the creator chooses or is able.

As the property grows, so do the memories of a life now departed. He will have visited his family over and over looking for some form of forgiveness, which he may or may not have found.

But now he's gone, and all is left is this shell which will continue to rot to nothing, his energy going into creating a new home. For these houses are living things that have had their energy supply cut off.

Though what remain are memory signatures, that leave open a gateway, whilst the property remains. An entrance to the minds of the mother and daughters who were the main focus of his attention.

So our squatter comes along and takes up residence whilst the going's still good. Not because of a love for what he's done with the place but because it gives him access to the minds of those damaged by the sins of the father.

That's how they get in to someone's mind, take up residence and find a way to remain earthbound.

This usually only lasts whilst the energy of the property holds strength, but it's long enough to create mental instability in the host.

Then, once the energy has become too weak, he'll look for another empty property to move into.

One of the individuals on Level Two who do

little more than steal energy from the living
and those departed in order to live some half
existence as an alternative to ascending.
Normally when an energy evolves they clean
up after themselves, leaving nothing for third
parties to feed on. But that's not Level Two;
they haven't learnt sufficiently, need their
backsides wiping. Leaving behind energy
that they really need for themselves.
Remember the more energy we hold on to
the more we create.
I felt sick and wanted out of there.
Still, the squatter didn't look too healthy so I
guessed the family weren't such easy
pickings after all.
Maybe someone granted my wish.
I was back on the street.
New revelations. Music and light.
Hall and Oates filled my ears, hadn't listened
to them for awhile. Back beyond the café
and the countless other homes out there. I
was aware of a light that seemed to have
such an intensity that I felt myself pulled
towards it.
Then another voice behind me.
'What are you doing here you silly arse?'
I turned, my heart doing a double flip.
Hailey, as I remembered her on the tube,
maybe a little younger.
No makeup this time but flawless skin, a truly
healthy glow.
Two others with her. A white haired lady and
a bald headed man.
A trio of angels was my immediate thought.
They were head to foot dressed in white. No,
not clothes. They were human shaped balls

of energy. Angelic faces, with long flowing locks. Hailey's blonde look suited her. She was breathtakingly beautiful, no matter how she looked.

'What are you doing here?' The best I could muster.

'No. what are YOU doing here?' Not a rebuke, she already knew the answer I was certain. If she did, she knew better than me. She was playing her teasing game again.

'We're here to clean up the mess made by others. And deal with any ne're do wells we come across along the way. Like your man in there.' Indicating with her head towards the house where the squatter was blissfully in residence. 'He's been upgraded to a pain in the arse, so he'll be coming with us.'

'Where?' I imagined there must be a hell, and they knew the general direction.

'You needn't trouble yourself with such frivolities. Can't stand here chatting, time to wake up.'

Which I did. Head and abdomen shaking as predicted.

It was three thirty.

It was going to be an age before I would get off again so I made a cup of tea and wrote down everything I could recall, which was almost everything.

Chapter Thirty: Level Three Energies, The Fourth Key.

'We take our last breath. Our energy lifts
from the physical shell, and we are drawn
towards and all consuming light....
Where our emotional guides are waiting to
help us cross over.
No unwelcoming grey skies or falling down
houses, and no interlopers out to steal energy
and sneak into our loved ones minds.
We are safe.
As a child in the arms of their parents, we are
embraced by those who have helped us get
this far and are equally ready to help us
move on.
Our Spirit guides.
We will go through, more or less, the same
ritual as a level two energy. The difference
being, when we form our living space it will
be a house we create and not a single room.
We are stronger than our level two
counterparts; that's how we've managed to
bypass that level in the first place.
If we are too ambitious in our designs, then
our loved ones can help out by offering us
some of their energy.
And if a partner has gone on before us, the
house will already be there, if we want to be
with them of course.
We will also have a recreational area, or a
garden if you like. Created in the same
manner as the house. It could be anything
you desire, and can be altered at any time.
What may take on the appearance of a rose

garden today could be transformed in to a beach setting tomorrow, and vice versa.

No need to go on holiday, the holiday comes to you. Though if you choose to leave the comfort of your own back yard, you are quite welcome to do so.

You want to go to a 70's disco, a 50's tea dance, a 60's style music festival, they will all be available to you. There's going to be thousands of energies sharing the same desire.

Going back in time to when, individually, your life was most memorable. This can be recreated by collective energy. All those thousands of people sharing the same thought and a higher force will create the means to party for eternity.

All the fun without the exertion. Dance all night, or as long as your energy allows. Eat, drink, fornicate even, though the eating and drinking are totally unnecessary and sexual excitement is created through emotional energy. Good news guys, size no longer matters in the afterlife.

Back to our home and take a seat next to the swimming pool you've created.

All that's missing are family and friends to party with.

So send out the invitations. Think about those you would like to share your space with and if possible their energy will materialise before you.

They might not be able to come for a number of reasons.

Level two energies can't jump to level three before they are ready. Others might be recharging, having run their 'battery' down. Simply, they may reject your offer to party because they have other commitments, or they may be working.

Yes, we are eventually expected to work for a living.

Those that want to be there, and can, will put in an appearance.. Reminiscing about old times and having harmless fun.

This is the easiest way to collect more energy, by interacting with others.

There is a word of warning though. Just as with every other level, abuse and violence will not be tolerated. Falling out in any way results in that Groundhog Day, reliving the events that caused the problem until we overcome our issues. Wasting energy along the way, which takes time to get back.

Positive interaction creates good energy. Moaning as we do in this life will drain us very quickly.

Just as we send out mental invitations, we cannot just turn up at someone else's home without an invite. If you want to go see your Grandma you have to mentally ask if it's convenient to drop by. If you get the green light, you think of Grandma and you'll be at her home.

Time becomes irrelevant.

The afterlife is a series of events, one running into the other. The more adventurous or creative these events are; the quicker your energies run down, and you go into 'sleep' mode to recharge. At this time you won't be available to anyone.

Though it's not required for someone to be

fully recharged to function, it obviously helps.
As with level two, this new world has an
atmosphere.
This isn't made up of constant grey skies,
thankfully, but there are shades of light and
dark.
Sunshine is created by our energies being
fully charged and the sun doesn't rise or set,
but dims as our energies run down.
Though you might be sat in bright sunshine
whilst your partner, sat on the next sun bed
by the pool might be seeing dusk on the
horizon because they are getting ready to
recharge. Even if you rest at the same time, it
might not make a difference, because they
may have collected more or less energy than
you to start with having passed at a different
time. You can of course offer some of your
energy, but surely you don't want to be
popping everyone else up for eternity. There
was enough of that when you were alive.
Likewise, collective energy having fun will be
shrouded in constant sunshine irrespective of
individual energies strength, only dimming if
there is a falling out or arguments ensue.
You see despite the belief that we become
all knowing in the afterlife; we're still learning
on level three, and people aren't much
different from their physical lives.
If you parents had issues with colour and
sexuality, well they aren't yet in a position to
see the error of their ways, so such issues are
still relevant.
If someone didn't believe in the afterlife
when they were alive, suddenly faced with
the reality that we do go on afterwards, well

that doesn't necessarily change their attitude, oh no.

The new belief becomes,' Well I was maybe wrong about that, but there'll be nothing beyond this!'

Surprisingly perhaps, many groups remain alienated from each other, mainly through religion.

Remember you will only be part of a group if you are willing to share energy. Just as you are helped out when you arrive, you will return the compliment later.

So at this stage we have the same prejudices we had on the Earth plain.

Faiths will flock together; those with a closed minds will happily share their stunted beliefs, and your parents may well continue to complain about the behaviour of your partner, both in spirit and the earth plain. Though you may well have been happily married for thirty odd years, he/she is still alive and taken up with someone else, so they have to have been right about him/her all along. Totally ignoring the fact that you're happy he/she has found someone else so they don't grow old alone.

So, as with everything we create, there are pluses and minuses.

The biggest difference, though at this stage no-one's aware, is that there are no power bases.

All physical links are severed so no-one's fighting over oil, or trying to control the drug trade, and no-one has need for a nuclear deterrent.

Those responsible for war crimes and other

atrocities aren't anywhere near here, so
whilst there will always exist natural leaders;
the word is 'love' and not 'hate.'
No one group as an advantage over
another, there is no longer a 'third world.'
The only benefit from being in a large group
is that, by sharing energy, they have the
ability to create larger communities.
1,000,000 Somalians collectively will have the
advantage of building a greater
environment than 100 white supremacists.
Though I'm talking semantics, and that's not
the point.
Irrespective of colour, creed, sexuality, faith
or nationality, the bigger the group, the more
we can create.
Eventually, the aim is to bring everyone
together in love and harmony, but we're still
learning so that moment for us isn't in the
now.
That comes later.
Let's go back to our home and our family.
Our own community will usually be made up
of family members.
Ascension is a personal journey of discovery.
There is no 'time' limit.
One spirit could evolve very quickly.
Some even bypass all these levels for various
reasons, good and bad.
So your parents might very well have moved
on, leaving you behind for now, whilst your
great great Grandparents might still occupy
space on this level, simply refusing to evolve.
The learning process can take an eternity for
some. If you're blissfully happy then why
would you want to change what you have

created for something new?
The truth is, often they think this must be
heaven when they aren't even close.
Picture yourself on a street. It could be
anything. Open plan, lawns, parks, ponds,
your family and friends have created this. All
those that live in your community.
Where you may see a pond, another may
see a pile of earth, or a woodland. The street
scene will change depending on each
individuals choice.
Certain things stay the same though.
Each house remains in the same space. It
could be any shape or size depending on its
creator. As grand or austere as they choose.
Animals roam around freely, searching out
potential masters. For us it would be usually
domestic animals. If you were from West
Africa your taste would, likely as not, be
influenced by more exotic breeds, lions tigers,
snakes, apes.
That's not to say we cannot choose an exotic
breed as a companion, personal choice.
Whilst dogs, cats, birds, rodents, are the norm,
think of an orangutan and that's what you'll
get. Just be aware that once you've made
an energy connection they become part of
you for eternity.
On level three almost everyone has at least
one animal companion.
There is no need for street lights or vehicles.
Everything is powered by individual energy,
so we create our own light and power.
If you want to drive, you can. Given the
choice of the streets and something more
adventurous, like a racetrack or rallying, well

all your dreams can come true.

Again collective energy creates the track and the individual energy provides their own vehicles.

All the fun and none of the pain. You may very well crash but well you can't die twice over once you're here.

Let's go back to looking at property.

My advice in this world is to have as many different experiences as possible. Visit as many different countries as money and time will allow. Listen to all forms of music, don't dismiss any experience.

Because we carry them over into the next life.

You go and visit your Grandmother.

Her home is the same as the two up two down she lived in for sixty years. Brought six children up and saw off two husband who she chooses not to be with here.

In those sixty years, she never left the village, other than to go shopping in the nearby town. Never ventured abroad, never saw the sea.

So when she steps out of her home she can only create what she, herself, experienced in life. No beach front home for Grandma. She can only recreate what she has experienced to this point.

That's not to say her loved one's can't share the experience of Pacific Oceans with her if they visited during their lifetime.

You can access your memories, recreate scenarios. A piece of music, a film, a rerun of your favourite television series. Fifty years of Coronation Street replayed before our very eyes; God help us.

Anything you stored in your subconscious is carried over with you.

You've built your home, learnt how to function, making the most of your environment. Reacquainted yourself with your families, but a certain group of people may be missing.

Perhaps those we cherish the most and want to know are well. Children we may either have lost, or were never born.

They may well have already evolved to a much higher level, and usually have.

Children do not have the same restrictions as adults, particularly if they were never on the Earth plain in the first place.

They don't have to undertake the same learning process, as innocence truly can be bliss.

People often refer to children in spirit as 'Our Little Angels' and are much closer to the truth than they can imagine. On that scale of one to eight they are already a six, or a seven.

They will evolve into 'adults' faster than on Earth and be able to work wonders.

They will visit those that created them in the first instance, Mothers and Fathers. However, the strength of that bond will rely on how close an earth bound connection there was.

A child aborted or miscarried may very well not have a strong a link as a child who passed as a five year old and loved them very much. They will appear as children and have the ability to flit in and out of their loved ones lives when circumstances allow.

Higher energies, however, cannot share

energy with lower energies easily as the vibration is too great.

Also, lower end energies cannot visit beyond their level for the same reason.

They only way to be properly reconnected to your lost child is to ascend to the same level as them.

If that's not encouragement enough to want to ascend, I don't know what is.

After awhile that brightest of lights will begin to appear to the East. Only not East of some town or city, nor some great plain or mountain. This light won't take you away from your loved ones, and everyone welcomes it with open arms.

It engulfs the back of your home and instead of passing through; you bathe in its beauty.

Unlocked by **The Fifth Key, it** takes us through another door, yes, but one that enables you to make contact with those loved ones still earthbound.

This light allows you to become a Spirit Guide and find gainful employment if you so choose.

There are no rules connecting spirit with earth time.

Such is the increase in vibration that it may feel that a number of years have gone by, yet in physical terms only a few days have passed. Alternatively spirit's version of time can appear to be frozen. Each spirits sense of timing is individual, based on their unique circumstances and needs.

Passing through this light will happen faster for some than others. The thing is though, even if it feels like an eternity before you attain this level, you'll still be in time to witness those that loved you sharing in their grief and you will attend your own funeral. For that is where the last of the ties are severed and where your true spiritual journey begins.

Chapter Thirty-One: The Field, The Beach, And The House Of Mystery.

The dreams I most coveted as a child involved those people and places I have already described.
And I'm back.
Is it the writing of this book that's brought me here, or some greater source drawing me in?
So much as come to light in such a short space of time.
I have had the book in my head for nine years.
I have been writing on and off for two and a half years.
Yet, these eureka moments can be condensed into but a few weeks.
To begin with, I was loathe to write about my life in any form, couldn't understand why I was compelled to do so. Now I realise that, without my experiences, there would be no book.
Imagine sitting an exam. My guides are providing the information that would make up the written part of the process whilst my dreams and experiences go to make up the practical.
Whether the two compliment each other is for the reader to decide, but I realise now that without one there wouldn't be the other.
Fortunately I remember these dreams with such clarity, but they are no longer dreams you would associate with a normal nights sleep.

For a long time now my sleep patterns have been taking on a life of their own. I can sleep solidly for nine to ten hours a night. If I set an alarm, I wake as though I've hardly slept at all, and I am drawn back in to my dream state, picking up exactly where I left off. As though a cycle has to be completed before I can face up to the waking day.

Anyway I'm back in the field I last visited on a never to be forgotten Christmas Eve in 1973. And the grass is once again brushing against my legs.

There's disco music pounding in my head and I want to dance. Really want to dance.

My mind is that of the fifty year old overweight man that I am.

My body, defying logic, is that of the eighteen year old dancer that I was.

Didn't I mention I could dance once upon a time?

As a teenager, before meeting my wife and my 'normal life,' I danced. Every evening I could be found tripping the light fantastic.

Those memories are stored amongst some of the very best of my life.

Some would say I was good. Some would say not so. The latter were jealous, because I was that good. To my mind anyway.

But it was a form of escapism. Nothing could hurt me on that dance floor; I truly felt like a king.

Of course, age, alcohol, and far too many take always take their toll. Although the tenth of the talent that still remains could give many a run for their money. Well for five minutes anyway, did I not just mention I'm really overweight.

So I'm thankful to those that have lent me my old body for the purposes of this dream.

But I still don't rise to the challenge. Even though it's Dan Hartman in my head, one of my all time favourites.

The eighteen year old Keith would have put on a display for anyone. Thirty two years can make a man question his dignity.

Even though it's only a 'dream.'

I know where I'm going even though it's been so long. The grass seems longer, lusher, coming up to my waist in places. Enticing me, tempting me into the dance.

My mind is distracted by the sound of the sea sneaking up on me.

I start to run, all thoughts of dancing brushed away, though the rousing music remains.

The beach.

Gypsies, children....and Hailey.

Everything was the same. The clearing, the dirt track, the road running adjacent to the beach.

Then everything was different.

Not the scene in itself. There were still the caravans. The clear lack of any horses to pull them. People still sat in their groups. Talking, smoking, drinking, dancing. Children still played by the waters edge.

But the numbers of these people had swelled a thousand fold. Maybe even more. From left to right, as far as the eye could see, there were travelling people and children.

I'd never noticed before, but the children outnumbered the adults.

Quite a few looked my way. The adults

stared, the kids waved, but only for a moment until their attention wavered.

Disappointment ran through me. If Hailey was here, well I had no chance of finding her amongst this lot.

'If she was here she'd find you.' My Mother's voice.

But she was nowhere to be seen either. Just a few words in my head blocking out the music temporarily.

I tried to step forward onto the beach, but some invisible force field stopped me. A bit like standing on the edge of a cliff, knowing one pace forward and your going to take a tumble.

Mother again, 'You haven't been invited. You can never go where you're not welcome.'

On that note, I found myself back on the tree lined street, heading towards the house I knew I would be allowed to enter. It dawned on me that I'd been here maybe a hundred times over the years. Not just in dreams but meditations too. At one time, about ten years ago, I could close my eyes and transport myself there in an instant. Though that amphitheatre was no longer open to me and I never ventured much further than the front lawn and the lower halls.

I hadn't been more recently.

Adventures in alternative realities and experiences relating to ascension have taken precedence. Again without them there would not be a book.

I go through the open gate.

There is the lady in black, complete with veil,

sitting on her bench. She is there every time I visit. I have no idea who she might be.
I have never been inclined to approach her and, she has never acknowledged me.
There are always women playing tennis, dressed for another age.
The music hasn't stopped but somewhere changed from Dan Hartman to the Crusaders, 'Streetlife.' That 1970's disco feel remained. The desire to dance not so.
I go into the house, the large double front doors opening out before me.
I almost expect the butler from the Adams Family waiting to greet me, but no, there's never anyone there.
Only that once during a meditation, sixteen, seventeen years ago when I was greeted by the bespectacled man.
Upstairs I can see the dozen or so room side by side in what can be best described as a horse shoe shape.
I feel drawn to the stairs but go into the familiar drawing room to my right instead.
I always sit in the same wing backed chair, and I always close my eyes....and dream.
Now how can you get a dream within a dream?
It happens. But I believe it's more like a meditation within a dream, or a dream within a meditation. The two things are not that far removed, but there is a subtle difference.
I'm walking up the garden path of my old childhood home.
There's a rough looking lawn on either side of the path surrounding the most beautiful rose bush I've ever seen. And boy did that bush

turn out some flowers in summer. Beneath the front window I can see the old blue bench. The paint's still flaking after all these years, I thought.

Mother's sat on the bench, knitting.

Behind her, the front windows gleamingly clean. To one side there is a television Aerial hanging down the side of the wall. God I'd clear forgotten about that.

This is the house as it was in the sixties. Before Mother and Danny died. Before our first colour television when they had to put an aerial on the roof. Before dad cut down and uprooted the rose bush, because it had become a 'nuisance' for him to prune and look after.

It was always his mother's rosebush anyway. Danny and dad aren't around, just mum and her knitting.

There is no conversation, just a middle aged man in a younger body staring at the woman who was taken from him as a boy.

She looks up, smiles….and I open my eyes. Back in the drawing room, sitting in the wing backed chair.

Only I'm no longer alone. There's a man wandered in at some point; he's staring out of the window, his back to me. Only he's doing what I didn't have the courage to do, his hips are swaying from side to side. And he's much older than me.

'Can you hear it, the music?' Aware of me but not turning.

'The Crusaders.' I replied.

He turned, bemused. 'Joe Loss, of course. Don't you know music?'

'We have different tastes I think.'
'So you can't here it then?'
'Not what you're listening too, no.'
Different strokes for different folks and all that.
'I've been visiting my daughter. She has her problems, but we're getting there. She'll be joining me and her mother soon. Have you been visiting anyone?'
'No-one in particular.' The only response I could muster.
Again, the man looked bemused.
'My daughter was murdered. They still haven't found her body. She's stuck because her friends and family over there won't let go. Four years and they still cling on to hope. She gets close to ascending, then someone always seems to pull her back. She's only just beginning to understand what happened to her, the trauma you see. It's stronger over here, harder to deal with because there's no time. Oh well, nice meeting you.'
The man leaves the room.
I find myself following.
He goes up the staircase whilst I watch.
He goes to the fourth, maybe fifth, door. The door doesn't magically open as I imagined. A swathe of light appears around the frame, coming together until the door is replaced by a brightness that is hard on the eyes.
The man walks into the light.
For a second it feels like all the energy is being sucked out of the hallway. I can't breathe. Then the light vanishes and I'm once more staring at a closed door.
And the music's gone from my head.
And with that I wake up, the words 'I love

you' coming from my lips as a block of ice pulls away from me, and it's as though the freezing cold sensation was never there.
An event within a dream within a meditation?
I slept well after all that. Woke up with more to ponder than the previous day. Should have spent the day writing, but instead sat thinking, probably with some dumb look on my face.
Over the years I've had my theories about the house I visit. Have doubted my mental competence a few times as well. I'm sure my sanities as intact as my theories, but I wanted to know the answers and not speculate.
The new found clarity to my dreaming has started to help in one aspect of my life.
Over the years I have become involved, usually, not through choice, in the search for missing people and uncovering the identity of those responsible for abduction and death.
Unfortunately, whilst the police claim to be open minded to psychics and mediums I find that, particularly more recently, the authorities don't want to know.
In many ways I don't blame them. Most psychics/ mediums don't know half of what they think they do. For every abduction or murder there is over a hundred self professed seers come forward within mind boggling theories and solutions to every crime. Most, if not all, of these leads go nowhere.
Even I've done it. Passed on information that led to nothing or got misconstrued as something else entirely.

Not for awhile though.

I realise now that what I understand today is different from ten years ago, and there's little point coming forward because I'm only going to get labelled with the rest of the idiots and time wasters. I'm sure most of these people have good intentions and get frustrated when they are ignored, but it's a fact that you will usually only see part of a much bigger puzzle, and the rest will not make sense to the authorities nor anyone else.

There are reasons why there is so little success in these matters and it's to do with both the victim and the medium.

The victim will be confused having suffered a great trauma. So their ability to vocalise will be distorted.

Ask a murder victim what happened to them and you will get flashes. Moments leading up to and during the event, but rarely the whole picture.

If the authorities gave me access to a crime scene, I would possibly piece things together very quickly.

The victim leaves an energy signature behind, as does the perpetrator. The longer time passes the weaker the signal becomes. The essence of everything in creation, energy. We have the ability to tap in to it to do so much good, yet we remain ignorant to the potential.

From a medium's perspective, and this is where things are changing, my ability to retrieve the details of what occurred are improving.

Why?

Human nature ensures we sanitize our bad experiences, we block out most, if not all, of the really bad stuff.

So if a spirit does happen to show me exactly what happened, well my conscious mind would react by putting up a barrier to protect me from the experience.

Take the scenarios from earlier. The young man shot in Ireland and the young woman shot in that Paris basement.

Now I did experience their demise because it seemed to be about me, but what if the executions had been tied in to recent events and the victims were trying to point the finger at their killer.

Whilst my subconscious mind worked hard at giving me the complete picture, my conscious mind may very well have me jumping up and down on a bouncy castle playing with pink bunny rabbits.

Protection.

But you see, in order to see with clarity the events that centre around my writing, I cannot afford the luxury of either rabbits or bouncy castles. Anyway the horrors of the nightmare might be more enticing as I'd look bloody ridiculous.

So the nature of my dreams and meditations has slowly changed. The fantasy elements, conscious interference, pushed aside.

So next time I'm shown the nature of someone's death, the chances of success in catching those responsible rise dramatically. Also it is my intention to revisit old cases I've been involved in to help bring peace of mind

to the families of the missing and dead.
I just need help in getting the police to listen
instead of paying lip service to my face and
probably having a laugh behind my back.
See, I do get frustrated and have a
rant....occasionally.

Chapter Thirty-Two: Level Four Energies, The Fifth Key.

Earth times passes.
Spiritual time can stand in one place for an eternity, depending on how quickly an energy progresses.
Imagine there are only weekends and you have the ability to live this time over and over forever. This may be an idea of heaven to some, but eventually you will get bored, move on, and look for new interests.
The longer you stay around this level the more family, friends, friends of friends, will come to join your group.
If you choose to stay for eternity, the numbers continue to swell, but you'll no longer know anybody because they were probably born after you died. You might not even like or get on with these strangers.
Those closest to you will probably have moved on.
This level allows us to experience one scenario after another, each created for the individuals satisfaction and enjoyment, but how much of a good thing can we take?
An awful lot apparently, which leads to problems at this level.
I actually wonder, if God in hindsight, got things a little bit wrong. For which I'm likely to get a spiritual slap any minute.
I'll come to this anomaly presently, but let's first look at other things that happen to spirits at this level.
I mentioned the ability to work.

Most take on the role of spirit guides at some point.
Though I hardly think of eavesdropping on loved ones as hard work. Waiting for another slap off of some spirit guide now.
Twelve years ago, I spent time with a psychic fair for a few months. A group consisting of the good, bad, and indifferent, and they are still going much to my surprise.
Ironically I was in Harrogate at a hotel on the street where I now live. The hotel is gone, turned into swanky apartments.
Anyway, this young lady came to my table. It was quiet, teatime; she'd just finished work.
I was talking about her partner, picked up that he was mad on judo but not much else. She felt she'd lost him, would never get him back, they were no longer together, though to her they were still a couple. I commented that he must be mad for letting her go at which point there was an almighty 'thwacking noise' and pain exploded in the back of my neck.
Everyone in that room clearly heard the noise, and that's when I came to realise that her judo loving ex-boyfriend was only an ex because he'd died. A spiritual slap!
I don't think I was fit to work for the rest of the evening.
There are sprits that are around because we have them in our thoughts constantly, and those whom we hardly ever think of who do the hard work of keeping us on the straight and narrow.
There are guides who are 'collectors.'
Storing new knowledge. Be it the latest

technology, archiving historical events, collecting new music, even every new film and every television programme in production. Each new fashion trend, design in furniture. Everything that is physically created is collated and processed.

Once we have it here they can have access to it there.

Many spirits refer to it as, simply, going shopping.

Collectively, shopping precincts exist. With a flick of a switch in the mind they can be transported there.

I know using the word 'mind' suggests a brain, but I use the word to describe a process where energy is moved from one place to another with a minimum of effort.

Certain items we would purchase individually for ourselves. Other items can be bought for a community to share, so the cost is shared. This cost is energy of course. Everything we have/build takes away from our energy pool. We could say, connect to the latest episodes of our favourite television programmes and pass them on once we've finished with them, or we can simply remove them from our energy.

There are higher energies that serve as guides to try and affect the nature of the base elements, in order to help us grow and keep the planet safe.

And energies even beyond this level that oversee every universe in creation and try to juggle, with great difficulty, the respective energies to maintain balance and avoid potential disasters.

Eventually, albeit there are always exceptions, we will become guides of one form or another. It's a fruitful way of advancement and helping us to evolve through the realms.

Which leads us back to the problem. God's faux pas if you like.

Beyond this realm there are other levels of existence, necessary if we are to get to heaven.

So the obvious question is, what comes next? Sprits on this level, unfortunately, aren't asking the same question. They aren't moving on as intended and are creating a blockage.

First of all a yo-yo effect occurs.

They are trying to ascend but keep being pulled back by those earthly connections that can't let them go.

In order to come to be around their loved ones in a physical sense they have to slow their vibration, and whilst they collect energy during the visit, there is a limit to the length of their stay. If they keep exhausting those energies, little else will get done.

So ascension is slowed down by our loved ones who can't let go of their grief. I'm not saying we shouldn't think about our dear departed, but let them see you with a smile on your face. Let them move on just as they would, hopefully, want you too.

Second part of the problem is that ascending from this level involves leaving behind your spirit family for a time and experiencing a rebirth.

Maybe a little hard to swallow if you've been with your family and friends for the equivalent of several hundred earth years. It can be almost impossible to say goodbye.

However, that's exactly what you must do to ascend from here. There are exceptions where couples, or families, have got to the same level and ascend together, but the next journey is for the individual and so you must still find it in yourself to say goodbye. Eventually you will come back together. New and improved. The lives you then share will take on a different dimension; the love and peace accentuated a thousand fold.

A client came to see me several years ago as she'd just lost her father.

He was in my head immediately.

He had been a publican. This particular morning he woke up and went down to get ready for opening. He didn't recognise the bar, wondered why no-one else had turned up to work. However, as was his nature, he got everything set up and opened the pub. Dozens of people came in as if they'd been waiting for him, which they had. Family, friends, old customers. All those departed whom he had shared aspects of his life with. This man had been a landlord for over fifty years. He passed in his sleep on the Wednesday as he was due to retire on the Saturday. Now just as there's no need for food and drink over there, neither is there a need for most of the day to day professions we have here.

If you are a builder and you want to build, then that's what you will do. Though your efforts will be wasted and your time better served trying to guide, inspire, a living person to be as good as you were.

You want to have a bar or a club, great, happy days.

Collectively your group could equally create the same environment as a meeting place and ask you to exist there. A saving on energy for yourself in many ways.

People will work if they want to work, but some professions are redundant. The individual just as to come to realise this.

So it is hoped that eventually they come to the realisation that ascension is the only true way forward.

Energy will have been collected at a constant rate. At this time, the ratio will be function for a year, recharge for four months. With this will come the obvious realization, that you are starting to leave your loved ones behind anyway. Your vibration will be so that you will become less easy to visualise to those around you. Your image begins to distort, then vanish altogether. Vocally, your audio responses attain a higher pitch than registers with others.

Not just you, but the animal spirits that have become apart of you as they meld even stronger to the essence of your spirit.

Once you ascend your animal spirits will be your only connection to those you leave behind. Travelling back, from time to time, to check in. To let everyone know that they are not forgotten.

Another problem is that spirits fight this process.

'Well we can't die; we have a choice, and that choice is to stay put.'

So they never fully recharge making sure they can be seen and continue to communicate cohesively at all times. Alternatively, some will fully charge and then share out that energy until they reach a more manageable level. With ascension comes the understanding that we no longer need to have an appearance.

We discover we can be pure energy and no longer need a form.

Taking on an appearance is still preferred throughout the realms for communication and for the purposes of enjoyment, but not whilst working.

It has distinct advantages and benefits. Conserving energy allows them to function for even longer periods. Moving too and from scenario to scenario faster, appearing to be in several places at the same time.

Thus, much more can be achieved.

The time to move on draws near, and that light in the East begins to beckon again. Not in their own backyard this time but a journey away.

Many are undergoing this transition for the first time, having bypassed level two, but the same rules apply. They are the only ones who witness the event. The light gathers in strength and eventually draws them in. Whether they fly a thousand miles or walk ten paces they come to that all consuming light where they use **The Sixth Key**, leaving behind those who want to believe that home is heaven.

Though, like a rubber band, their earth bound loved ones can, and will, pull them back from time to time.

To the spirit, this moment will pass in an instant and they will return to their learning. Also, that seemingly endless well of good intentions starts to run dry.

Beginning to understand the way of the universe, it soon becomes apparent that the dramas created by loved ones, in both worlds, are not relevant to the bigger picture. We are essentially selfish and live for our dramas. We put ourselves in the centre of our universe, yet we offer nothing positive to help the cogs turn.

One day, maybe not on this plain, we will come to realise that we have wasted opportunities and missed the point of our purpose here altogether. All because we want to be more in every way but are only able to achieve it through self delusion.

Anyone who knows their purpose is blessed by an advantage over their peers.

Those that have the tools to fulfill their purpose are closer to heaven than they may realise.

One other point of interest before we move on.

Once this book is finished and gathering dust on a bookcase somewhere, well anything we have here they can have there. So maybe this work has a dual purpose. Not just to help us here in this realm but to help everyone in every realm of every dimension, both physical and spiritual.

What holds them on that level when so much more is open to them?

I asked the question some time ago.

The answer was simple, love.

That overwhelming feeling that we all search for. That place of belonging. Of feeling contented and excited simultaneously. Collectively that is what spirit share on this level.

Imagine a clear running spring that will never dry up, and when we drink from this particular body of water we are overcome with pure joy.

Yes, they have love on tap over there.

So why would you want to evolve when you feel you have utopia anyway?

What lies beyond and how can it be better?

Chapter Thirty-Three: Love.

It's quite simple really.
We all want the things we can't have, human
nature.
We are brought up to believe there are
certain principles, which we can translate
into the emotional, the physical, the spiritual,
or all three.
Such feelings can be associated with anger,
lust, boredom, and lethargy, to name but a
few.
But surely the strongest feeling of all is love.
Most of us know we really want it.
A certain number of people may think they
have never felt it.
More people than you imagine will not truly
know what love is. Confusing this most basic
emotion with sins like pride, jealousy and
obsession.
Love isn't about control.
It isn't about being fixated or being hooked
on that emotional heroin.
It's about two people having an extremely
positive connection that draws them
together.
Some would say it can equally pull them
apart, but that's only when other negative
influences are added to the mix.
Love should be about the joy of sharing. Not
loss, nor compromise. Put the right elements
together and two become one.
That's the love two people share who are
destined to be together.

There are other equally important forms of love of course.

Parental love. Brotherly love, though I'm sure that's meant to include sisters as well.

Friends can share love. I regard a few of my friends as family and love them dearly.

Love travels in many forms and guises. Multi-layered, and sometimes hiding in plain sight. My personal experiences with regards love as all the makings of a relatively short chapter, but there's a story to be told all the same.

Remember my earliest psychic/spiritual memories. That time from losing my mother to the Christmas of 1973. Three years that gave me my grounding and I believe without those events I would not be sat here writing now.

I asked about that time, the occurrences and experiences. The answer was simple and came from mother. 'We were getting you ready.'

There was a little resentment from me at this answer. Referring to the royal 'we.' Danny and Bill were around, yes, but the most important person of all was missing from my life.

'That would have been cruel on us both. Do you really think I wanted to leave you to grow up on your own?'

Of course she didn't.

All I wanted was my mum. Had my wish been granted I would probably have been more successful with that razor blade and then, well God would have been a right old mardy arse about that one I imagine.

It was because she loved me that she couldn't be around. Far too painful for both

of us. My mother couldn't return to my life until the time was exactly right, and of course it was her visit that set me on this path.
Back to Danny and Bill.
One upstairs, the other banging on the pantry window. Calling my name, trying to warn me. Would they have tried to intervene in my life if they didn't love me?
Their warnings went unheeded, yes, but I was still a child after all. The same sort of warning today would be dealt with differently, I'm sure.
A little voice in my head laughs and memories of Doncaster in my thirties comes back. The turbulent days when I became lost within myself.
The half a dozen or so times where a voice shouted my name with a resounding urgency.
Every time I thought I knew better. On each occasion I ended up getting into scrapes, always alcohol related, bumps, bruises, and still a few scars to prove it.
I keep telling myself I have learned and that warning voice has had nothing to do for over ten years.
It's warming to know they are out there somewhere keeping a watchful eye on me. For the best part, at times, it feels like they keep me going. They certainly give me purpose.
But what of real, physical love?
Well actually there's another step between spiritual love and physical love. It connects the two and is intended to bring out the best in all of us.

Music and particularly dance.

Irrespective of style, genre, tempo, music does something for all of us.

Most of us cannot sing. We may like to think we can, but our delusions get the better of us. It doesn't stop the music being in our heads. Doesn't detract from the fact that it can shape our moods, helping us find a calmer place in our minds, or press us to get on with things.

Everyone can dance. You might have two left feet and your whole routine might involve little more than shuffling from side to side, but it's still dancing.

If we think about this shuffling gait we adopt, well it's what we choose as the least obvious way of getting noticed. Let go of your inhibitions and you'll find your meagre efforts fast become a full-blown Michael Jackson impression in no time. There is only one rule to achieving this. Stop being self conscious and giving a damn what other people may think. The truth is, they don't care because they are too busy getting on with it themselves.

Music is a 'gift' from heaven.

Dance is a way of giving the spirit space to breathe.

In fact I would say that dancing is the closest you can get to being a medium without the effort of having to tune in.

When we dance we self tune, the aim being to become as one with the music in order to attune our spirit to our physical efforts.

In a sense we are allowing the spirit to come out to play.

The more freedom of expression, the more

open the movement, the happier the spirit
will be. Physically we may become tired, but
at least we'll find an inner peace, and if we
connect properly, those feeling can be
closely related to love.

I've always wondered where my sense of
rhythm comes from. Considering my size and
age, I can still lose myself in that moment.
Don't care what other people might think,
not usually aware of them. Though ten
minutes and I'm done for the night these
days.

A good friend, he's seen me do my Fred
Astaire, put a comment on my face book
page. It read: Next year: sell 100,000 copies
of your book and win Strictly (Come
Dancing.)

Of course there's no chance, but it would be
fun. He's got more chance being a bit of a
minor celebrity.

So though we may not always experience
love as a constant in our physical lives, we do
have a placebo, if we can dig down within
ourselves and find it.

Dancing also works the entire Chakra system.
The sense of movement starts in the brain
and then works its way right down to your
toes.

Something that is enjoyable from an
emotional perspective and works the body
both physically and spiritually. You really
can't ask for more, and everyone can
dance.

It answers so many question relating to my
teenage years. I had left the voices behind,
had no confidence with girls, but boy did I

look good on a dance floor. Nothing else mattered when the music took over.

Just like most things in life it was a phase. A time I would love to recapture. It's just that thirty years and eight stone make a difference. The memories and the reality will have altered, and I doubt whether the placebo effect would be the same.

We never love two people in quite the same way.

I've spoken of love and love lost, touched on marriage. A desire for children that remains unfulfilled. I have been guilty of fixation at least once but fortunately came to my senses quickly.

The bottom line to all this was that the only times I've truly felt loved, well they are both in sprit and to this point I don't know who Hailey is.

Mum loved me the way any mother would, but she was taken too soon.

Hailey is but a dream, a living dream maybe, but our physical connection is the most tenuous imaginable. Yet I hold on to our few tender meetings and have replayed them over the years just as one might revisit a favourite place or occasionally dig out that all important piece of vinyl that we've kept hold of our old stereo for.

So about two years ago I asked the question: What does love truly feel like?

I met a lady, quite frankly the nearest I've come to thinking; I want to be with this person.

Yes, many of my friends are very attractive. I'd go as far as to use the term stunning for some of them. That doesn't make it plausible that a relationship would work. Two people have to connect. Not one thinking there's something there whilst the other is oblivious to your desires.

I know this, but it's exactly what happened. Normally I would have controlled my emotions in a more appropriate way, but my guides chose this time and this circumstance to answer my question.

I knew her as a client, but we became friends. She'd just come out of a disastrous relationship, and whilst I felt very attracted to her I knew she wasn't ready for anyone else, and she had shown no interest in me anyway. This was purely platonic.

For a time I would go to her home and help her with meditation.

Now. I'll reiterate this, she never gave me any encouragement, showed no interest in anything other than friendship but it didn't stop that lot upstairs injecting me with 'Emotional Heroin.'

Simply they answered my question, choosing this lady as the vehicle to do so.

It was a weekday evening I'd been having those flip-flop feelings in my stomach all day and she rang and invited me round for a pot of tea.

Then it happened.

She became enveloped in a golden light that radiated out towards me. Unaware of this I'm sure; my friend carried on as normal. That light connected to me and I was literally carried away, or so it felt.

Those flip-flop feelings began to travel

through my body embracing every nerve, every sinew, flooding my senses with the strongest emotions imaginable.

I recall crying, unable to control myself. Making up some excuse for my erratic behaviour.

I don't know how long it lasted. Probably no more than a few minutes, but it stayed with me for a long while afterwards.

What is love?

Well they gave me my answer.

The problem is that whilst I should be competently able to deal with these feelings, I give advice on such things on a daily basis after all; I found myself self-imploding.

I knew she wasn't interested but then why did I suddenly feel this way?

Emotions that were new to me had taken root in my head and were torturing me. For a few weeks, I took to drinking more, confided in friends I perhaps shouldn't, though never fully able to explain the whole story.

It culminated in a drunken kiss and unwanted advances from my part. An e-mail that wasn't really welcome and the end of a friendship.

And those feelings eventually abated.

She now has a partner and seems very happy. She always says hi in passing and continues to express warmth.

I can't apologise for how those feelings took me, I just wish there had been a different way of answering my question.

What is love?

If it's right, there's no other feeling like it in creation.

If it's wrong, well it holds the greatest pain of all, emptiness.

Getting in divorced in 1991, I asked the question 'Who will I settle down with next?' I was given a detailed answer about how and where I would meet someone but all these years later nothing relating to that situation as ever happened.

My faith keeps me optimistic.

Chapter Thirty-Four: Checking In.

I'm in the foyer of a hotel.
It's huge; I can tell from the size of the
reception area.
There are many people moving through,
heading off in all directions. Men and
women, all different nationalities. Some
couples but mainly single people. Everyone
seems to be doing their best to ignore/avoid
one another. Some seem surprised by the
cultural clash that ensues.
There is a short queue at the reception desk
though there are half a dozen men and
women dealing with arrivals and requests.
I'm stood watching but not joining in.
I focus on one petite blonde receptionist
speaking German to a man who nods
amicably and moves off.
Next in line is an African woman, seemingly
carrying her life on her head. She has a box
of belongings balancing on a flattened grey
afro. She made me smile, though seemed
oblivious to everyone around her.
The receptionist's language changed from
German to something I didn't recognise so
effortlessly; I couldn't begin to guess what her
native tongue would be.
I noticed that, despite height and body size,
all the receptionists had a similar look. They
were handsome people. No flaws or
blemishes, ageless.
The female receptionist started talking
Australian to the man next in line, 'Room

3130. We hope you enjoy your stay.'
Room 3130. What was this place?
What hotel had so many room?
I was aware of no entrances or exits. Could
see no restaurants or bars, just this reception
area and the every decreasing number of
people waiting to check in.
A number was in my head, 4421.
That's when I realised it was one of my
waking dreams.
4421 was my old works number from my days
at British Coal. A number I could relate too.
On auto pilot, I set off to my left, knowing I
would find room 4421 with ease.
People wandered around, still keeping to
themselves.
I noticed no lifts or stairs yet surely there
couldn't be thousands of rooms on one floor
could there?
4421, 4421, I was there. Pure thought took me
to my destination. The door was open. I
looked around but there was no sign of
another room. Just walls either side of the
door and behind me. A structure that
appeared to go on forever.
I entered.
There was a bed against the wall to the right
of the door. There was a window opposite
the bed and a second window to the far
right. A leather sofa and matching chair filled
a space between the window and the bed.
Now, a question. How can pitch black look
so beautiful and light?
Impossible you might say, but that's what I
faced.
Either outside the windows it was the middle

of the night or there were black blinds blocking out the view.

The walls were white, as was the ceiling. The bed was, well a bed. The sheets and pillows shared the same deep pool of black as the windows. However, they seemed to vibrate encouraging me to lie down, enticing me towards blissful sleep.

Even though that's where I already was. In my own bed in my own room.

Once again, a dream within a dream. It's mind boggling really.

I moved towards the divan, started to pull back the black top sheet, then withdrew. Someone else was already sleeping, enveloped beneath the covers.

My initial instinct was to wake them up, after all this was my room. I needed this bed.

'You're not meant to be here, this isn't for you.'

The words, crystal clear, from a prone male figure ran through my mind. No spoken words, just pure telepathy.

I couldn't see him, his body immersed in black, but there was an uncomfortable familiarity that put me on the back foot. My last thoughts were, but it's my number....and I was transported to a different room.

Clean, bright, airy. A place I'd dreamt of many times before.

No black sheets or blinds, but instead gleaming bright light filled the room. What's more, I could distinctly hear the sea.

Dimensionally the room was the same. As was the furniture and the placement of the windows. But the sunshine shone through both windows simultaneously, one facing south, the other east, so technically impossible, but occurring all the same.

I stepped into the hall. Room 126. The number of the house I grew up in.

No-one else was stood in the hallway.

A flick of the switch in the mind and I'm in the reception.

Much smaller than the last check in, in fact only manned by one person. An elderly gentleman, yet a picture of health with the same flawless skin and seamless tone. The only give away was the thick head of lustrous white hair.

He smiles, 'Good afternoon for a stroll, Sir. See you later.'

I must appear ignorant because I remember having this experience on several occasions but never once replying to the man.

I step outside into a side street, just up from where there is a promenade, miles of pleasant beaches, calm seas, and countless people of all ages passing time.

No vehicles, no bars or cafes. No fast food outlets, 'kiss-me-quick' hats. No litter bins needed here either, everyone behaves.

I say there are no vehicles, a man makes me out to be a liar by riding by on a penny farthing. He is dressed like Sherlock Holmes, complete with deer stalker hat.

There are a few groups but mainly single people minding their own business.

There seems to be a 'no children allowed' policy as there are only adults wondering up and down. Bizarre dress sense mind. We have everything on show going back over a hundred years.

On the beach, you'd find everything from the beach huts circa 1920, to 'Itsy bitsy teeny weeny yellow polka dot bikins' to g-strings and thongs. One or two are even 'au natural.'

What's for sure is that whilst it all looks out of place it doesn't feel so, and no-one seems to be offending anyone else, irrespective of preference.

It's almost as though each person has their own individual space and no-one is aware of anyone else.

Maybe I was the only one who could see everyone, who knows?

I realised I was the only one still living in a physical realm.

I was also aware that if I chose to walk just far enough I would come to a place where Gypsies made their home and just further up there was a tree lined avenue that would lead me to the house of mystery.

The place that kept drawing me back more and more, through dreams and meditations. A place that posed so many questions and so few answers.

Chapter Thirty-Five: Level Five, Rebirth And The Sixth Key.

Why was I shown the hotel reception and the vastness of the biggest hotel in creation?
They take the journey east, embrace the light, turn **The Sixth Key,** and this were they find themselves.
Nothing Earth shattering perhaps, but only until you understand what this turn of events leads too and what this place represents.
Back to the bedroom in all of its pitch black beauty.
In a physical sense we can be afraid of the dark, and what it represents, so it's hard to explain its better qualities.
In this room you will feel as safe as if you were still in the womb. And in a way that's what it represents. A place of absolute safety that is for you and you alone. No-one can enter, interfere, or mess with that energy. You cannot even invite someone else in.
So how come I was in room 4421 when someone else was in that bed?
Why did I have this dream when I'm very clearly still alive?
I hope there is an answer there somewhere or some, myself included, will be very disgruntled.
Several voices are laughing in my head, 'All in good time.'
So you are allocated a room, and from what I know, you'll be drawn to the bed immediately.

Now the rate of vibration means we are pure energy, don't need our earthly shape anymore, so it's strange that we are drawn back to a physical form so quickly.
The answer lies in symbolism and also the new journey the spirit is about to undertake.
The bed becomes a womb, or cocoon.
Becoming enveloped into the bed which, despite its color, bathes you with light.
Which in turn radiates outwards towards the two windows...and returns you to your early earthly life.
Childhood.
Many return to those days when they relied on their parents for protection. To that time of innocence where maybe not such good things were lurking round the corner.
Not everyone, but many will relive part of their formative years.
Everything here is about completing cycles. For those that had to grow up before they were intended to, suffered abuse of some kind, felt unloved, well here's the opportunity to enjoy all that was missed.
Children who aren't born, or don't get to grow into adults start off here. There is no need to go through the lower levels usually. The exception may be if a parent and child pass together, then they'll more than likely share the lower levels together.
The unborn get to meet the family they never knew once they've completed the cycle.
Throughout our physical lives we carry baggage from our childhood, sometimes never coming to terms with the tragedies and pains inflicted on us. This is the first step to

rectifying those issues. For to get to heaven such things need to have been dealt with. You aren't necessarily going to relive your childhood. You will create, collectively your own playground with like minded children, sharing the same interests. You will go back to school but not to learn anything that has no meaning. You will be shown how to fulfill any potential that got lost along the way or was never encouraged.

If you had anger issues, you may well have carried them over, though they become suppressed as an adult.

You will get to work through these issues, though the general principle applies. Cause problems and you have to replay the day over and over until you get it right.

For many it's about freedom, and learning to express themselves properly. Endless days of sun and fun in a chosen environment.

Chaperoned by spirits on their own learning curve living out alternate lives.

Back to the beach and countless children looked over by Gypsies.

And there was your parents telling you not to trust such people. Imagine everyday being playtime until you could play no more.

Having the experience of food and drink for the first time even though it's no longer necessary, sleeping under the stars, creating a make believe jungle full of pink elephants that take you for long rides.

Hey, it's a child's energy; he/she can do whatever they like.

No-one and nothing can hurt you; it's just pure bliss.

Allowing you access to everything you were genuinely deprived of in your physical life. Imagine your ideal childhood, if you didn't have it, well that's your reward for ascending to this level and letting go of your loved ones for now.

Remember, it's only a transition, and you will all come back together eventually.

But this is only the beginning of, what will be, a long journey.

we can no longer measure in physical time. Remember you will have built up your energy resources and will be functioning for at least a year before you get to this place, and the idea of this vast hotel is very simple.

To maximise those resources.

The less energy you need to create houses and environments to live in, the more you have to build on, and the longer you can function.

So from here on in your living arrangements are provided, the energy to create them, collective. It's like suddenly being asked to pay a small amount in board and lodgings instead of a mortgage.

So you will live out your childhood years, in physical terms, free of trauma, though you will have to learn the lessons related to anything practical or emotional that you missed.

All the while cocooned in your new home, your energy being used to help the process move along smoothly.

It must be a bit like being in a coma. The physical form is incapacitated, but the mind still functions leading us on journeys we will not consciously recall later.

One thing is sure. This cycle, as all others on this path, will need to be completed before we move on.

Between every cycle we get 'down time'. You have just relived parts of your childhood of which you now fully understand the purpose. Then imagine having the ability to replace the images in that window with any destination you desire. Being able to go on holiday without restraints on time or the cost of getting there. It might not even be an earthly destination. It might be that jungle full of pink elephants.

Whatever you desire is your reward for completing this task, though, on the whole, there's been nothing arduous to endure.

Whilst relaxing or partying to your hearts content, your animal guide can go visit your loved ones. Checking in, if you like.

Whatever your animal guide captures within their imagery, it's stored away to be played back at your convenience.

The second part of your journey is maybe less pleasant for some.

Revisiting the sins of your physical life.

Every nook and cranny of every illicit act is explored.

It might be that you were a school bully. You stole, cheated on your partner, the list is endless, though we're not including the really serious misdemeanors.

Those guilty of grade A crimes are not likely to be found anywhere, anytime soon. Not by their families, nor their victims.

For everything you have ever done you will

be brought to task.

No-one's going to beat, or brand you. There's no snake tongued demon with horns and cloven hoofs set ready to cast you into hell. The only weight of justice that will bare down on you is made up of your own guilt and emotion. You will be made to feel what your victims felt at that time.

Bullies will know what it feels like to be the victim. Cheats will know what it feels like to be swindled, the boot will be firmly on the other foot.

Of course, nothing's ever straight forward; there are many shades of grey.

What if the bully was being mean because he received the same treatment elsewhere. The swindler had cheated once having been a victim themselves many time over.

Weights and measures. Comparisons between the good and bad we have endured in this life. Feeling the weight of emotion from all sides for every situation we've created or endured.

A mixture of guilt and relief, reliving the scenarios, then confronting or being confronted by our victim/antagonist.

The end result is to achieve forgiveness.

On this basis my advice is to get closure in this life wherever possible. We're never going to cover all the bases, but we can make the journey easier later on.

After that task, you'll need a welcome break. There is one other factor here that involves time and how out of synch it becomes in spirit.

I've explained that everyone's time is

different anyway, but consider this.

You are exploring your 'weights and measures.' There phrase, not mine.

Coming together with half dozen different people you have crossed swords with on the earth plain. Reliving these scenarios, drawing a line under them and moving on.

Now you are on level five, but those other energies could be anywhere on the ladder. They may even be still on the Earth plain!

So how can we come together with someone still living?

Because what we experience now, they will experience once they get to that level. The same scenario will unfold, scene by scene, word for word, with the same resolution.

Just in an alternate time frame.

Hard to get your head round, I'm sure.

We have to dispel time as we understand it here on the earth plain and understand that once over there time takes on more surreal qualities.

Task Three caught me by surprise.

Still thinking about all the people I need to make my peace with before it's my time.

Replay your life and think about all the times you were at a crossroads. Then consider all the times you took the wrong path.

Further consider the occasions when you made wrong decisions you weren't even aware of.

Now you have the opportunity to set everything right.

This journey can take several lifetimes, but we do have eternity to play with, and that old father called time can be confusing.

We dream and within its scale and grandeur we believe we've been there for hours, yet only five minutes might have passed when we open our eyes.

Another point. I called this God's Faux Pas. My thoughts edged towards the idea that we should experience these levels first, before we reacquaint ourselves with our loved ones. There were no thunderbolts and lightening; I haven't been inflicted with some rare decease for daring to question the most omnipotent.

'Death, for some, is a difficult enough transition without having to face up to the past straight away. Some would really think they were in hell.' Also; one must build up their reserves of energy before undertaking this particular journey.'

I consider myself humbled. Though it is always good to question in my opinion.

So back to this new challenge.

Imagine you are eighteen years old, going abroad with friends for the first time. You are shy as hell so when the best looking guy/girl in the resort shows an interest you literally run a mile, and then some more. You spend the entire holiday desperate to spend time with them but too afraid to even look in their direction. The holiday comes to end. You go your separate ways destined to never meet again.

What if you were meant to spend your entire lives together. Marry, have two kids, live on some paradise Isle.

Gutted wouldn't come into it, but what you never knew can't harm you.

Well now you get to relive that entire part of your life over again, only this time the way fate intended.

This new experience can be whatever you want it to be.

For your new partner, well they may absolutely adore you for fifty years and live out each day in earth time.

On the other hand, you may find aspects of the relationship not to your liking, and wish to 'fast forward' through certain events.

Everything doesn't, strictly speaking, speed up, but you can bypass certain parts of the experience, and your better half will never know.

If only the physical realm gave us that option.

Remember, I talked about certain people who never seem to quite fit with the rest of us because they always conspire to miss their fate points, well this is set up for those individuals to get back in synch.

Every fate point missed, whether we think we are aware of them or not, will be revisited, experienced the way they were intended and become part of us.

Some will have hit every fate point throughout their life, and so this experience will be bypassed.

Others may have a very limited amount of experiences to explore.

Whilst, for some, it will be the equivalent of living a dozen or more lifetimes. Each experience to be savoured or hurried through depending on its make up.

We won't, unless we have masochistic tendencies, dwell too long on experiences that may have been less pleasant.

We have to have a taste of everything we missed out on that was intended for us, good and bad, in order to help us work out our life's purpose.

Even at this stage many spirits may be blissfully unaware that there ever was such a thing. But with experience comes knowledge and as we get a more complete picture of who we were on the earth plain we will, hopefully, begin to come to conclusions as to what it was all about.

There is a fail safe in place just in case. Having completed this journey we will be visited by higher energies that will point out the obvious if need be.

These higher energies also bring **The Seventh Key,** and whilst you won't be leaving your room anytime soon your new journey is intended to set you on the path to joining them, and becoming one of them.

An Angel.

Chapter Thirty-Six: Changes.

I suppose I asked for this.
Somewhere in an unspecified place in one of
the many dimensions that exists out there,
before I was 'a twinkle in my dad's eye' as
the saying goes, someone gave me a
purpose to pursue in this life.
It's no secret, this book's part of it.
'The Message' is the book's title, so whilst I'm
not the Messenger, It can be said that I'm the
Messenger's mouthpiece. Sent to spread the
word, though the book speaks for itself.
What if we had proof absolute to back up
the books contents?
That's not possible at this very moment; I
haven't the spiritual strength to do more, not
yet anyway.
Book the book wasn't possible a few years
ago.
Everything in its time.
As with most books I laid out the contents, the
subjects they were going to thrust at me.
It was going to be 250-280 pages in length.
We have already way surpassed that.
Every chapter was planned only for that draft
to sail straight out the window on each
occasion. Replaced by softly speaking voices
guiding me through the content they wish to
share. Their thoughts translated into my
words.
At times my fingers feel like they've taken on
a life of their own.
I read words I have little, or no, recollection of

writing. Yet, to me anyway, they make sense. Any lack of clarity is down to my weakness as a writer, where the thought and the written word lose cohesion.

The journey's coming to a close and I wanted a moment to step back into reality. A bit like being on dry land having spent six months on a submarine beneath the oceans, yet knowing the most crucial part of the adventure is still ahead.

A few moments to breathe. Take stock of where I am, what I've learnt.

I, as yet, don't know how this ends either for myself or for creation.

You know what I know.

It's Sunday 16th October and my inner compass tells me I need two more days. The phones are off, have been for a week. I've just got over a bout of flu, without this inconvenience I may be already at the finishing line.

Though, I have no doubt that if I'm finished in another day, week, month, or year, it will be when they want it finished, not of my choosing.

I have been little more than their servant from day one.

I don't' mind. How can I complain when I been allowed access to the wonders of the universe?

They've taught me well, though I don't feel I've necessarily been the best of pupils over the years.

Thankfully they have persevered. Developing me slowly but only because too much too soon and my mind would have melted.

The number of times they have worried me with their antics.

Waking up in the middle of the night to see shadows of spirits moving across the walls.

Pressure on my bed, where I physically feel them sitting with me, sometimes blowing on my face to get my attention.

Someone sitting in the room, at last I assume they are sitting, scribbling notes onto a pad. They are using pencils. I know because of that unmistakable noise a pencil makes when it is pressed against paper.

That has been ongoing for at least three years. I have often wondered if they were actually writing this book, the words being stored in my subconscious for a later date.

Then there was the shaking and the vibrating. It started with my bed rocking from side to side. Not just at night, but during the day. Random times, no structure.

Then it transferred itself to my body. During meditations I would often start to shiver, a cold front passing through me, over and over.

The results were amazing.

For years, those that came to speak to me were in my head, but whatever was happening to me changed the way I work. Suddenly the spirits were taking up space in the room. So you would have Mother's side of family in one corner, Father's side in another. Those departed connected through relationships and friends off to one side.

Sometimes odd links would sit at the side of me, talking in my ear.

Working in your head, you can only really

have one channel working at any given time. This way I could have up to five channels running simultaneously, and whilst it's noisy at times it's also less draining. They had begun taking energy from the room and not directly from me.

Even then they hadn't finished.

That shivering sensation altered.

It became more pronounced and more aggressive. Instead of an all over feeling it started tapping into my main chakra points, replacing the shivers with a direct vibrating sensation.

Imagine putting your mobile phone on vibrate and pressing it firmly against your chest whilst it rings. That was more or less the feeling.

All this was preparation.

Altering my own vibration to allow these higher level energies to communicate without any diverse effect on my physical form.

I want to suggest there's much more to come, but it's only a sense at the moment.

I would like to develop physical mediumship, I mentioned it earlier, show the world what is possible. And whilst there will always be cynics, at least give them something to ponder on.

Certain people will always ultimately have to be proven to be right, even when they are obviously wrong. For a cynic to question their failings is to question the very fabric of their existence.

There will always be someone who doesn't believe. Still, it would be nice to shake things

up all the same.
I've paused, reflected, taken in the journey
thus far and feel ready to climb back on
board, finish the quest.

Chapter Thirty-Seven: Level Six Energy. The Seventh Key.

Remember, there are two windows in the 'hotel room'.
Whilst our physical life has been dissected in high definition before our very eyes, there is also a window/screen to our right.
To this point redundant, at least until now.
What took on the appearance of a bed is now but a pool of bright light, containing the essence of your spirit.
And as the size of the spirit grows so does the size of the room with it. Lights of various colors, created by the nature of the journey you have undertaken.
Emotion and experience garner knowledge and for the first time, there is the makings of a giant jigsaw puzzle forming before you.
Speaking metaphorically of course.
When we pass many imagine our life is at an end but for most the puzzle is little more than a quarter complete.
Add the pieces collected through the journey's you've undertaken in this room and you might be half way to finishing..
So what comes next?
Well you've exhausted your physical life cycle, exploring every avenue from every perspective, possibly as many as fifteen life times if you've missed every fate point.
Whilst one screen represents your existence and the path you've followed, the second screen allows interaction with third parties.

They are new guides.
No longer a family connection or close friend,
it may be that you've surpassed everyone
you ever knew, so they can hardly be best
placed to further assist with future
development.
No, this new guide will be an angel.
Whilst appearing to you as an individual, an
angel is made up of multiple spirits, with one
chosen as the spokesperson. An angel's
appearance is A-sexual, so gender is
insignificant. The voice may be male or
female, but will never sound out of place.
Angels can vary in size and stature. Two spirits
combined, technically, are classed as an
angel. On the other end of the scale, we can
be talking about millions of spirits connecting
together to carry out certain types of work.
Angels who work with ascendents can vary in
number depending on the individual and the
nature of their purpose.
The purpose of life can differ vastly from
person to person.
One person's role may be that of parent.
Nothing more or less.
Another's may be to lead nations to peace
and prosperity. What's for sure is that there
will be many more of the former and very few
of the latter.
'Yes, there are always more water carriers
than Generals. But without water the general
would not have an army to lead.'
Whatever your given purpose, no one person
is seen, spiritually, as being greater than
another. It's just that people are given
different tools to work with to help add to

their strengths.

Be it physical attributes or a more intellectual strength. Some have the role of entertainers, others protectors, others messengers. We all have a given role and an end product.

What if someone is intended to be a great performer?

In the vastness of space and time, not a great purpose, some may say. They won't save the world from starvation or stop wars. What they may do however is inspire that one person who can achieve those goals.

So if they go through life without fulfilling their purpose, they may indirectly add to the problems in the world.

You get the picture, but that question raises its head again, how do I know my purpose?

It's not always obvious. Go through life being positive, taking the direction that most inspires you, and you won't be far off the mark.

There are those lower energies that may get in your head and try to throw a spanner in the works, but the answer always remains the same. Positive attracts positive.

Each path missed or ignored would have taken you some ways to completing your cycle so by the time you've explored all your avenues you should have the answer.

There will be those who have had an essence of their spirit reincarnated; possibly many times over. That small portion of energy left over to grow with the elements and later be reborn with the same purpose, just possibly a very different path.

Well by this time that individual may also

have passed into spirit.

If they have passed, there may be an essence of their energy that has had to be left behind.

The cycle continues.

Male or female, you will connect with this energy, if they have passed. The idea being to add more pieces to the puzzle. For you are part of the same energy, connected through soul. You will be able to see their entire life as though it were your own. Experiencing the relevant parts of their journey to add to your own knowledge, just as they will be able to do so with you once they have ascended to the same level.

This is **The Seventh Key**.

No all consuming light to follow this time, because you have become part of that light. Once that part of your reincarnated spirit begins its journey east, the light it follows will be the light that emanates from your room and you.

Of course, there many more spirits not reincarnated than are but everyone has an angelic creator, so there is always a light to entice us towards ascension.

So you've connected with that essence of energy long ago left behind. But what of the light you've been following until now, who does that belong too?

Imagine your life's meaning is so complex even the highest placed angels have trouble explaining its true purpose. Potentially a journey, maybe, a thousand years in the making.

Whilst each of those energies retains their

individuality you are also part of a collective.
Each as their own room, their own private
space, but these are the people that have
been guiding you towards ascension and
through this third party screen you gain
access to their lives.
You can go all the way back to the
beginning of creation, experience each life,
as they can access and experience yours.
Again it is a learning process that provides
more pieces to the puzzle, but imagine the
magnitude of this particular journey if there
are literally hundreds of people to get
through.
Don't worry, I'm talking extremes here, usually
there's no more than half a dozen energies in
a chain before a purpose is complete.
And for most of us these experiences will not
apply.
We arrived, did what was set out for us, and
moved off into spirit, job done.
At this point, we reconnect with our creators,
and we in turn learn to create.

The Eighth Key.
You join a group.
They could be made up of any given number
of spirits and are split into two sections.
For those that have been reincarnated,
everyone comes together to interact as one.
For those that have completed their task and
have no such links, they come together with
the angelic hosts that set them on the
physical path in the first instant.
Imagine each group, sat around a round
table. The centre is made up of a chasm of
light energy which exudes from those

present. So everyone's energy is connected.
In that moment everyone around the table is
as one.
The goal is to maintain balance.
All the physical lives of those around the
table are taken into account.
'Weights and Measures.' The phrase
whispered in my ear again.
Not just the lives we originally lived, but the
experiences of what could/should have
been. Everything is taken into account.
The results will dictate the purpose and paths
of new life, yet to be created in the physical
world.
The group will come together with the
purpose of creating new life and may have
no further contact with each other from one
gathering to the next.
It could be that the group is made up of
reincarnated energies and their purpose is
complex and nowhere near reaching a
conclusion. The energy left on the earth plain
floundering in the same manner as everyone
that's gone before.
So the group will assign new energy to help
complete the task. The same subconscious
purpose programmed into one or more new
babies born to the Earth plain.
 Likewise, the second group will have a new
mandate.
New goals and fresh challenges, the cycle
beginning again.
It could be that, once measured out, the
balance amongst the group is out of synch.
Either too much positive or negative energy.
This will dictate what happens to newly

created souls, the sort of life they will be born into.

Too much positive energy and the new life is born into a life where perhaps there will be more difficult obstacles to overcome.

A negative measure dictates that the new life may be born into circumstances far less challenging.

As it is your first time in the room you will dictate what happens. The others, some here many times before us, know what their measures are, the unknown elements is formed by what you bring to the table.

Just as future generations will become that unknown element when they first arrive.

In extreme cases, more than one new soul may be assigned to this world. If the balance exceeds certain levels it may take more than one new person to complete the task at hand.

It's rarer than winning the lottery but if these two energies come together, become a couple, well that is soul mates in its purest form.

There is also another major factor to consider when new life is introduced in to the physical realm.

Reincarnations evolve from the same world. They are connected by a time line, usually having graced different generations from each other.

If we were given life by the second group, angelic creators, then there is likely to be a number of versions of us created simultaneously, each sent out to alternate realities in parallel universes.

The number will depend on the creators themselves, and where they originated.

Five angelic creators sat around the round table with you.

Each creator might be sharing energy with any number of other versions of themselves from different dimensions.

You aren't sharing energy because you're the first one of your type to get this far.

But each of those creators might have links to a dozen or more alternate realities.

So when a new energy is created for the earth plain, there will be an alternate created for these other realities as well.

The same aims and goals. An identical purpose just modified for an alternate environment.

It's no good for your purpose to be a computer wizard, if in the next reality computers are still a figment of science fiction.

Purposes are always being modified, but remain intact at the very source of what they represent.

For each alternate reality represented there will be version of you born into that world. Irrespective of where that place may exist the same rules apply.

There could be a dozen versions of you out there, all with the same issues, an essence of your energy reincarnated over and over.

You have completed the journey to this point, but are now waiting for the other versions of you to catch up.

But for the first time you have been made aware that there likely exists these separate individuals, whilst singular in purpose, also a part of your energy.

The Ninth Key.

Back in our comfort zone, our light shines bright. We have been part of creating new life and designing its purpose.

The first true task of an angel.

Our own journey isn't complete though, not by any means. That jigsaw puzzle still has quite a few missing pieces because whilst we are as complete as we can be, there are still parts of us trailing behind.

The essence of our reincarnated energy may have caught up, but anything beyond we will have to revisit when the moment allows.

As for our alternatives, well that's another story.

We will connect to each of them individually once we ascend to their level, or them to ours.

First we will learn about their world and them ours.

The teacher will usually be our spiritual creator whose origins lie in that particular world.

This is vital in that forewarned is forearmed. What if the world we step onto has been ravaged by disease or devastated by war? I have written of examples of these world as experienced in my dreams and the differences can be vast. A world where everyone speaks double dutch might be quirky, but a world where everyone is reduced to living in bunkers is horrific.

The Ninth Key gives us access to these worlds, the ability to witness an alternative version of our lives had we been consciously born in a parallel universe.

From birth to death if we so choose. The entire experience played out before us, complete with out takes or reliving those missed fate points as we did with our own lives.

For each alternative reality there will be new experiences to explore as part of learning who we are. These alternates are truly part of us, and us of them.

We will not stay connected, unless we grow a strong bond and choose to be, but we will connect at the end of every cycle when the time comes for us to carry out our role as angelic creators.

What if there are five versions of you out there.

Three have completed their ascension to the angelic level.

One is staying on level four, convinced they are in heaven.

The last has begun a cycle of reincarnation not quite having fulfilled their purpose but is personally ascending.

Well those three versions will continue their journey onwards and upwards, but will revisit the other two as and when they arrive.

We are capable, have an ability to encourage the others to catch up. But our efforts are limited because of free will, and the fact that, at this stage, they don't know about us.

All we can do is send out that welcoming beacon of light, hopefully encouraging them to move Eastwardly and reap the rewards

that await.
Meanwhile, we are now about to begin the work of angels where the real business begins.

Chapter Thirty Eight: The House, Revealed.

I'm sharing time with Hall and Oates, surprising because as much as I'm a fan, the album is 'Private eyes,' which I probably haven't heard since the 80's.

The track is 'Keep my head above water' though I know I've been listening from the beginning.

I'm on top of a snow covered mountain, well outside my comfort zone, with a large group of people either carrying or wearing skis.

Not for me thank you very much.

Others can be seen sitting in deckchairs, basking in the sunshine. One or two are dressed for a poolside afternoon of sunbathing. Swimwear and sunglasses which considering where we are seems bizarre.

The track changes, something I don't recall ever hearing. 'Tell me' I think is the title. I want to fast forward but am apparently stuck with the track all the way through.

I know I'm dreaming, not sure what this scenario means.

The air is clear and clean. The temperature no different to the beach front scenario I arrive at so often.

Not to hot or cold. In fact as temperate, I imagine, as you choose it to be.

Does everyone have an awareness of temperature in dreams?

I'm not sure I always do, just my special experiences.

Like the beach, there is a distance between

myself and the rest. An invisible cordon that keeps us apart.

To further confuse, and add to that 'something's not right' feeling, a young woman comes into view wearing a blue nightdress. She dances in a sensuous manner, the clothing too short to leave much to the imagination.

I know who she is straight away.

A case I began to get involved with. A missing woman, who had disappeared well over a year ago. The police don't want to entertain me, even though they admit they have nothing to go on. Certain members of her family refuse to admit she might be dead. I met some of her friends and colleagues. I came to the conclusion that no-one really knew her. A fact that isn't exactly a secret. And she's here in my dream, before me for the umpteenth time. Surprising, because her body isn't buried half way up a mountain, that's for sure.

She has worn this dress and danced for me before though.

A flick of the mind and we're in the lounge of the big house.

Still wearing the blue night dress, still dancing. Had I invaded her dream, or her mine.

I suddenly realise she's not just dancing for me, but for a small audience.

There are two other women, a man, and a little boy, standing around the room watching.

I begin to feel slightly embarrassed. Did I not say that her clothing left little to the imagination?

Whether or not she heard me in some telepathic way I'm not certain, but she was suddenly no longer in the room.

The others remained, staring in my direction.

'Hello.'

No answer.

'I'm Keith..'

Hopeful, but getting no response.

It suddenly came to me.

The young lady in the blue night dress was aware of my presence, trying to get my attention, but these others could no more see her as they can see me.

A different energy connection.

The boy and one of the women seem nervous around the man. The second woman seems less likely to take prisoners. For his part the man remains quite, guarded even.

Their clothing is old. They look like land workers, farmers maybe. Eastern European perhaps. The man holds a wide brimmed hat almost in reverence to the others in the room. He is a good size with pork chop sideburns. He speaks in some Slavic dialect I couldn't begin to comprehend.

The boy runs to the woman, maybe his mother, and holds on for dear life. The other woman replies, harsh words. You didn't need a translator to know there was a mixture of hate and fear in this room.

The man keeps himself in check, unwilling to be anything other than calm.

'He killed them. A long long time ago. He worked their farm whilst their husband was away in the war.'

Though the voice was clear, I couldn't put a

face to it.

A man's voice, authoritative but kind.

I picked up on the phrase, their husband. Did these women share a man? In what society and when?

'He robbed them and had to take their lives when he was surprised. He escaped and lived out his life with the guilt. Now he has to face up to them in order to move on. He wants forgiveness, but it won't be coming any time soon with the feel of things.'

The group vanishes from sight and I'm seemingly alone.

Save for the voice.

'You've been here many many times now. More than you realise, more than you perhaps should. But we understand.'

I woke up.

I felt I was on the cusp of learning things and I bloody came back to consciousness.

Off to the bathroom, back to bed.

I couldn't get back to sleep. Decided to try a meditation.

Honestly, I couldn't tell you if the rest of the experience was one thing or another.

'What exactly is this house?'

I remember visualising the room and hoping the voice was still there, listening.

My forehead suddenly felt frozen, icy hands started pushing down on either side of my temple.

There was no vocal reply to my question but, as when I'm writing, the answer to my question was suddenly there.

It's the only way I can describe it. One moment I was scrambling for answers, the next there was a certain clarity to everything, like I was ready to know. Which was a bonus as I was getting to a point in my writing where someone had to show their hand in order for me to continue.

It took a short while to let things sink in though.

Well, just as time isn't a factor and carries unusual properties over there, space can throw up a few surprises as well.

This house doesn't exist on any recognised level; its unique vibration allows it to move through all the levels but particularly welcomes lower end energies who have been so scarred emotionally that they are in spiritual limbo.

The murder victim whose family won't accept her as gone, who is somewhere no-one would think to look. Buried in a pipe or conduit underwater. Her killers still free to roam. Yes, there's more than one person responsible.

Multiply that one person by the many more whose deaths are never solved. Their ascension on hold until their killer passes over to give the individual a chance to find closure.

Well this is a home for those individuals.

They don't belong on level two, don't have the vibration for level three. So they are given a pleasant environment in which to pass the period of waiting.

I am limited to what I witness because I shouldn't be even aware of this place, never mind making it my regular nighttime haunt.

At that moment I remember thinking; I only

want to help.

The amphitheatre is a holding area for those that have died in disasters, or where a large number have passed before there time.

The tsunami hit on Boxing Day 2004. Reports estimated the number of deaths at approximately 8,500 with a further 4,000 missing.

All those spirits passing simultaneously. Whilst spiritually the disaster couldn't be averted and a percentage would have been marked for passing anyway, there would still be as many as a quarter to a fifth who passed before there time.

No-one to meet and greet them, confused by their new surroundings, well these victims might not have arrived at the big house, but their souls would have been redirected to some South East Asian equivalent. Where no doubt there would be an amphitheatre with an open area and a door without hinges. Surroundings that may appear austere and unwelcoming but necessary to assist in the passing process.

Not just lower end energies and premature passings pass through here.

Those upstairs rooms give access to every spiritual level. There is even a doorway through to the earth plain.

That voice again,' How do you think you get here?'

'I usually start in a field or by the beach.'

'That's the point you become aware of your surroundings. You always begin and end your visits here at the house. You don't return to the field or the beach to get home now do

you?'
Drat and double drat. I'm giving up on the questions. If I was a fighter pilot I'd get shot down at every turn. Ok, I keep missing the obvious. Maybe I really am still a child when it comes to understanding what's before me on this plain.

Those that are required to work through their childhood years often stay around here.

Those that, like myself, were born as water elements, drawn back towards the sea.

Hence, the comfort of the beach environment nearby.

Could the girl in the blue dress have been born an air sign or did she like to go skiing?

I don't think those answers lie in this book but are to be revisited at a later time.

'The answers will come.' That assuring voice once more.

So the beach children are a mix of those that were never born to this world, passed at an early age, and ascending spirits completing those childhood experiences that passed them by.

The common factor they all share is the elemental sign they would have been, or were born under. Water.

Back at the house and the recollections of a man visiting his traumatised daughter.

Spirits can visit their loved ones here. Stay as long as their vibration allows. Usually only in ones and twos, not too much stress for the patient. Anything that encourages the individual to learn who and where they are. Everything happens at their pace; nothing is ever forced.

That phrase again whispered in my ear,'
Eternity is a long time.'
Some simply refuse to accept anywhere else
as home once they arrive. I refer to the
woman sitting on the bench.
Dressed all in black, including the veil.
Someone must know who she is, how she got
here. Her loved ones have long gone on
leaving her behind. No-one visits and she
refuses to converse with anyone who tries to
help. She's been here a long long time, and
the house has been here, in one form or
another, as long as there's been a universe.
Quite simply, anyone spiritually traumatised is
drawn to this place. Almost like a respite
center, a time out from the hustle and bustle
of spiritual life.
Even higher end energies can become
traumatised.
Once they begin to connect to their 'other
selves' and maybe have experiences that
are unexpected and less than pleasant.
There is always a fail safe to serve as
protection from such events, but even the
smartest amongst you will get burnt
sometimes.
What if one of your other selves spent a
lifetime being tortured and beaten?
You tap in to that energy, believe you can
handle the experience, and then become
consumed by your own spiritual ego. By the
end you've actually gone backwards in your
development and ascension is on hold until
you fully recover.
There can be thousands of scenarios being
played out here at any given moment. The

protagonists only become aware of each other once their issues begin to clear.

The healthier their spirit becomes the more they will want to interact with others.

I recall seeing the tennis courts in the distance, to the right of the house as I face it. Many people interacting there, though I've never been able to get up close and personal.

Or sitting by the river bank, often with my mother, watching groups of people go by aboard different types of boats. Whilst no-one ever acknowledges us, they don't see us I realise now, they do seem content with their lot.

I suppose, considering what the house represents, none of you will ever want to come here. It's always better to visit than to be a patient.

My latest experience showed me that 'The Damned', their words not mine, come here seeking forgiveness for their sins.

I have more questions but have become loathe to ask. Because I feel obliged to write everything down and I keep getting spanked with the answers.

But here goes, 'Do 'The Damned' go to some form of hell? Are they then brought back to face those they tormented to the very end? Could the face off that ensues be part of hell itself?

Questions abound.

I get an answer, not as obvious as I thought, so I don't feel so stupid this time.

Though this does lead us away from the house, for now.

Chapter Thirty-Nine: Level Seven, Angels.

Connect two spirits together. Give them a
task that needs equal effort from both
parties. You have created an angel.
They come in all shapes and sizes.
From a biblical sense, we have angels with
names such a Michael, Raphael, Peter, to
name just a few.
In mythology we had the Greek Gods,
examples being Aphrodite, Zeus, and
Poseidon.
Then there were the Norse variations, maybe
less known deities of Germanic origin, Thor,
Odin, and Freyr.
I can't think of any female angels in the
bible, but that doesn't matter, we can no
longer ignore our female counterparts like we
did all those many years ago.
Whatever your religious faith, or belief system,
biblical angels and gods are one and the
same. Multiple energies, male and female,
come together to carry out universal work.
Be it two, two thousand, or two million, the
energies will mix and match depending very
much on the task before them.
So the angels may have names; there might
even be a Peter or two working under the
banner of that angel, but it is only a given
name, not a person.
You could give an angel any name; it
doesn't really matter.
A spirit with four or five alternates will likely as

not have four of five different names, a mix of male and female.

What is common is that each angel has a spokesperson, So when that group is being addressed it is usually the name of that person that is used.

Teams of angels are usually picked for their diversity and balance.

Our angelic creators will not just usually come from parallel universes; they will culturally and politically be diverse from one another. The room will be a mix of male and female, black, white, and yellow. That's before we start to consider every other race in existence, the possibility that there may be hermaphrodites in some worlds and half a dozen colours and creeds beyond our comprehension.

The bottom line is that by the time we have finished experiencing and learning, we no longer have a need for prejudices of any kind, because we truly are a right royal spiritual mix.

When we join a team to be assigned work, the usual number is no less than four. That number again.

Each person assigned will represent a different element, and when not together their energy will take up different space In the universe.

Remember as you ascend you travel in the direction dictated before birth. You will follow your astrological chart as you ascend into the heavens.

A team of four gives elemental balance as well as an all round ability to carry out any task.

A bit like the A-Team. You will have the spokesperson who leads the group. The mind, the body, and the spirit. Or if you like, a leader, an intellect, a soldier, and a religious figure.

The group is picked for its individuals as well as how they might work together.

Remember, we retain our individuality through out eternity. Once an intellect always an intellect. If you've always had the heart of a warrior then that's what you will always be. Just with the rough edges honed down.

The work of an angel ranges from taking care of groups, sometimes even individuals, on the earth plain. Averting the potential for disasters throughout all the universes.

Maintaining balance between the elements and their impact on each world.

Once we start to carry out elemental work, we further progress and this is representative of **The Tenth Key.**

First though there is a major problem. Remember that blockage on level four? Everyone convinced they are already in paradise, refusing to ascend, not wanting to be apart from those they are most familiar with.

Because of this blockage there is a shortage of angels in key positions.

Also, these groups are endangering the very fabric of spirituality itself and the necessity to create new universes.

If twenty people are the minimum number necessary to run a production line, then it's pointless expecting three people to do the same work. Then suddenly if that production line became a matter of life and death, we have trouble in paradise.

So, somewhere on high they had to find a solution to this problem. It's nothing new apparently, it's been this way forever, but it creates a fine line between creating and averting disaster.

We talk of unborn babies or still borns as going off to become little angels, well literally that's what happens.

They haven't had a life to mull over, don't have knowledge of family, though they do have a connection and spend a short time with grandmas and aunties who may have already passed.

They live out their childhoods in pure bliss but then ascend much more quickly than someone who's lived a full life and has reincarnations and alternates to come to terms with.

So, they fill some of the vacancies left by those that refuse to evolve. It's still not enough, but in times of need they make do, even in the afterlife.

These spirits still have to learn, understand right and wrong, experience the life they would have had, but it passes in a flash because they are ascending from the moment they arrive.

Sadly without miscarriages and abortions there might not be a world for us to live in. Though the anguish someone goes through having suffered such a loss can be unbearable so I apologise for any offence I may have cause with that point, however necessary.

An answer to my latest question, regarding 'The Damned.'

When starting out, many angels take on the role of warders, or guardians, as I'm told they prefer to be called.

Guardians watch over and take care of those spirits that in the physical realm carried out crimes that put them into the 'evil' category.

Though, on this point, I'm told they prefer the term 'misunderstood.'

We know whom we're referring too, no need to name names. There have been figures of disgust and hatred through out the centuries that will have passed on to find themselves here.

Remember my reference to God's Faux Pas and my gentle chastisement?

I was told that if we came immediately to our assigned room when we died it would prove too much for us and the vibration wouldn't sustain our energy.

Well that's what happens to the 'misunderstood'.

The black bed beckons, then engulfs them. Their life is played out like the rest of us. Only we skip childhood and go straight to facing up to our misdemeanors. A procedure that can take many lifetime's because the process is so slow.

The levels vibration means they can only actively function for a short time.

Imagine having to recharge every two hours, then to reawaken once more to come face to face with all those they tormented in this life. Taking on the role of victim over and over until they have nothing left to learn.

It's like trying to run through wet tar, it can take forever.

Respite comes from places like the big house where they are allowed to visit from time to time, though no-one else will be aware of their presence.

They can no longer do harm; their energy subjected to a cleansing that eventually eradicates the 'evil' within them.

They are assigned angels whose job is to monitor their progress. Not too much pain, nor pleasure, this is about learning not punishing.

Once this task is complete, and it can take the longest time, the spirit goes to level three where they meld with their reincarnated form, the original version buried deep within its energy.

Family and friends are connected to the reincarnated version but will have no knowledge of the original.

That's just one basic job that angels carry out. By now they have so much energy they can multi-task.

Angels always travel as pure energy; their source is always based in their assigned room, and their tasks carried out on the screen before them. Though, by now, these screens have multiplied three or four times.

One screen might show you spending time with your loved ones on a lower level. Simultaneously you may be working with your team to try to change the direction of an oncoming storm on the earth plain. Your animal guides might have come together to work their way through the list of jobs you have to prioritise, travelling from site to site collecting information.

You might be working on several jobs at one time, spreading your energies more thinly than you might like.

As ever, the more energy you use the faster you will need to recharge. Though whilst working as an angel all of your collective energy is pooled, and you pretty much can gauge just how much can be achieved.

There are things angels can and cannot do. They can manipulate people for the greater good.

Bend the elements to try and avert disaster and death before it's time.

The bigger the group, the more energy and the further ahead they can see what is to come. Good, bad and indifferent. They have access to all the different paths leading too and from an event. What the event means, how best to deal with it, and the maximum amount of good that can be achieved set against the minimum amount of bad.

What if the death of a child means that millions will be saved at a later time?

We mourn for the child, chastise God for letting this happen to an innocent, but we only see what's before us. Not the knock on effect, not the whole picture.

What angels cannot do is interfere directly with an earthly situation involving people's individual choices.

They can try and manipulate through positive

means. Inspirationally.

Hitler found an escape through his artwork, which was spiritually inspired, but it didn't stop him becoming a tyrant.

The angels would have seen what was to come so why didn't they smite him down before he had the opportunity to introduce the atrocities he did on this world?

Because it's one of the few rules they have to adhere too.

No smiting on the earth plain.

They can introduce a natural element, like a plague of locusts, to torment us, but not provide the gun or it's bullets with which to hurt each other. That has to come through personal choice.

And every decision, big or small, has to go through the big man anyway.

God. The ultimate energy.

Every energy of every realm, known and unknown, all interconnected, all as one, God.

We hurt a fly, we are hurting ourselves; we are hurting God.

Everything in the universe is connected. So we can hurt each other, or we can help. The more positive an environment we create the more we can achieve. We have the ability to heal the sick and feed the starving, but we won't because we live under the illusion of every man for himself. Whilst we have to love and look after ourselves before we can love and take care of others, there is enough love and understanding to go around.

Why can't we create angels in a physical

earthly sense? Teams of the finest minds working for the planets better good instead of some corporate giant's profit margin.

The good new is that there are parallel universes in a much worse state of health than our own.

The bad news is that we are heading the same way. The strong stomping on the weak and big corporation's manipulating governments to strengthen their power bases.

We have presidents and prime ministers, meant to run their respective realms, but they are only as strong as those pulling their strings from behind closed doors.

It's not about the little people. it's about the scraps that are remaining once those in power have picked over the carcass.

We are only allowed meagre rations, but made to believe every day is a feast.

Continue in this vein and the world will not survive more than a few generations. There will be nothing for our children's children but war and famine.

And beyond that the light of our world will be no more.

And if there are no universes, there will be no heaven, everything will cease to exist.

The angels are losing a battle that has been raging forever.

'We've always been losing. Nothing unusual there.' The voice returns.

But this has become serious.

No matter how many angels there are, the numbers need to swell dramatically to put everything in its place once more.

That blockage needs to be cleared and quickly.

The plan is for a new universe to be created as an old universe dies.

From the day of inception the time is set; the length of life known.

Natural death of the earth will come once the sun gets too close, and we burn up, that's the theory.

Before that happens a black mass will enter our universe, like a hole and swallow up everything in its path.

Don't panic, it's thousands of years away. We're more likely to destroy our world long before then.

The bottom line is that our neighbours are destroying their worlds faster than we can hope to create new ones.

Whilst we cannot do a great deal to help them, we can help ourselves.

The angels will do their bit; we have to do ours.

Chapter 40. Hailey And Christian.

Today I will finish writing.
I know because I have the answer to many of the mysteries of my life thus far.
Am I surprised? Yes.
Is it what I expected? Nowhere bloody near!
I've been like a child in a sweet shop. Too busy mulling over the vast choice before me to notice the child catcher from 'Chitty Chitty Bang Bang' waiting in the background with his net.
To explain, I was exhausted when I got my head down at 8:30 last night. My visit to the house, my new understanding, the revelation of its purpose, came to me around 2am.
The next four hours were some crossover between sleep and meditation. A mish mash of experiences I didn't want to let go of.
So I have some answers, and I'm too tired to write, yet too excited to sleep at the same time, so I'll tip tap away until I'm finished, or the tiredness finishes for me.
Back to the big house.
I'm content in the knowledge that I understand what happens to 'The Damned.'
Then I'm drawn into the hallway.
I don't know what I expected, my friend in her blue nightdress perhaps?
But not spirit orbs.
Large ones, each a myriad of colors drifting over the banister and approaching me.
I'm thinking; they should be rising towards the ceiling, like bubbles, or balloons, but no, they

had me in their sights.

Three of them levitating ever closer.

As they approach the hallway floor they begin to change, their form becoming more substantial, their appearance human.

Two women and a man.

Of course, I have seen them on several occasions, the blonde woman and the bald headed man.

Hailey looks more beautiful than I have ever seen her.

If she whisked me up now and swept me away, I would put up no resistance. There would be no arguments.

That long raven hair, wicked know it all smile. For the first time, whilst perfectly in proportion, I notice how much taller than me they are. I stand over six feet tall, all three of them stand at least 6'6" or 6'7".

Trying to kiss her now would probably require the use of a stepladder, not that I'd mind one iota.

'Nosy parker, just can't stay away, can you?' I heard her words but was too busy gawping. All three had shrunk by 6" or so to be my height. To make me more comfortable, I presumed.

No comment was made about this. Maybe I should have asked.

I was wrapped up in the beauty of what was in front of me. Those breathtaking feelings of love I'd felt some months ago returned, as strong as ever. I think I was crying. I noticed her hair had reverted back to its dark coloring, but this was trivial.

Hailey, herself, shed a tear or two whilst the

others looked on impassively.

'You're getting older love, but you have a young heart and that twinkle still blesses your eyes.'

There was no repost. It felt right to do nothing but listen.

I had this thought, odd under the circumstances, but very human. I'm middle aged and grossly overweight; she's as stunning as ever, she can't still be interested in me.

They all started laughing, reading my mind, finding my fears hilarious.

I felt a momentary pang of anger, but it passed without a pause.

'Come and sit with me, let's put things to rest.'

Taking my hand, Hailey led me into the lounge.

We sat together on the sofa.

The others don't follow, either waiting outside or perhaps dealing with other pressing matters.

'You are a silly arse, Christian. You truly are. But you're my silly arse and I'm stuck with you.'

My first words, no more of a thought, why do you call me Christian?

She puts her hands across my face; that icy cold sensation envelops my head, and I come back to consciousness.

Not another anti-climax, not now. Panic began to set in. I closed my eyes. Lay on my back, on my right, my left, nothing.

Then I was outside the hotel room, 4421.

This is a full blown dream because I only

remember later. At the time, it's as real as writing this.

I have two simultaneous urges. One is to enter the room; the other to run away.

I choose the former, open the door and enter.

A different scene from my first visit.

What was a bed is a now a deep pool of the brightest light imaginable. So bright I can't look directly at it.

My attention is taken by the screens where two scenes are being played out simultaneously.

If I'd have been having this experience in the real world, I would probably have freaked.

Though there are no horrors to be witnessed here and for the second time love envelops me.

The lyrics of a Michael McDonald song fill my head as I write this. 'I was tossed high by love and almost never came down.'

That's what I felt at that moment.

The screen in front of me is set in the lounge of the big house. Hailey has her hands gently caressing a man's face. He seems lost to her touch. He is tall, slim, smooth features, no wrinkles to speak of. Shaven headed, extremely healthy looking. Dressed in white, just as they all are.

Ageless, I remember thinking, surpassed by the pangs of jealousy that suddenly overcame me.

The screen to the right of the bed showed a different scene. As though the room was wired for sight and sound, the image was of me standing in this room, staring at myself, wearing my boxers and a T-shirt.

I let out a little laugh, maybe of nervousness.
Do I never dress properly for these events? No
wonder people ignore me; they must think
I'm a resident.

I turn to the pool of light, want to jump in,
immerse myself in the light.

I must have come close because I awoke,
yet again.

Back in the lounge, my face being stroked,
the transition from my bedroom to this room,
flawless.

I'm him, and he's me. Realisation ran through
me.

Hailey doesn't see me in my underwear,
maybe doesn't see me at all. She sees this tall
dashing shaven headed man called
Christian.

'Of course I see you. I see all of you, every
part of you, earth bound and angelic. You
are the one that doesn't see 'himself.'

Well the last time I looked in a mirror I had
hair and a large belly that had trouble
behaving itself. I also have too much body
hair, and he's as smooth as a new born
babe.

'She's right.' The voice in my head, him, my
other self.

Thank god that in the context of what I was
experiencing my mind could take it with a
pinch of salt.

I returned to my bedroom again. Nearly 4am
and it was bloody cold, like an ice box. So
much spiritual energy in the room, I had
Goosebumps on goosebumps.

A part of me wanted no more of this. Forget

it, bad dream, wake up tomorrow feeling like crap, feel sorry for myself for a few hours, I'll get over it.

Not this time, Pandora's box was well and truly opened.

I didn't sleep again; I was aware of being laid on my bed for the next few hours, but every time I shut my eyes I was transported to that house where Hailey remained on the sofa, either me or my other self with her.

No -one spoke, but the voices were Haileys and Christians, sometimes singular, other times, as one.

They were neither of them born to this world. Both miscarried at a time when such things were common place.

Well over two hundred years ago, but that's just my feeling, nothing more.

They quickly evolved to become angels, but more importantly they found each other.

Those that don't find love in this world can certainly find it there.

In earth terms, they were together, 'joined at the soul' for over a hundred years, their choice of phrase.

Lived, loved, worked together, ascended all the way to heaven.

Could have helped create a new universe but were asked to stay behind.

There are others, scattered, not just throughout this world, but all of the dimensions in existence. Their job is to try and clear the blockages. Thinking of new ways to encourage spirits to ascend, a job made near impossible because they can't force change.

However, they have carte blanche to deal with those disruptive level two energies and the mess they leave behind.

They move from scenario to scenario, up and down the levels, doing the best job they can. Finding a place of belonging for the misplaced, helping the misguided see the error of their ways, placing the damned out of arms way.

But all of this was deemed not to be enough. God needed this work to start at the most basic end of the scale, on the earth plain.

So volunteers were asked for.

In this case Christian, the silly arse!

To be reborn onto the earth plain, with knowledge stored in their subconscious to help mankind overcome its problems. To show what we need to be doing to save ourselves.

To spread the word, be the mouthpiece.

Not just now but throughout history to try and influence the outcome of significant situations in favour of good.

No pressure there then.

Most fall by the wayside never setting foot on the right path to begin with. Others are killed, the boy in Ireland, the woman in France. They were never part of me, as I first thought, but angelic reincarnations that never came close to realising their potential.

Though I do sense there is more to explore there. A bigger, more colourful picture than I can currently see or grasp. Otherwise, those experiences have no significant meaning, and I've learnt that everything holds some relevance.

Others do exactly what they are meant to do, but not in an obvious way.

You see there is a danger with returning to the earth plain.

We obviously become human again. Live a life filled with pitfalls and pratfalls. Become accustomed to what we are told, and not how we feel. We have to work it out for ourselves without help and assistance from our celestial helpers.

There may very well be reincarnated souls out there, having already experienced heaven, who think all this is total rubbish. Not willing to explore the far reaches of their mind.

What's more, they will have to go through the process of ascension all over again.

Not a very good deal then.

So what's different this time?

Hey, it's taken until now for the bells to ring, and that's allowing for the fact that I may actually be stark raving mad.

First off I have no baggage. There is only me, so there are no outside influences to turn me one way or another.

Secondly, there is the Hailey factor to taken into consideration.

How can God truly expect two soul mates to stay apart?

I don't think he did. I believe it was part of his purpose all along.

I've been waking up for twenty years, but I've only truly opened my eyes today.

Though this explains so many things over those years.

What if my two minds have been in conflict

all this time?

There is no real reason why my body should be holding on to the weight I carry. I eat well, don't drink to excess, exercise, and yet don't lose a pound. I was ill sometime ago but have been well over that for awhile now. Before I got fat I was a good looking lad, so I'd like to think. I started with the weight problems when I started on my path as a medium.

What if subconsciously I have been using my weight issues as an excuse for not getting involved with anyone romantically, a way of warding off potential love interest?

There's another trait that suddenly becomes meaningful.

About nineteen ninety -four I lived in a bungalow in Doncaster. It was a decent size but I took to spending most of my time in my bedroom, using the other facilities as a necessity. One has to cook and bathe.

Later I moved to a fairly sizeable flat, but lived in the bedroom, only using the spacious lounge when I had guests.

And now I live in a studio flat with very little desire to move anywhere bigger.

I keep promising myself it will happen, but do nothing to change those circumstances. In fact I've just signed another six month lease.

Now they all have their size in common and all take me back to that room with its pools of light.

Have I cocooned myself because I'm subconsciously aware of my true self and his predicament of having to look on helplessly as I cock things up?

You see; I get it. This isn't as we die and we leave an essence behind to complete a task. This is someone giving over their very being to come back to carry out something of far greater magnitude..

A full blown angelic reincarnation.

Trust me, if I feel anything, it's uncomfortable. The idea was to write this book and then relax. I feel no different than yesterday. No, scrub that, I'm knackered, and I need a shower and a shave.

I'm sure I'll continue to have a good drink from time to time. I'll still swear when the mood takes. Share the same human desires and frailties as anyone else.

Alright, I talk to dead people and do it very well.

I am different.

But an angelic reincarnation is a lot to get my head around. Though it does answer many of the questions about my experiences.

When it's my time, what will happen?

Will I retain some form of individuality or be swallowed up by Christian's far superior energy?

At least I know there aren't half a dozen other versions of me out there in different spaces and times.

And why I can experience the emotions and feelings of being over there, in spirit, so easily.

Also, why I have had access to the house for nearly thirty earth years, I was there long before I took root on the earth plain.

As for the Christian dilemma, I'm not sure. I remain limited to what I can see.

I have to get fitter, healthier, attune myself

through further meditation to increase my
abilities.

As I've said all along, there is more to come.
My part of the journey, as far as this book is
concerned is almost over, but the meditation
was not, and maybe the most important
messages were yet to come.

I'm sat with Hailey; hours seem to have flown
by, but it's no more than the blink of an eye.
Tears fill the corners of her eyes once more.
That other voice sharing my head, Christian.
'There isn't meant to be any contact whilst
we're on the earth plain, too much
distraction. We are meant to teach and learn
in equal measures. To prove that there is
something beyond the physical life. That is
the remaining goal. To leave a mark that will
make people think, question their mortality
and what to do to improve their existence.
But you also have to live your remaining time
and not wallow. Have fun. Don't be afraid to
express yourself both emotionally and
physically. Let's enjoy ourselves.

Well God knows I'm known for my insolence.
My inability to leave well alone. I think he
chose well with this other me, because I
won't lie down and go away.

Though I'm not sure what mark is to be left on
the world, not yet anyway.

Then something happened in an instant.
Hailey and Christian are sat on the sofa
cuddled up together. I'm sat on an identical
sofa facing them cuddled up to another
version of Hailey. I say another version,
because it's definitely her, but somehow
different. Just as I am Christian and he is me,

but more obviously different. We are mirroring each other, sharing the sameness of the moment.

The two Hailey's speak in unison, as one. 'Did you think I would let you take the journey on your own? I'm out there waiting; you just have to let fate brings us together. One day soon my love. We'll even have a real family together. I turn my attention to the face of the young woman I'm holding so close.

A flick of the mind and I'm upstairs, on the landing, for the very first time. The place I always wanted to visit at the most inappropriate moment. Hailey and her reincarnation no longer accessible to me. Before me is a door, not the end of horse shoe shaped landing, one up from the end.

'Open the door.'

Would you do as you were told under such circumstances?

It had to be almost tea and toast time, and I'm trying to deal with one revelation at a time.

I didn't open the door, but politely knocked. I expected a ball of light to consume me as it had the spirit I'd seen come up here more recently, but nothing of the kind happened. I was transported into another hallway that led to large set of double doors.

I felt I'd been here before but couldn't recall. Too much to process, I was never going to remember everything. Though it seems I haven't done a bad job.

I was just thinking I had better knock this time, when the big double doors opened before me.

I entered the room.

The man I refer to as Buddha and his three associates waiting to greet me.

A group of four elements, one angel. Rooted to the earth plain with the sole purpose of saving our planet. Fire, Water, Earth and Air. Joined together as one.

My core guides and now it made the most perfect sense.

I know there's a limit to what I can achieve without much more intensive development and the constraints on a physical body are limited.

I still found myself asking the question, 'What next?'

The answer is simple, in the most complicated way.

Running along either wall of this great room are many more doors leading off to only God would know where.

'This is the font of all knowledge. Through each door lies a solution to a global problem. Not in a book but through a living experience based on a mix of reality and meditative communication. In a short time you will return. Once you have evolved sufficiently, and you will choose a door to go through.'

I'm back to my bed. Bathed in sweat, dry throat, needing to start writing it all down.

For all I have learnt; a journey that I thought was almost over is only just beginning.

I always maintained there would only be this one book, but it seems, with all the questions I myself want answered there has to be a continuation. Once I've rested, taken stock of these revelations and discovered what tortures await in order to further develop my abilities.

I want to further explore alternative realities, parallel universes, their history and impact on our own world. As stated before, if a world ends four doors down it will have an impact climatically on our world.

And of course the many doors in the room of knowledge. What is held within and what it means for us all.

And what of the possibilities of a living, breathing person put on earth for me to love? An angelic reincarnation of Hailey. Plenty to ponder on.

But enough for now.

Chapter 41. Heaven.......

You will reach some invisible magic point that only God can measure, and your life's journey will be complete.

All of your alternates and reincarnations will be on the same level of ascension.

Your purpose will be recognised, your tasks complete.

Each part of you remains as individuals, coming together only at the times of angelic creation, in order to maintain balance.

Appearances can deceive, and what I was first led to believe to be a room in a hotel is anything but.

That pool of energy could probably power level three for an eternity, which gives you some idea of how powerful Hailey and her 'warriors' are.

There are now too many screens to keep track of as you multi-task your way through countless scenarios and journeys.

Then all of those screens dissolve into one bright light, one more all consuming light that takes us to the end of our quest.

The Eleventh Key. Heaven.

Where exactly is this place?

To the right of the centre of all the universes.

Not a planet as we would perhaps imagine, but a huge black mass that vibrates.

Once welcomed into this mass we experience utopia, creating our own personal paradise consisting of absolutely anything we desire.

Any environment, any home, to be shared with family and friends for eternity once they choose to make the transition and complete their own journey.

That's one cast iron guarantee. If we follow the path to ascension, we will always get to heaven eventually.

Those feelings of love, a constant reminder of what we have achieved.

Negative energy is no longer present, constituting another need for a physical plain. When measuring balance, the earth plain does get the short end of the stick.

If there is only a positive vibration in the realms of heaven, then the negative energy that counteracts it has to exist elsewhere at the other end of the spectrum.

Here on Earth.

So essentially we are fighting an uphill battle to begin with, the promise of real spiritual reward coming much much later.

....And Beyond, The Twelfth Key.

They still work in heaven by giving up a some
of their energy for the greater good.
To help create environments like the hotel
and the big house, places of necessity.
Your family and friends group increases.
By now you should be reunited with those
you love and have missed the most.
Husbands, wives, children, and parents.
No more falling out, no more prejudices. Just
the pure bliss of being all knowing, all seeing.
Work on the principal of six degrees of
separation.
The idea that every person on the planet can
be interlinked by six people knowing one
another.
So imagine all of us settling in heaven. Along
with the generations before, and those yet to
come.
Even the biggest of black holes will fill up
eventually.
Imagine a litre glass bottle. Put a rubber hose
in to the top but then seal the bottle so
nothing can escape.
Now fill the bottle with water.
The bottle is the black hole and spiritual
energy is the water.
The bottle is full, but we keep pouring the
water into the vessel. We all know the
outcome; the bottle will shatter.
So keep introducing spirits into this black mass
and something has to give.
The smashing of the glass bottle is the

equivalent of the big Bang.

Two events occur simultaneously. One universe is swallowed up by the black mass to maintain balance; whilst the overflowing spiritual energy is thrust out.

The effect on our spirit is little more than a slight interference to our vibration. But we have been propelled in a new direction.

The Twelfth Key.

We have created a new universe.

Printed in Great Britain
by Amazon

75773210R00244